THE VALUES OF
ECONOMICS

Economics has often been accused of losing its connection to some of the basic characteristics of human behaviour: commitment, emotion, deliberation and the different forms of interaction through which human actors in economic life provide for themselves and for others. With an aim to bring caring back into economic theory, Irene van Staveren draws upon the work of Aristotle and Amartya Sen's notions of capability and commitment to propose an alternative methodology to utilitarianism that is not normative.

In his *Ethics*, Aristotle argued that human beings try to further a variety of values by balancing them, stating that people try to find a middle road between excess and deficiency. The author develops and applies this idea to the values of economics, arguing that in the economy freedom, justice and care are also balanced to further ends with scarce means. Freedom is furthered through market exchange, justice through a redistributive role of the state, and care through mutual gifts of labour and sharing of resources in the economy. This book argues that economics is, and has always been, about human values, which guide, enable, constrain and change economic behaviour.

The Values of Economics will appeal to advanced students and professionals with an interest in economics, philosophy and gender studies.

Irene van Staveren is Lecturer in labour market economics of developing countries at the Institute of Social Studies in The Hague. She won the Gunnar Myrdal Prize 2000 for her dissertation *Caring for Economics: An Aristotelian Perspective*, from which this book evolved.

ECONOMICS AS SOCIAL THEORY
Edited by Tony Lawson
University of Cambridge

Social theory is experiencing something of a revival within economics. Critical analyses of the particular nature of the subject matter of social studies and of the types of method, categories and modes of explanation that can legitimately be endorsed for the scientific study of social objects are reemerging. Economists are again addressing such issues as the relationship between agency and structure, between the economy and the rest of society, and between the enquirer and the object of enquiry. There is a renewed interest in elaborating basic categories such as causation, competition, culture, discrimination, evolution, money, need, order, organisation, power, probability, process, rationality, technology, time, truth, uncertainty, value and so on.

The objective for this series is to facilitate this revival further. In contemporary economics, the label 'theory' has been appropriated by a group that confines itself to largely asocial, ahistorical, mathematical 'modelling'. *Economics as Social Theory* thus reclaims the 'theory' label, offering a platform for alternative rigorous, but broader and more critical, conceptions of theorising.

Other titles in this series include:

ECONOMICS AND LANGUAGE
Edited by Willie Henderson

RATIONALITY, INSTITUTIONS AND ECONOMIC METHODOLOGY
Edited by Uskali Mäki, Bo Gustafsson and Christian Knudsen

NEW DIRECTIONS IN ECONOMIC METHODOLOGY
Edited by Roger Backhouse

WHO PAYS FOR THE KIDS?
Nancy Folbre

RULES AND CHOICE IN ECONOMICS
Viktor Vanberg

BEYOND RHETORIC AND REALISM IN ECONOMICS
Thomas A. Boylan and Paschal F. O'Gorman

FEMINISM, OBJECTIVITY AND ECONOMICS
Julie A. Nelson

ECONOMIC EVOLUTION
Jack J. Vromen

ECONOMICS AND REALITY
Tony Lawson

THE MARKET
John O'Neill

ECONOMICS AND UTOPIA
Geoff Hodgson

CRITICAL REALISM IN ECONOMICS
Edited by Steve Fleetwood

THE NEW ECONOMIC CRITICISM
Edited by Martha Woodmansee and Mark Osteen

WHAT DO ECONOMISTS KNOW?
Edited by Robert F. Garnett, Jr

POSTMODERNISM, ECONOMICS AND KNOWLEDGE
Edited by Stephen Cullenberg, Jack Amariglio and David F. Ruccio

THE VALUES OF ECONOMICS
An Aristotelian perspective
Irene van Staveren

HOW ECONOMICS FORGOT HISTORY
The problem of historical specificity in social science
Geoffrey M. Hodgson

THE VALUES OF ECONOMICS

An Aristotelian perspective

Irene van Staveren

London and New York

First published 2001
by Routledge
11 New Fetter Lane, London EC4P 4EE

Simultaneously published in the USA and Canada
by Routledge
29 West 35th Street, New York, NY 10001

Routledge is an imprint of the Taylor and Francis Group

© 2001 Irene van Staveren

Typeset in Palatino
by Curran Publishing Services Ltd, Norwich
Printed and bound in Great Britain
by Biddles Ltd, Guildford and King's Lynn

British Library Cataloguing in Publication Data
A catalogue record for this book is available from the British
Library

Library of Congress Cataloging in Publication Data
Staveren, Irene van.
The values of economics : an Aristotelian perspective / Irene van
Staveren
p. cm. – (Economics as social theory)
Includes bibliographical references and index.
1. Economics–Philosophy. 2. Economics–Moral and ethical aspects.
3. Aristotle. I. Title. II. Series.

HB72 .S674 2001
330'.01–dc21   00-068430

ISBN (Hbk) 0–415–24182–0
ISBN (Pbk) 0–415–24183–9

CONTENTS

List of figures		viii
List of tables		ix
Preface		x

1	The missing ethical capabilities of rational economic man	1
2	Paradoxes of value	25
3	*Liberté, égalité, fraternité*	58
4	Beyond the highway of modernist economics	88
5	Hypotheses on economic role combination	108
6	Toward an Aristotelian economics	145
7	Institutional mediation between value domains	174
8	Conclusion	202

Notes	209
Bibliography	221
Index	238

FIGURES

2.1 The relations between economic value domains   48
2.2 Some characteristics of economic value domains   57
6.1 The relationship between capabilities and virtues within
     an economic value domain   154
6.2 Excess and deficiency in value domains   161
7.1 The mediating role of institutions within each value
     domain   180

TABLES

4.1   Dualistic reductionism in neoclassical economics   90
4.2   The classes and the virtues   95
5.1   Time-use in paid and unpaid work for women as a
      percentage of men   113
6.1   Externalities spilling over from each value domain   164

PREFACE

Somewhere along the route of modernisation economics has lost its connection to the most basic characteristics of human behaviour. It has come to disregard human motives, emotions, evaluation and the different forms of interaction through which human actors in economic life provide for themselves and for others. With this neglect the discipline not only lost much of its charm but also became less persuasive.

In the days of classical economics, actors in economic life were regarded as individual men and women interacting closely with each other to 'truck, barter and exchange one thing for another' (Adam Smith, *Wealth of Nations* 1776 [1981] Book I, II.i: 25); they were viewed as citizens who agree that the economy should 'supply the state or commonwealth with a revenue sufficient for the public services' (Book IV, introduction: 428); and they were considered vulnerable, interdependent fellow humans 'who stand in need of each other's assistance, and are likewise exposed to mutual injuries. Where the necessary assistance is reciprocally afforded from love, from gratitude, from friendship and esteem, the society flourishes and is happy' (Adam Smith, *Theory of Moral Sentiments* 1759 [1984] Part II, II.iii: 85). However, in today's neoclassical economics *Rational Economic Man* does not care at all.

This book started as a dissertation that attempted to bring human caring, as well as other values underlying economic behaviour, back into economic theory. The consequences of my inquiry turned out to be dramatic. At an earlier stage I thought I could get around the axiomatic methodology of modernist economics by doing empirical research on the role of care in the economy. But I soon found out that I lacked a conceptual framework to do so. Moreover, there were no data to be found except for a few case-by-case time-use studies: nothing to help me understand what caring means in economic life. Yet a theoretical approach was not possible without any empirical insights. The research therefore includes some fieldwork, though not in the familiar form of the testing of hypotheses. The empirical method has an inductive purpose, to generate hypotheses that would inform my theoretical inquiry. This theoretical research required me to demolish doors that had been closed firmly over the past one-and-a-half centuries. I was forced to use unconventional epistemological methods in order to proceed, methods that I had to borrow from virtue ethics, anthropology and chaos theory. Together they gradually came to form a web coherent enough for a conceptualisation of care in economics, next to other values that play a major role in economic life (see on methodological pluralism Bruce Caldwell 1994; Andrea Salanti and Ernesto Screpanti 1997). This book is a reworked version of my dissertation (van Staveren 1999) and argues that economics is, and has always been, about human values, which guide, enable, constrain and change economic behaviour. The reader of this adventurous journey is forewarned about the many turns this book will make to uncover the values of economics.

During my research I felt encouraged by the acknowledgement given by the discipline to other turns away from the highway of the mainstream, as expressed for example in the Nobel Prize 1998 awarded to Amartya Sen. During my research I found out that more and more economists had come to the conclusion that neoclassical economics is 'the same sort of error as to mistake the highway which may be the easiest way of getting to your house or lands for the house and lands themselves' (John Stuart Mill, *Principles of Political Economy* 1848 [1917] Preliminary Remarks: 6).

I could not have pursued this unusual inquiry away from the highway without the support of many people and organisations. The epistemological foundation that I needed to bring caring back into economic theory was the experience of caring myself: giving care and being cared for. Therefore, first and foremost I want to thank my children Sam and Paula and my husband Pablo Curutchet who helped me to understand what caring is. It is only in its daily practices that one begins to understand the value of care. For the same reason I thank my relatives and friends who understood and accepted my ambitious project, on the implicit promise that my individualistic retreat would not take longer than three years. Special thanks go to Hans Schermer, who read through all draft chapters and gave his refreshing comments while re-affirming our friendship.

I thank my supervisor, Arjo Klamer, for his wise, respectful and sympathetic guidance; without his stimulating support, I would certainly have lost my way. Moreover, if he hadn't come back from the United States this dissertation would not have been written. My gratefulness also goes to Deirdre McCloskey and Marian Verkerk who inspired me with their unorthodox ideas on, respectively, economics and ethics. The discussions that I had with them helped me to persevere in my inquiry at the times when I doubted where it would lead me. Thanks go also to all those who commented on my papers at conferences, who discussed the methodological problems that confronted me, and who undertook the work of reading through one or more unclear and unfinished draft chapters: Hans Abbing, Drue Barker, Ton Bevers, Wilfred Dolfsma, Nancy Folbre, Regenia Gagnier,

John Groenewegen, Susanne Janssen, Barbara Krug, Fieke van der Lecq, Ann Mannen, Judith Mehta, Fenneke Reysoo, Selma Sevenhuijsen, Olav Velthuis, Karin Willemse and P. W. Zuidhof. Finally, thanks go to the three anonymous referees who helped me bring out my argument more clearly and address unresolved problems, and to Tony Lawson who has given invaluable advice in the reworking of the text from the form of a dissertation to this book. I am proud that it makes part of his series of *Economics as Social Theory*.

My ideas on this project began more than ten years ago, before the combination of the words 'feminist' and 'economics' grew together to form a sub-field in the discipline. The ideas of feminist economists – as expressed through the first international conference in 1993 organised by Edith Kuiper and Jolande Sap in Amsterdam, the International Association For Feminist Economics (IAFFE), our Feminist Economics Network in the Netherlands (FENN) and later also the Routledge journal *Feminist Economics* – were an enormous help to me. It was the pioneering work of women economists like Diane Elson, Nancy Folbre and Julie Nelson that finally brought me to the subject of the values of economics. Also my work in the field of development policy appeared helpful indirectly: it taught me to keep my feet on the ground, to keep the study close to economic questions and not to drift away into philosophising *about* economics. Therefore, I also thank my former colleagues at the Ministry of Foreign Affairs of the Netherlands who pulled me back into reality every time, Antoinette Gosses, Rita Rahman and Bart van Zwieten. Furthermore, I want to thank the women's movement for keeping on asking me practical questions to which I often did not find an answer but which nevertheless guided this theoretical research. I learned much from the women who spoke so freely in the group interviews. And my engagement in the women-and-development movement through WIDE in Brussels made me realise how urgently we need more human economic policies, more human economic models, more human economic theories. I want to express my gratitude to everyone with whom I have had the opportunity to work along the parallel roads of my activities over the past few years.

I also needed funds to support my project. I hereby want to thank all the organisations that assisted me financially, starting with Erasmus University, whose Faculty of History and Arts provided me with hospitality from 1996 until 1999. Thanks go to my present employer, the Institute of Social Studies, in The Hague, where I was able to rework the text in the summer and autumn of 2000. I also thank the Hanneke van Holk Fonds for funding costs for the interviews in 1997, and the Catharine van Tussenbroek Fonds for funding my participation in a conference on culture and economics in Exeter, summer 1998. Thanks go to the Association for Evolutionary Economics (AFEE) for issuing a prize that included a sum of money with which I was able to buy much needed books. I thank the Vereniging Trustfonds Erasmus Universiteit Rotterdam for funding the costs of travel to Chicago in January 1998 for the AFEE meeting. Thanks also go to the Netwerk Algemene en Kwantitatieve Economie (NAKE) of the University of Amsterdam for subsidising half of the costs of a Ph.D. course in 1996. Furthermore, I want to thank the organisations and people who helped me organise the interviews: CEEWA in Nairobi, the British Council in Yemen, the Dutch embassy in Costa Rica and the staff of the Vrouwen Alliantie in the Netherlands.

Finally, I owe many thanks to the publishers of the following journals where parts of chapters appeared. Part of chapter five was published in *Feminist Economics*, vol. 3, no. 2, 1997 by Taylor & Francis Ltd (http://www.tandf.co.uk); parts of chapter seven have been published in the *Journal of Economic Issues*, vol. 33, no. 1, March 1999 by the Association for Evolutionary Economics and the University of Tennessee.

1

THE MISSING ETHICAL CAPABILITIES OF RATIONAL ECONOMIC MAN

The writer of a book such as this, treading along unfamiliar paths, is extremely dependent on criticism and conversation if he is to avoid an undue proportion of mistakes. It is astonishing what foolish things one can temporarily believe if one thinks too long alone, particularly in economics (along with the other moral sciences), where it is often impossible to bring one's ideas to a conclusive test either formal or experimental.

(John Maynard Keynes 1936: Preface)

A deficient conception of economic rationality

In 1848 a new railway was built in New England (USA). Phineas Gage, a dedicated 25 year old foreman was seriously hurt in an accident with explosives.[1] A 1.10 metre long iron bar weighing six kilos pierced his skull from the left cheek and passed through the front of his brain and the top of his head, landing thirty metres away. Gage lost consciousness only for a short while. He soon stood up, walked, and was able to describe what had happened in a clear and understandable way. The wound was disinfected, high fever was overcome and two months later Gage was declared cured; it seemed he had only lost an eye. More than a century later, a similar type of brain damage happened to a patient named Elliot, an intelligent and successful employee of a business firm in his thirties. He developed brain damage after an operation on a tumour in the front side of his head. The operation was successful and Elliot was sent home.

However, both patients' characters appeared to have undergone dramatic changes. The polite, precise and committed colleague Gage turned into a rude, blasphemous, stubborn and capricious personality, using obscene language and refusing to accept any advice or objections. He lost his job, broke with his family, and ended his life as a vagabond, incapable of planning ahead or earning a living. The other patient,

1

Elliot, seemed just as intelligent and physically strong as before the operation. But he could not function any more in his job; after being fired he tried several other positions, without success. He lost his savings in several ill-fated investments and went bankrupt. His wife divorced him, his children could not cope with him, and a second marriage ended soon in divorce.

At first glance, these men did not appear to have lost their rational capabilities. Gage was able to read and talk, to remember and process information, and to direct his hands to a task as before. He travelled and for a while earned his living as a circus performer, with his inevitable iron bar. The intelligent Elliot (with an above average IQ before and after the tumour) was still good at arithmetic, he kept himself up to date with politics and the world news, he had a reliable memory and could recall every detail about his unfortunate life after the tumour. In short, these patients, like others with damage in the prefrontal cortices of the brain, had not lost their rationality as it is commonly defined in economics.

Yet something seemed to have gone wrong. Personal relationships were broken up and behaviour in the market failed consistently after the brain damage. Loss of jobs, inability to set targets or to keep to them, inefficient time management, foolish investments, bankruptcy and inability to learn from mistakes characterise the economic life of frontal brain damage patients. Gage had become so foul-mouthed that it was impossible to work with him. According to his former colleagues, his presence became particularly offensive for women, who had to put up with ceaseless sexual intimidation. A century later Elliot made himself impossible at work, too. He could spend the whole day calculating the costs and benefits of a new method of ordering files: chronological, or thematic, or according to paper size. (This pattern is reflected in another case where a patient was unable to decide between two proposed dates for a new medical appointment. He endlessly added argument after argument in favour and against both dates without any feeling of inappropriateness. When his doctor became impatient and finally picked a date, the patient happily accepted.)

In a gambling experiment, Elliot consistently lost his money, whereas players without frontal brain damage soon moved to a strategy with low risk. Elliot and the other players received a loan of $2,000 at the beginning of the game. The game consists of a player taking one card at a time from four decks of cards. Some cards result in gains, others in losses. The player does not know how long the game will last, nor what the distribution of the cards over the decks is. He or she is not allowed to keep accounts, nor to make any notes. 'Winning' cards in decks A and B yield approximately a hundred dollars, whereas cards in decks C and D only yield about fifty. But the losing cards in A and B sometimes require payment of over a thousand dollars, while those in C and D impose losses of less than a hundred. These hidden rules are never changed, and the probabilities are impossible to calculate without keeping accounts on paper. Healthy players move within thirty rounds to decks C and D and come out with a net profit. Elliot and similar frontal brain damage patients, in contrast, kept picking cards in A and B which led them to borrow extra money halfway through the game. Elliot lost every game.

The cases of patients Gage and Elliot have been described by the neurobiologist Antonio Damasio (1994). In a way, the patients are the real-life clones of *Rational Economic Man*, in possession of all the conventional characteristics of rationality. They follow their self-interest, they calculate costs and benefits of alternative actions, and they are consistent in their chosen strategies (Shaun Hargreaves Heap *et al.* 1992). After further study of their cases however, their rationality appears deficient. The frontal brain damage patients appear to lack some basic characteristics of rational human behaviour. These shortcomings are brought out in their individual activities and even more so in distorted relationships with others, such as their partners, children, friends, employers and colleagues. Gage and Elliot were somehow unable to function adequately in social and economic life and they failed to make meaningful choices that would improve their lives or, at a minimum, that would provide them with a sufficient livelihood. This deficiency of *Rational Economic Man* has been clearly recognised by feminist economists, for example by Julie Nelson:

> Economic man, the 'agent' of the prototypical economic model, springs up fully formed, with preferences fully developed, and is fully active and self-contained. . . . He interacts in society without being influenced by society: his mode of interaction is through an ideal market in which prices form the only, and only necessary, form of communication. . . . Yet humans do not simply spring out of the earth. Humans are born of women, nurtured and cared for as dependent children, socialised into family and community groups, and are perpetually dependent on nourishment and shelter to sustain their lives.
>
> (Julie Nelson 1996: 31)

Having studied the cases of Phineas Gage, Elliot and other frontal brain damage patients, Antonio Damasio recognises that they lack any notion of ethics that healthy humans have, such as the conception that people tend to have of their lives, meaningful interactions with others, responsible behaviour, judgement and human will:

> Unwittingly, Gage's example indicated that something in the brain was concerned specifically with unique human properties,

among them the ability to anticipate the future and to plan accordingly within a complex social environment; the sense of responsibility towards the self and others; and the ability to orchestrate one's survival deliberately, at the command of one's free will.

(Antonio Damasio 1994: 10)

The neurobiological cases are revealing. They suggest that the assumption of human behaviour in standard economic theory, which ignores the ethical dimensions of rational behaviour, is not a neutral theoretical tool. In fact, the cases support the critique that the standard rationality assumption in economics is a scientific error (Deirdre McCloskey 1996), contributing to the discipline's reputation as a 'dismal science' (Marcel Peeters 1987). The neurobiological cases show that the assumption of *Rational Economic Man* is selective, including some characteristics and excluding others, without an apparent empirical basis, as has been argued within the economic discipline for some time (Marianne Ferber and Julie Nelson 1993; Nancy Folbre 1994; Tony Lawson 1997; Harvey Leibenstein 1976; Genevieve Lloyd 1984; Shaun Hargreaves Heap 1989; Hargreaves Heap *et al.* 1992; Robert Heilbroner 1988; Arjo Klamer, Deirdre McCloskey and Robert Solow 1988; Uskali Mäki, Bo Gustafsson and Christian Knudsen 1993; Jane Mansbridge 1990; Philip Mirowski 1989; Nelson 1996; Amartya Sen 1977, 1981, 1987, 1993a; Amartya Sen and Bernard Williams 1982; Mary Zey 1992). Moreover, the selectivity of the rationality concept in mainstream economics is biased in favour of a narrow mechanistic view of man and against the experiences of men and women in real life: people with needs and with capabilities. Mainstream economic rationality is restricted to a white, western and masculine interpretation of reason. In this construction, reason, self-interest and calculation, all captured in distinct masculine metaphors, are opposed to emotions, other-regarding motives and intuition, which are almost by default connected to the feminine (Susan Bordo 1986; Ferber and Nelson 1993; Folbre 1994; McCloskey 1985; Nelson 1996; William Waller 1995). The gender critique is confirmed in Damasio's study. He found that the missing components in frontal brain damage patients' rationality are moral, emotional, deliberative and social, together shaping an individual's ethical capabilities, regardless of one's sex.[2] What follows from Damasio's empirical research into the substance of human rationality is that *Rational Economic Man* seems to represent a pathological case and not an abstraction of healthy, ordinary human behaviour.

The increasingly full critique of the neoclassical economic rationality assumption provides the starting point for this book. The chapters that follow will therefore *not* present a summary or a discussion of the literature that criticises the rationality concept, nor will this book add to it, since the subject has been treated extensively and thoroughly already. I will largely take the existing critique as given and build on that.

From this starting point, the purpose of this book is twofold. First, I will undertake an inquiry into the missing ethical capabilities in the rationality construct of neoclassical economics, capabilities that will suggest a very different notion of rationality, not merely some 'add-ons'. In other words, I intend to seek an understanding of economic rationality that does not present an image of a human being that has an iron bar stuck in the head. Second, I will analyse the consequences of such an alternative notion of rational economic behaviour for other central notions in economics, without, however, implying another micro foundation for macro behaviour. Acknowledgement of morality (Daniel Hausman and Michael McPherson 1993), of emotions in economic behaviour (Jon Elster 1998; Robert Frank 1988), of endogenous preferences (Samuel Bowles 1998), of interdependence of economic behaviour (Maarten Janssen 1993; Thomas Schelling 1978), of the embodiedness of economic behaviour (Susan Feiner 1994; Ferber and Nelson 1993; Folbre 1994; Jean Gardiner 1997; Gillian Hewitson 1999; Edith Kuiper and Jolande Sap 1995; Nelson 1996), and of other elements of human nature that were still part of political economics in the days of Adam Smith, help to sketch a more realistic picture of rationality, making possible more realistic explanations of economic behaviour (Lawson 1997).

Recognising the extent and relevance of the critique of the conventional rationality concept, we are in need of a different terminology to refer to healthy rational human beings without the pathologies of *Rational Economic Man*. In my search for a better terminology I have rejected the term 'agent' because it has a strong legalistic and individualistic connotation. I have also rejected the notion of 'economic man' because of its masculine and dichotomous implications. The idea of economic man suggests that he (*sic*) should naturally be distinguished from a stereotypical 'economic woman' or, alternatively, that he should be set against a 'social man'.[3] I have opted for the term 'actor', following Harvey Leibenstein (1976: 71). The word 'actor' embraces all participants in economic life and it expresses the idea that economic behaviour implies inter-acting with others in the social realm, rather than disembedded and disembodied individualistic actions on spot markets. Also, use of the word 'actor' later on enables a smooth link with the position that actors take in economic life, or their 'roles'.

Now that the deficiency of the conventional rationality concept has been recognised as having an ethical dimension, we need to find a theory of ethics that will help to fill the gap. The next section will argue for one such theory: Aristotle's theory of virtue ethics. I will start with a brief summary of his theory, that I hope will help the reader to recognise the Aristotelian approach taken in subsequent chapters.

The ethics of rationality

It is perhaps not a coincidence that Damasio's identification of missing ethical capabilities runs parallel to the major lines of critique by economists on the conventional notion of rationality. This suggests that an alternative, inclusive notion of rationality should address the ethical capabilities of rational human behaviour. In Greek philosophy, such a perspective can be found with Aristotle. His *Nichomachean Ethics* (*NE*) not only includes the ethical capabilities that are missing in *Rational Economic Man*, but actually builds on these elements.

Aristotle's theory of ethics, also called virtue ethics, is explicitly phrased as a theory of rational human behaviour, of 'practical wisdom' (*phronesis*), which is 'a true and reasoned state of capacity to act with regard to the things that are good or bad for man' (*NE:* 142). For Aristotle there is no dualism between reason and emotion, between calculation and intuition, between individual and collective behaviour. The main reason why such dualism is absent in his ethics, and why the neoclassical rationality assumption is defective, is that human beings pursue ends that are important in themselves, intrinsic ends, rather than exogenous preferences instrumental to some undefined 'utility'. In other words, Aristotle argues that human beings have commitments, rather than preferences:

> If, then, there is some end of the things we do, which we desire for its own sake (everything else being desired for the sake of this), and if we do not choose everything for the sake of something else (for at that rate the process would go on to infinity, so that our desire would be empty and vain), clearly this must be the good and the chief good.
>
> (*NE:* 1–2)

Being virtuous implies being committed to what is good, while the pursuit of the good makes one virtuous. The definition of the good is human flourishing, or *eudaimonia* (*NE:* 12), according to Aristotle. This is not singular, or commensurable as in utilitarianism, but plural: 'But of honour, wisdom and pleasure, just in respect of their goodness, the accounts are distinct and diverse. The good, therefore, is not something common answering to one Idea' (*NE:* 9–10). On the contrary, the good is plural and valuable in its own terms, 'self-sufficient', as Aristotle puts it (*NE:* 12). Moreover, the good is contextual, not absolute: 'Now different things appear to be good for different people, and, if it so happens, even contrary things' (*NE:* 58). There are no universal standards of the good. It is in the context of daily activities that virtue is practised (*NE:* 28): in the household, politics, the labour market, the military, friendship and in any other 'sphere of actualisation' (*NE:* 31). Therefore, in the absence of absolute standards, the good, or virtue, has to be sought through trial and error, in between excess and deficiency, as between rashness and cowardliness in the case of the virtue of courage. In other words, virtue is a mean between extremes, a mean that can be found only in practice, in relation with other human beings and the context of practices. 'These acts cannot be prescribed exactly, but must avoid excess and defect' (*NE:* 30) is all that Aristotle is able to give as advice on how to become virtuous. There exist no prescriptions, no behavioural laws, and hence, no moral rules as they appear in most other ethical theories. In order to clarify this contextual character of Aristotle's ethics, I will quote Aristotle's account of the virtuous mean at length:

> But though our present account is of this nature we must give what help we can. First, then, let us consider this, that it is the nature of such things to be destroyed by defect and excess, as we see in the case of strength and of health (for to gain light on things imperceptible we must use the evidence of sensible things); exercise either excessive or defective destroys the strength, and similarly drink or food which is above or below a certain amount destroys the health, while that which is proportionate both produces and increases and preserves it. So too is it, then, in the case of temperance and courage and the other virtues. For the man who flies from and fears everything and does not stand his ground against anything becomes a coward, and the man who fears nothing at all but goes to meet every danger becomes rash; and similarly the man who indulges in every pleasure and abstains from none becomes self-indulgent, while the man who shuns every pleasure, as boors do, becomes in a way insensible; temperance and courage, then, are destroyed by excess and defect, and preserved by the mean.
>
> (*NE:* 30–1)

Thus, according to Aristotle, human beings have ends that are of a pluralist ethical character, as ends in themselves, as commitments, if, and only if, humans succeed in pursuing them well, which is by no means guaranteed or easy. Merely having commitments to human values is clearly not enough. In addition to commitments, therefore, Aristotle refers to emotions. He calls our attention to the positive emotion of pleasure that one enjoys as part of virtue, as belonging to the pursuit of the good: 'so the pleasures intensify the activities, and what intensifies a thing is proper to it, but things different in kind have properties different in kind' (*NE:* 258). So virtue is not a hardship but pleasurable for those who pursue valuable ends well, with different emotions experienced as different virtues are pursued. In fact, the emotions help human beings to become virtuous, but they should not be confused with virtue itself, 'because we are not called good or bad on the ground of our passions' (*NE*: 36). Emotions thus appear to have a supportive role in the human pursuit of valuable ends.

The same is true of deliberation, another characteristic of virtue mentioned by Aristotle. Deliberation is part of virtuous behaviour since it indicates *how* to pursue virtue, namely, as a voluntary act of human will, as a deliberate choice. 'Moral virtue implies that the action is done by choice: the object of choice is the result of previous deliberation' (*NE*: 53). The ends, as I have indicated, are defined by the good, by human flourishing. Thus deliberation is not so much about ends as about means, or the 'how' (*NE*: 56). Unlike neoclassical economic rationality, deliberation is different from constrained maximisation. It is an act of human will, real choice, rather than the determinate outcome of an algorithm, depending on external constraints: 'choice is deliberate desire of things in our own power' (*NE*: 55).

The final ethical capability that Aristotle recognises is the social aspect of virtue. He refers to virtue throughout his book as 'in the eyes of other men'. Hence virtue can only be achieved at the social level, since it has no meaning without others. Human beings can act virtuously only in relation to others, as they are social beings. This is clarified in Aristotle's examples of virtues, which all involve one's attitude toward others; they include responsibility, temperance, liberality, friendliness, truthfulness, ready wit and justice (*NE*: 62–106). Aristotle's *Nichomachean Ethics* thus, as I have indicated far too briefly earlier, is built on, first, a commitment to moral values, second, emotion, third, deliberation and, fourth, human interaction.

The implications of Aristotle's ethical theory have not completely gone unnoticed by economists. Amartya Sen, for example, in *On Ethics and Economics* (Sen 1987), has referred to Aristotle arguing that economics is necessarily about ethics (ibid.: 3, 6, 9), when discussing human ends as commitments (ibid.: 6), when arguing against utilitarianism (ibid.: 46), or when defining ends as functionings that together define human well-being as flourishing and consisting of capabilities (ibid.: 46 and 64). Others have referred to Aristotle's *Nichomachean Ethics* as well, including John O'Neill (1998) in his critique of markets and Robert Solomon (1996) on the role of virtue in corporate life. However, the best known economic interpretation of Aristotle's ethics is that of Scott Meikle (1995), entitled *Aristotle's Economic Thought*. His book is a detailed discussion of book V.5 of the *Nichomachean Ethics*, which deals with justice in exchange. Meikle argues that Aristotle rightly separated use value from exchange value, as belonging to different categories (Meikle 1995: 8 and 17). He explains that Aristotle derived his distinction between use and exchange value from metaphysics, or ontology (the theory of being). In Aristotelian ontology, there is a clear distinction between substances and their attributes.[4] Therefore, Aristotle maintained, goods simply cannot be defined by their use value and by their exchange value at the same time. '"Use value" as a collective term collects substances as substances, that is, the things they are by nature, and so use value is necessarily quantitatively differentiated and heterogeneous' (Meikle 1995: 17). Again, a major difference from neoclassical economics becomes apparent:

> The metaphysical gulf Aristotle establishes between use value and exchange value makes it quite impossible, consistently with his metaphysics, to achieve the object of the neoclassical theory of Jevons, Gossen, Walras, and Menger. That object was, in Schumpeter's words, to show 'what A. Smith, Ricardo, and Marx had believed to be impossible, namely, that exchange value can be explained in terms of use value'. To achieve such a merger, it is necessary to reject the Aristotelian metaphysics of substance and attribute.
>
> (Meikle 1995: 18)

Nevertheless, various neoclassical economists have portrayed Aristotle as 'the father of subjective, utilitarian, or neoclassical value theory', as Meikle observes, referring, among others, to Mark Blaug (1991).[5] In neoclassical economics, fair exchange and actual exchange are assumed necessarily to coincide, because contracts are agreed voluntarily. But for Aristotle this was not necessarily the case: there could be unfair exchange, by the unjust man, as Meikle notes. The far-reaching conclusion which Meikle derives from his study of a small part of the *Nichomachean Ethics*, namely that for Aristotle ethics and economics are separate (Meikle 1995: 109, 196), is however surprising and unjustified (see also Steve Fleetwood 1997). Meikle himself has acknowledged that Aristotle not only linked the concepts of exchange and justice, but also that he did so in a clear, convincing way. He has also recognised Aristotle's view that the virtuous man cannot only be found in politics or private life, but in economic life as well. I agree that Aristotle did not come up with a theory of exchange value (Meikle 1995: 42), partly due to a lack of a notion of labour and commensurability. But it goes too far and is in fact unnecessary to claim that therefore Aristotle did not make any contribution to economics. I would rather accept Amartya Sen's interpretation referred to earlier, that Aristotle did say important things about economics, and indeed made important, though implicit, links between ethics and economics (though not between use value and exchange value).

Aristotle's ontology, distinguishing between substances and attributes, and the application of this idea to virtues, has an essentialist flavour which in these postmodern days tends to be met with fierce critique, and often rightly so. Again, we meet with a factor that distinguishes Aristotelian rationality from the neoclassical notion of rationality. Whereas in neoclassical economics human actors are pictured as disembodied and disembedded individualists who only have subjective preferences that cannot be compared between individuals, Aristotelian ethics implies that there is a shared though differentiated human nature. Human beings share ethical capabilities that are not found in other animals and that distinguish them from other animals, Aristotle claims (see also Philippa Foot 1978). 'The character, then, must somehow be there already with a kinship to virtue, loving what is noble and hating what is base' (*NE*: 271). It is important to note, though, contrary to the interpretation of many critics of Aristotle's essentialism, that Aristotle only claimed a *shared human tendency to become* virtuous and *not* a virtuous human nature. 'Neither by nature, then, nor contrary to nature do the virtues arise in us; rather we are adapted by nature to receive them, and are made perfect by habit' (*NE*: 28).

Critics of Aristotle's essentialism do have a point, though less so on the *Ethics* than on his *Politics* and, even more so, on his works on biology. In these studies, Aristotle displays a type of essentialism that is expressed at the inter-human level. He held that human natures differed between free men and slaves, between men and women, and between inhabitants of different cities (such as Athens and Sparta). Feminist scholars in particular have criticised this dimension of Aristotle's essentialism, and rightly so, because of its misogynist nature (Jean Bethke Elshtain 1981; Aafke Komter 1995; Lynda Lange 1983; Susan Moller Okin 1979; Arlene Saxonhouse 1985; Elizabeth Spelman 1983; for a feminist economic critique, see Drue Barker 1995). Cynthia Freeland (1998) puts the point very clearly:

> it is hard, after all, to forget such notorious assertions as the claim that a man's virtue is to command, a women's to obey; that women have fewer teeth than men; or that we contribute nothing but matter to our offspring.
>
> (Freeland 1998: 2)

John Stuart Mill already recognised and rejected this form of essentialism in Aristotle:

> Aristotle held this opinion without doubt or misgiving; and rested it on the same premises on which the same assertion in regard to the dominion of men over women is usually based, namely that there are different natures among mankind, free natures, and slave natures.
>
> (Mill 1869: 137)

Recently, feminist revisions of Aristotle have gone beyond wholesale rejections of Aristotle's work (Cynthia Freeland 1998; Ruth Groenhout 1998; Martha Nussbaum 1998). Ruth Groenhout, for example, rejects Aristotle's inter-human essentialism, but admits that:

> there is a sense in which the proponent of an Aristotelian or virtue-oriented theory will need to accept some degree of essentialism with respect to human nature. A theory that relies on a conception of human flourishing for its development is dependent on some account of what humans ought to try to become if it is to have any content at all.[6]

(Groenhout 1998: 180)

But there is a thin line between accepting basic characteristics of human nature by defining human rationality, and listing specific ends for all humanity. The first seems necessary for any meaningful theory of human behaviour, including economic behaviour. The second however leans to universalism and absolutism, the other extreme *vis-à-vis* post-modernist and neoclassical economic relativism and subjectivism. For example, Martha Nussbaum's well-intended listing of human capabilities runs exactly this risk of presuming or prescribing universal moral values, even though she claims not to do so (Nussbaum 1995). On the list, Nussbaum states that: 'My claim is that a life that lacks any one of these capabilities, no matter what else it has, will fall short of being a good human life' (ibid: 85). The list of ends, or functionings, that Nussbaum has made includes for example the fulfilment of sexual desire (Nussbaum 1995: 77), which however may not be a necessity in everyone's life.[7] Given human differences, it is not only impossible but also undesirable to develop an exhaustive list of capabilities for human beings everywhere at all times. Rather than trying to define these in such detail, we need a more open-ended account of needs, ends and capabilities, one open to continuous transformation (Lawson 1999). Aristotle's ethical theory seems exactly such a theory, balancing between the extremes of, on the one hand, subjectivist and relativist theories of human behaviour and, on the other hand, theories that assume universal needs and ends, and rule-based ways in which these are connected. In other words, Aristotle's virtue ethics seems a theory of human behaviour that seeks a mean between under-determination and over-determination (Mark Granovetter 1985; Lawson 1997).

In the next four sections, I will briefly discuss each of the four ethical capabilities that are missing in the neoclassical notion of rationality but have such a central place in Aristotle's virtue ethics. I will do so with help of critiques of the conventional rationality concept that have been raised within the discipline.

11

Moral commitment

Rational Economic Man is assumed to follow his self-interest. He sets out to realise his strictly individual and subjective preferences straightforwardly. These preferences are instrumental to only one final end: utility maximisation, subject to constraints. This cost–benefit based behavioural assumption does not allow for adaptation of the individual's ends in response to social needs or personal re-evaluations. Nor are ends shared with others: individual utility is independent of the utilities of other people, and cannot even be compared to them because of the presumed subjectivity of individual utility. The ends which *Rational Economic Man* pursues are only valued as long as they contribute to his own utility (including the emotional utility of doing good or the utility resulting from preventing shame). This assumption of self-interested utility maximisation rejects ends as valuable in themselves. But how can *Rational Economic Man* pursue valuable ends without having any notion of what values mean? Or, in other words, how can he provide for himself and allow others to provide for themselves without understanding the importance of the ends in his life?

The frontal brain damage patients lost their sense of human values and the responsibility involved in a commitment to these values. They forgot what it was to function as a good worker, dedicating time efficiently to productive tasks in a fruitful relationship with other employees. Instead, Gage made himself insufferable among his co-workers while Elliot wasted his employer's time on useless arrangements of files. Employers could not keep them on; the patients' attitude had made them unproductive. These patients were no longer endowed with a sense of politeness, reliability, zeal, or fairness. They had lost every sense of appropriateness; they had lost their commitment to the human values they had been raised with and that were shared in the community in which they lived and acted. The frontal brain damage patients behaved disrespectfully and irresponsibly, not only to others but also to themselves: they were no longer able to provide for themselves.

They failed not only in their personal lives but also economically. This seems odd: the patients' rationality parallels the prescriptions of rationality in economics but none the less they failed to maximise their utility. Apparently, rational economic actors need to have valuable ends to pursue rather than a set of indifferent functions. Also the assumption of 'self-interest' does not suffice to guarantee utility maximisation: it does not clarify anything about actor's identity – 'self' – nor what would really be in his or her 'interest' (Mansbridge 1990). That is why alternatives have been proposed such as expressive rationality (Hargreaves Heap 1989), purposeful agency and purposeful choice (Folbre 1994), or situated rationality (Lawson 1997). Self-interest can include anything and is therefore conceptually self-defeating. Amartya Sen has illustrated this incapacity with the notion of the 'rational fool'. The rational fool provides a striking analogue to patients like Gage and Elliot. Sen illustrates the irrationality of the conventional rationality assumption based on self-interest when applied to an ordinary question.

> 'Where is the railway station?' he asks me. 'There,' I say, pointing at the post office. 'And would you please post this letter for me on the way?' 'Yes,' he says, determined to open the envelope and check whether it contains something valuable.
>
> (Sen 1977: 332)

Sen argues instead that people act upon their commitments rather than for instrumental ends (Klamer 1989), even when they compromise their own well-being from an instrumental point of view. Their commitment 'drives a wedge between personal choice and personal welfare' (Sen 1977: 329). Another illustration of the relevance of commitment rather than self-interested, instrumental ends is that of a man who is determined to stop a fight even if he gets hurt in so doing (Sen 1992). Even in an ex-post evaluation, this man's behaviour can be judged as rational, no matter what the outcome of a utilitarian calculation of physical pain versus psychological satisfaction would turn out to be. Stopping the fight was the only reasonable action for the man in question, motivated by his values (see also Richard Langlois and László Csontos 1993). Self-interest provides no meaningful explanation for his behaviour.[8]

Commitment to values that are, at least to some extent, shared within a community does provide an explanation for such unselfish behaviour, since the motive resides in the value itself: commitment has intrinsic value and intrinsic motivation (Bruno Frey 1997). The ends that economic actors value are valued for their own sake and are self-rewarding: the ends are pursued because they feel right (see, for example, Daniel Batson 1997; Daniel Batson *et al.* 1997; Nelson Goodman 1983; Martin Hollis 1987; Samuel Oliner and Pearl Oliner 1988). In the labour market, intrinsic motivation may be found in fairness involved in the work relation, the quality of work relationships, the quality of the task, and participation and responsibility in the decision making process about one's work. Where these dimensions of working life are rewarding, a direct appeal to self-interest through higher external rewards can even be counterproductive. As Bruno Frey (1997) argues, it crowds out the intrinsic motivation inherent in commitment: increasing external rewards can undermine the very values that motivate actors. External rewards only tend to reward production outcomes, *not* the eventual social good, the teamwork and the creative processes that make the outcomes possible. Monetary incentives, then, can only partially explain behaviour, and very unreliably so.

13

The intrinsic motivation of commitment should, however, *not* be confused with altruism. Commitment is not the opposite of self-interest. Commitment is neither self-interest nor altruism and does not conform to the dualism that has been constructed between these two motives (for a critique of such a dualism, see Paula England 1993; Nelson 1996). Rather, it refers to the valuation of ends in themselves, not for one's own benefit nor for the exclusive benefit of someone else (see also Folbre 1994: 28). Hence, the valuable ends that economic actors pursue cannot be pictured in terms of interest, nor are they instrumental. To return to Sen's example of the fight: the person stopping the fight acts on the basis of a commitment to peaceful conflict resolution or some other value, not to increase his pleasure (self-interest) nor to please one of the fighters (altruism); he may not even know or want to know the men involved in the fight.

Commitment refers to a value, not to a person who may benefit from pursuing it, although furthering a value involves support for the people who share it. To extend freedom, for example, helps those who care about freedom. By contributing to a value, economic actors further the value for the whole community in which it is shared, including him- or herself. Commitment thus contests the dichotomy between the self and the other: the one implies the other when shared values are the ends that actors seek to pursue.[9] But an individual's contribution to the furthering of particular values can only go so far. The actor's commitment is sustained by the hope or belief that others will also contribute to the shared value (Robyn Dawes, Alphons van de Kragt and John Orbell 1990; Elster 1983, 1992). In other words, this hope or belief supports the intrinsic motivation belonging to each value. When others no longer share a particular value and no longer contribute to its furthering, intrinsic motivation may depreciate for everyone until in the end hardly anyone will be committed to the initial value. At the same time, values are contested in a community by those who seek to change their meaning or who adhere to different beliefs (Barbara Herrnstein Smith 1988). Values, and individual commitments to them, are not universal givens; they change from time to time and from place to place and between different groups of people. At the same time commitments are developed, maintained, justified and challenged in the dynamic evolvement of human interaction.

> All value is radically contingent, being neither a fixed attribute, an inherent quality, or an objective property of things but, rather, an effect of multiple, continuously changing, and continuously interacting variables or, to put this another way, the product of the dynamics of a system, specifically an *economic system*.
>
> (Herrnstein Smith 1988: 30, emphasis in original)

14

When fewer and fewer people share a particular value, the contributions to it will decrease. Consequently the hope that others will continue to contribute will also decrease, which will further undermine the value. New values may arise or different expressions of the same value may take the place of the old, leading to different and partially shared commitments among actors in social, political and economic life.

Rational Economic Man cannot do without commitments. He needs to have them in order to be able to behave rationally in economic life, to earn his living and to allow others to earn theirs. However, commitments do not stand on their own; they need to be perceived, expressed and sustained (Avinash Dixit and Barry Nalebuff 1991: chapter 6).

Emotion

Rational Economic Man is endowed with given preferences that he seeks to satisfy. Yet he does not seem to feel emotionally attached to them; it is as if they appear arbitrary to him and do not matter substantially. His preferences are exogenously attributed to him and he is assumed to be indifferent to them. Why then does he put so much effort into satisfying these particular preferences when a different set of preferences would be easier to satisfy? In other words, why would he stick to an arbitrary set of preferences if he does not really care about them?[10]

Gage and Elliot saw their relationships with friends, partners, children and colleagues collapse and made no effort to sustain the bonds. They did not feel sorry or embarrassed when interactions went awry. In a test of patients' capabilities for emotional evaluation they watched a slide show and were asked to report later what they saw and how they felt about it. Most slides showed dull scenery or uninteresting abstract patterns. Some slides however showed disturbing pictures, such as homicides. The emotional reactions were measured by means of skin conductivity, which records changes in the autonomic nervous system. Participants in a control group had a distinct reaction, while frontal brain damage patients did not show any reaction at all. In the personal reports a significant difference between the patients and the control group appeared. Like the people in the control group, the patients were able to describe fear, disgust, or sadness related to the relevant pictures. But one of them noted that, in spite of realising that some of the pictures ought to be disturbing, he himself was not disturbed. The patients did not feel frightened, disgusted, or sad when looking at these particular slides. They somehow were not able to care, even when remembering from their healthy past that they ought to. A lack of emotion, however, hampers rational decision making since emotion is important to that process, as Damasio argues: 'feelings are just as cognitive as any other perceptual image, and just as dependent on cerebral-cortex processing as any other image' (Damasio 1994: 159).[11]

Exceptions to the neglect of emotion in economic analysis can be found in the work of Robert Frank (1988) and Jon Elster (1998), who draw attention to the importance of emotional attachment in economic behaviour. Frank argues that in economic life we face important problems that simply cannot be solved by the conventional construct of rationality. In his view, people do not simply act upon given preferences but feel emotionally committed to the valuable ends in their lives. The emotions that support people's commitments can be negative ones like guilt, fear, or disgust, or they may be positive like appreciation or the feeling of pride. We feel emotionally attached to our ends because they matter to us: we are committed to this particular set of ends and not to another (for this argument in sociology, see Émile Durkheim 1915: 207–8 and 1992: 112; the argument can be found in philosophy, for example, in Martha Nussbaum 1986 and 1990, and Justin Oakly 1992). When we find out that we were wrong in pursuing these ends, we will generally try to make up for the mistake and adapt our ends accordingly, consciously or unconsciously, as explained by the theory of cognitive dissonance (Leon Festinger 1957).

Emotions help attach us to our ends but they should not be confused with the ends themselves. People can be enchanted by their toddlers or proud of their adolescent children's developing talents, but it is their children in all their surprising developments who represent the parents' ends, not the emotions they evoke (though these are not irrelevant: such moments of delight seem needed to make parenthood bearable). Parents tend to melt with their son's first word or step, and they feel proud of their daughter's swimming diploma. But generally, people do not have children merely for the sake of these feelings. It is not emotions that represent the ends people seek. Rather, emotions help sustain people's commitments. They express one's care for one's valuable ends. Elster rightly argues for recognition of their role in our adherence to the ends we value in life.

> This, presumably, is why artists are artists, scientists scientists, and so on. They do not engage in art or science to get a thrill, but to 'get it right', and yet the thrill they get when they get it right strengthens their motivation to do this kind of work.
>
> (Elster 1983: 107)

For scientists it is a peculiar mix of emotions and rewards that seems to support their commitment to science, as Deirdre McCloskey asserts: 'The human scientists pursue persuasiveness, prettiness, the resolution of puzzlement, the conquest of recalcitrant details, the feeling of a job well done, and the honour and income of office' (McCloskey 1985: 46).

In their role of attaching the actors' wills to their commitments, emotions help also to express these commitments to others. Emotive responses serve as signals in interaction with others (as blushing can be a signal of cheating). The signals help to develop durable relationships and to build a reliable reputation in the eyes of others: they communicate actors' commitments to each other and help to build a reputation based on these commitments through signalling unconditional moves and the keeping of promises (Dixit and Nalebuff 1991: 143).

> Thus, when we see that a person has never been caught cheating, we have reason to believe that this behaviour is motivated, at least in part, by non-material rewards. And herein lies the kernel of truth in our belief that reputations matter.
>
> (Frank 1988: 84)

An example can be found in bargaining games. Those which allow for communication, which involve people who know each other, or where personal differences are expressed and respected, result in higher levels of co-operation than games which do not allow for such community characteristics to develop, as is the case in the Prisoner's Dilemma Game (Michael Argyle 1991: 52). Dixit and Nalebuff argue that these social characteristics have proven to be most effective in repeated co-operative bargaining games – more effective than Axelrod's famous tit-for-tat strategy. Most effective seem to be strategies that are forgiving, that is, strategies that express care for each other, or 'sympathy and benevolence' to use Adam Smith's terms.[12]

Emotions seem to be an integral part of rational behaviour, with links both to rational actors' ends and the methods they choose. This brings me to another capability that our poor *Rational Economic Man* lacks: the capability to deliberate.

Deliberation

Rational Economic Man calculates costs and benefits in the attempt to maximise his utility, under constraints. But given the nature of this calculative process he is in fact not able to choose. His free will is reduced to the mere following of an algorithm. There is a unique outcome dictated by the shape of his preference function and the position of the budget restriction. Rationality comes down to the calculation of a determinate outcome, with no acknowledgement of human will (James Buchanan 1969; Geoffrey Hodgson 1988; Langlois and Csontos 1993; Lawson 1997; Thorstein Veblen 1919).[13] Besides, *Rational Economic Man* is unable to perceive risks, let alone uncertainty, living as he is often supposed to do in a dream world of perfect information and certainty. When imperfect information is acknowledged the problem is generally solved with the aid of the additional assumption of rational expectations, which assumes probabilistic risks rather than uncertainty as expounded by Frank Knight (1921). Otherwise, *Rational Economic Man* is confronted in his models with multiple equilibria among which he finds himself unable to choose. In short, he is unable to cope with the contingencies of real economic life that cannot be resolved through constrained maximisation. Where then does choice come in? And how do economic actors choose between different commitments with intrinsic value that cannot be traded off against one another? How is choice possible if there is no single scale to measure the costs and benefits of each alternative, as is assumed in a utility function?

The brain damage patient who kept adding arguments in favour of and against two dates for an appointment neatly followed the algorithm. His problem was, however, that at each stage the information appeared imperfect. He did not feel the impropriety and futility of the extraordinary time use of his decision making process. At each stage he came up with new possible states of affairs as inputs for the algorithm, not put off by any inconvenient emotion. Ever more information was available. Endless reasons could be found to choose the early date, but an equal number could be produced in favour of the alternative. He stuck to the calculations, unable to make a choice for one or the other option. Making a choice demands deliberation, an expression of will power and drawing on context with a due sense of appropriateness, but the patient was not able to make such a choice.

When Elliot participated in a gambling game experiment he followed in each game the high-risk strategy of decks A and B and lost money. When he was asked about his strategy after the game he told the organisers of the experiment that he was risk averse. The other players, recognising the uselessness of looking for an algorithm, followed their intuition and made responsible choices. They may not have fully maximised utility but they were clearly better off than Elliot. In terms of non-monetary utility also, Elliot did worse than the control group. Non-monetary utilitarian gains would lie in a psychological satisfaction derived from risk-taking. The monetary costs of losing the game might be compensated by the psychological satisfaction of playing a high-risk game: the kind of utility sought by real gamblers. But there was no such rationale behind Elliot's gambling performance. He did not experience high-risk utility since he had expressed his dislike of risk: he described himself as a 'conservative, low-risk person' (Damasio 1994: 214). So, both in terms of monetary reward and of non-monetary utility (the fun of playing a risky game), Elliot's behaviour in the gambling experiment was significantly less rational than the behaviour of the control group in which participants relied on their intuition and made judgements relating to the contextual knowledge that they gradually developed on decks A, B, C and D during the game. Elliot was irresponsible to himself and unhappy with the outcomes of his strategy. His strategy did not seem to comply with a 'revealed preference'.

In real life, humans are mentally incapable of doing the calculations that the neoclassical rationality assumption requires, and they have only imperfect information to inform their calculations (Herbert Simon 1982, 1983). Economic actors cannot possibly calculate the algorithm assumed by standard economic rationality. They satisfy rather than maximise, 'reconciling alternative points of view and different weightings of values' (Simon 1983: 85). Here, Simon seems to refer to the commitment people have to their goals, commitments that are different but all valuable. 'The underlying assumption is that if these procedures are followed, then, in some long-run sense, the decisions reached will be tolerable, or even desirable' (ibid.: 90). Simon assumes that the problem is only one of bounded rationality, in which rules can do the job that utilitarian calculation cannot. The problem is, however, that rules may help but they do not always apply. And often rules are not available, since the weighing of values requires not principles but judgements (Hargreaves Heap 1989; McCloskey and Klamer 1995).

The ends that economic actors value are diverse; each matters in its own right and cannot be selected according to a set of behavioural rules (Hargreaves Heap 1989; Uskali Mäki, Bo Gustafsson and Christian Knudsen 1993), though rules may help in deliberation. Nor can the ends be selected on utilitarian grounds since they have intrinsic value (Stuart Hampshire 1983; Herrnstein Smith 1988) and derive from a mixture of motives (Mansbridge 1990). Each commitment of the various actors is valuable in its own right and therefore, taken together, they are incommensurable. There is no trade-off between different commitments since there is no single scale along which the different ends can be measured. Nevertheless, economic actors have to make choices, real choices in a world of uncertainty. They choose with help from the particular context in which they interact. They are guided by shared and contested values, without the certainty of moral rules. They follow their commitments, knowing the conflicts implied among different intrinsic values. Hence, they cannot and do not *calculate* but *deliberate*, using a mix of interpretation, reflection, tacit knowledge, rules of thumb and free will. Such deliberation is a careful process of intuitive reasoning rather than calculation, involving emotion rather than an algorithm, and evaluating pluralist commitments within changing contexts rather than following utility maximisation.[14] What counts are the valuations that constitute people's very being, their 'self'. Hence, deliberation expresses our selves, our identity, through the ends we pursue and upon which we act (Hollis 1987).

Finally, one more deficiency in *Rational Economic Man* needs to be addressed: he needs to interact with other actors in the economic process.

Human interaction

Rational Economic Man is supposed to further the ends that are important to him. It was argued above that he cannot do so without being committed to certain values, without emotion and without deliberation. Now he also needs to interact with others. In the complex social world in which he finds himself, he needs to communicate with others and to seek their willingness to co-operate. Ultimately, he needs to engage in relationships with other actors in the economy. It is at the social level that the economy operates, through the interaction between its actors. At this level *Rational Economic Man* would find that other people's simultaneous actions influence his own: actors in economic life are interdependent. The assumption that individual *Rational Economic Men* act bilaterally and sequentially ignores the social dimensions of human interaction. How can *Rational Economic Man* engage with others in economic transactions if he lacks the capacity for human interaction? How can he persuade others to interact with him without establishing and continuing any relationships?

Phineas Gage, after the accident with the iron bar, was good at 'always finding something which did not suit him', a medical doctor observed (Damasio 1994: 8).

> In fact, he moved around, occasionally finding work as a labourer in the area. It is clear that he was not an independent person and that he could not secure the type of steady, remunerative job that he had once held.
>
> (Damasio 1994: 9)

The use of the word 'independent' is important here. Paradoxically, people need to relate to each other if they want to become independent; that is, economically speaking they can only secure a living by *interacting* with others in the economy. Individual action presupposes the relationships of interaction, whatever form these interactions take: negotiation in exchange, the following of agreed distributive rules, or mutual sharing of gifts. The character of each relationship is different, depending on the particular context defining the interactions. A negotiating relationship between entrepreneurs is different from the caring relationship with those you are intimately affiliated with. But *Rational Economic Man* is not fit for any interaction. He is constructed as totally independent, disembodied and subjective, outside the social realm where economic transactions take place. He lives in a silent, asocial world of bidding. How could he engage in any economic transaction?

Several economists have recognised that economic behaviour is indeed interdependent, building on the relationships that actors develop and sustain with each other. The argument is at least a century old (see, for example, Caroline Foley 1893) and has been raised several times since (for a brief overview, see Edward Fullbrook 1998). Individual behaviour does not take place in a social vacuum. It is dependent on the behaviour of other actors: not only on the behaviour of one particular other with whom one interacts at a certain moment in time, but also on the simultaneous interactions of everyone else in the economy in different forms of relationships. Hence follows the argument that macro behaviour is not a simple aggregation of micro behaviour but the result of all interdependent interactions in the economic process (Janssen 1993; Schelling 1978). Schelling thus argues that macro behaviour is contingent behaviour 'that depends on what others are doing' (Schelling 1978: 17).

This view does not imply that individual behaviour is wholly determined by others, by an overruling authority or by a set of compelling norms, which would make choice a useless concept. Such a deterministic view is just as erroneous as the concept of *Rational Economic Man* as isolated and independent. Economic behaviour is neither purely determined from outside, nor purely subjective actions taken by unrelated, self-interested individuals (see, for example, Amitai Etzioni 1988; Folbre 1994; Granovetter 1985; Hodgson 1988; Lawson 1997). Rather, economic behaviour is the interdependent action of individuals in their social relations. It is a complex mix of the agency of individuals in their various roles, influenced by structures and influencing these structures in turn (intentionally as well as unintentionally). It is in this setting that actors in the economy persuade each other to engage in transactions (McCloskey and Klamer 1995). Without the capability to engage in and to sustain relationships Gage and Elliot found themselves terribly lost.

This deficiency in the frontal brain damage patients' rationality can also be illustrated with the help of a discussion on the deficient properties of utility functions (see for a discussion, among many others, Folbre 1994; Hargreaves Heap 1989; Hollis 1987; Nelson 1996).[15] Utility functions are incomplete when individuals are committed to values not for the utility thereof but because of their intrinsic motivations, for such valuable ends fall outside the definition of utility functions. The fact that values are socially shared can result in non-transitive preference orderings, assuming that these values could be caught at all in preference functions. In time, preference orderings become inconsistent when continuously changing relationships link people together around various shared and contested human values. Utility functions can be discontinuous when people include intrinsic value commitments as their ends in life, since different values are incommensurable. Is there, for example, any meaningful marginal trade off to be found between friendship and honesty in which both values are still perceived as intrinsically valuable? Once it is established that human interaction and activities influence each other, utility functions would take on discontinuous, non-linear shapes and multiple intersections.[16] Much of the neoclassical model would become infeasible.

21

The capacity to interact meaningfully with others must appear an unrealisable art in the eyes of frontal brain damage patients and for our poor *Rational Economic Man*. The interdependent interaction of actors in the economy cannot be dealt with in a smooth utilitarian world. Constrained maximisation of independent and subjective utility functions is unable to explain economic behaviour in which interaction is crucial. Economic actors need others, and would still do so even if they were concerned only about earning an independent living.

The ethical capabilities of rational economic human beings

Phineas Gage's and Elliot's behaviour appeared rational only at superficial glance. They failed tragically in their personal and economic lives after their brain damage. Due to the neural damage that affected the moral and social dimensions of their rationality, they lost the capability to understand values, to experience emotions, to deliberate on alternatives and to engage in human interaction. A similar kind of lobotomy seems to have been performed on *Rational Economic Man* after his nineteenth-century transfer from classical to neoclassical economics. The portrayal of rationality in neoclassical economic theory resembles the pathological form of behaviour described in some peculiar cases in neuro-biology. *Rational Economic Man* is stuck with an iron bar in his head. The damage to his brain prevents him from acting in a meaningful rational way.

The problem is not merely that neoclassical assumptions are abstract. Every theory implies an abstraction from the concrete, a simplification of relationships and the exclusion of secondary influences. The assumption of rationality in economics does not have to be, indeed cannot possibly be, a complete and concrete description of human behaviour. But it should reflect, although in abstracted form, real, healthy, ordinary human behaviour if it intends to explain the economic behaviour of human beings. The neoclassical defence of the moral and social deficiencies in the rationality construct is that the objective of economics is not explanation but prediction. The theory claims that economic actors behave *as if* they were *Rational Economic Men* (see particularly Milton Friedman 1953). According to this defence no realistic description or explanation of economic behaviour is needed. As long as the theory can do its job in prediction, the defence argues, it suffices to assume that economic actors behave *as if* they follow certain economic laws.

I have already indicated that in fact *Rational Economic Man* lacks the capabilities to act on these laws since much of human behaviour is not rule-based at all but contextual (Lawson 1997; Leibenstein 1976; McCloskey 1985: 15; Sen 1995). A major difference between the behaviour of bodies as studied in the natural sciences and the behaviour of human beings, as studied in the social sciences, is that humans act intentionally rather than in fixed, rule-governed patterns. Friedman's *as if* assumption however, ignores this difference and wrongly equates instrumental and intentional behaviour. For a reasonably adequate description of human behaviour, any theoretical abstraction requires certain minimum necessary realistic elements to make the abstraction work in theory. But, as the Lucas critique has shown, economic prediction based on neoclassical economic models fails (Robert Lucas 1981). The *as if* assumption apparently does not do its job as Friedman had hoped. The explanation of this failure however goes beyond the Lucas critique and points to the mistaken assumption that utility maximisation is an adequate description of intentional human behaviour. As a consequence *Rational Economic Man* cannot even perform the limited task to which neoclassical economics has confined him: constrained maximisation in a situation of exchange.

When we search for alternatives, one problem is that we tend to look for refinements and additions that would leave intact the utilitarian framework and methodological individualism; hence we posit a second type of rationality as 'social rationality'. In an influential volume on rationality, Hargreaves Heap *et al.* (1992) try to compensate for the deficiencies of *Rational Economic Man*, or *Homo Economicus* as they call him, through giving him a partner called *Homo Sociologicus*, who is supposed to take care of the ethical dimensions of human rationality. How these two forms of rationality should be reconciled in a non-gender biased way is not argued however, nor is the problematic assumption of schizophrenia if the two characters should live in the same individual. Likewise, Hargreaves Heap advocates complementarity between instrumental rationality, procedural (rule based) and expressive (duty based) rationality: 'the postulate of instrumental rationality is very useful; it just cannot be all there is' (Hargreaves Heap 1989: 10). On expressive rationality he seems equally positive: 'I want to claim that expressive rationality stands for a universal human concern with understanding the world in which we live' (ibid.: 148). He does not make a choice of one of these types of rationality but argues that they should be combined (ibid.: 172). The rationale for his choice is his assumption that instrumental rationality is about intentional behaviour whereas expressive rationality is not. This assumption is flawed. Not only is instrumental rationality *not* intentional – there is no human will involved in the following of an algorithm – but expressive rationality *is* intentional, since actors follow ends that are deemed important in themselves. Such choices clearly imply a human will, and hence, intention.

Hargreaves Heap's and several other economists' attempts to solve the problem of economic rationality reflect a methodological monism that prevents us from understanding the deficiencies of the rationality concept in economics thoroughly. It is not merely a matter of adding a *Homo Sociologicus* to *Rational Economic Man*; it is time to recognise the deficiencies, the incapabilities, inherent in the neoclassical rationality concept. Only then it will become possible to heal the wounds of the brain damage, to remove the iron bar and to recover the ethical capabilities that were acknowledged to be part of the discipline in the days of classical political economics.

Overview of the book

The book will build on a brief assessment of problems with the rationality assumption in mainstream economics as presented in this chapter. In chapter two, it will be shown that economists throughout the discipline have drawn upon values, emotion, deliberation and interaction in their economic analyses even when they claim their work is 'neutral'. Three values appear time and again in economic analyses: liberty, justice and care. This is no surprise when one realises that economists have recognised these three human values as dominating economic behaviour over time and across cultures: markets tend to express freedom, states to express justice, and unpaid labour to express care among human beings. Chapter three gives a very brief overview of how each of these values have been recognised in the history of economic thought. Chapter four then discusses recent attempts to integrate values in economic theory, but concludes that none of these attempts is very successful or persuasive. Chapter five develops some empirically based hypotheses on how economic rationality might be constructed around the three values distinguished in chapters two and three. It does so without invoking a behavioural law, but through the anthropological technique of focus group interviews. The hypotheses that evolve from interviews held in Africa, Asia, Latin America and Europe are then employed in chapter six to elaborate an Aristotelian perspective on economics. In this chapter, the Aristotelian idea of a mean between excess and deficiency is analysed in terms of individual economic actors' roles in the economic value domains of freedom, justice and care. Chapter seven then shows how economic behaviour is influenced by and in turn influences institutions, which are embedded in the three value domains. Together, these institutions help to create a balance between the market, the state and the care economy. Chapter eight is a concluding chapter.

2

PARADOXES OF VALUE

Value is a relationship between people.
(Joan Robinson 1962: 32)

The hidden values of economics

The four capabilities that *Rational Economic Man* lacks were identified in chapter one as having ethical dimensions. Commitment, emotional attachment, deliberation and human interaction all express human values. Such values are shared and contested among individuals in a society. To some extent, these values are also shared and contested among the participants of an economy that is embedded in society (Mark Granovetter 1985). The problem that now arises is: how can we address the role of such values in economics without, on the one hand, moving too far away from our discipline into sociology and without, on the other hand, reducing values to axioms that exclude any meaningful rationality, as is the case in neoclassical economics? In other words, we would first need to find out which values are particularly important in economic life compared to other values that may be important in other spheres of life. Second, we need to find out how these values are expressed in economic transactions. Finally, it may be important to know whether these values are somehow related to each other in the economic process. This chapter will suggest an initial answer to these questions. Not, however, by immediately jumping to heterodox schools. In subsequent chapters I will argue how important heterodoxy has been in the elaboration of values in economics. For now, it suffices to stay with the mainstream, at least for a while.

Neoclassical economic theory is not so value-neutral as its proponents claim. In fact, neoclassical economics is quite outspoken about one particular ethical value operating in economic life, which is eagerly taken up in economic assumptions, concepts and policy advice: the value of freedom, or liberty.[1] This assessment, which is by no means new (for an overview see Jean-François Laslier, Marc Fleurbaey, Nicolas Gravel and Alain Trannoy 1998), points to a first paradox of value in economics:

> *Paradox 1:* Neoclassical economic theory is presented as value-neutral, but many of its arguments are grounded upon liberal ethics, defending the moral value of freedom. This commitment to liberty is expressed in neoclassical theory as the free individual, free choice and free exchange.

It is a paradox and not a deep contradiction because the theory has been developed in a society that has been imbued with the idea of the importance of the value of freedom.[2] For those committed to this value, the theory may seem value-neutral: freedom does not seem a moral value but 'natural', as belonging to the state of being human; only other values are regarded as moral by many proponents of neoclassical economics. The hidden belief in the theory is that economic life should be all about our freedom to choose certain activities rather than being coerced into others. People should have freedom since 'the individual is sovereign', as was held by John Stuart Mill (1859). We should be 'free to choose', to cite Milton and Rose Friedman (1980). Such expressions of liberal values have come to be reflected in the very rhetoric of mainstream economics, which frequently presents itself as 'the study of choice' or 'the analysis of free exchange' (McCloskey 1985, 1994a).

As a consequence of the 'naturalness' of the moral value of freedom for neoclassical economists, contradictions between commitment to freedom on the one hand and value-neutrality on the other hand persist in the theory. *Rational Economic Man* is not committed to his ends out of free will but takes them as given; he does not feel attached to them so why does he not change to another set that is easier to satisfy; he cannot evaluate alternatives according to what he really values; nor is he able to persuade others to interact with him. In fact, *Rational Economic Man* does not know what it is to be free. Yet, his creators and supporters ascribe values of freedom to him. Has freedom become so perverted in economics that it has been reduced to a mechanical calculation of an algorithm? Has the human value of liberty degenerated in the discipline, as has been argued by Joan Robinson (1970: 118) into 'freedom to make money'? Or is freedom still cherished by many economists as an important value in itself?

To answer this question I will take a closer look at two exemplary economic texts that unveil a commitment to liberty. This will refute the cynicism of Joan Robinson's question: economists *do* appear to care about freedom as an end in itself. However, by exposing their shared commitment and their emotional attachment to freedom, and through their persuasive rhetoric, they prove Robinson right in her assessment that value resides at the social level, where it is shared with others: 'value is a relationship between people' (Robinson 1962: 32).

Freedom in economics

Freedom is deemed important in economics since it implies that 'no body of men interferes with my activity', as formulated by Isaiah Berlin, elaborating on John Stuart Mill's *On Liberty* (Berlin 1969: 122). This characterisation of freedom is a freedom *from*. Another characterisation is a freedom *to*, which consists in 'being our own master' (ibid.: 131). This positive notion of freedom is concerned with the ends that one values, chosen among other possible options, and with the quality and importance of these ends. The negative notion of freedom is concerned with an unhindered pursuit by people of their (given) ends. This dual understanding of freedom as positive and negative is reflected in economists' writings, where negative freedom features as an instrumental value and where positive freedom is understood as intrinsically valuable.

Next, I will briefly discuss two texts that celebrate the moral value of freedom in economics. One of these is Milton Friedman and Rose Friedman's *Free to Choose* (1980), which particularly supports the idea of negative freedom. First, however, I want to discuss a text that argued in favour of positive freedom. This is not a neoclassical text but an Austrian one, Friedrich Hayek's *Constitution of Liberty* (1960). I have chosen this text rather than a neoclassical one since it brings out the positive freedom concept very well and has been influential for the development of the ethics of liberty in the mainstream as well, reflected in Milton Friedman and Rose Friedman's work.

Friedrich Hayek

Friedrich Hayek positions freedom explicitly as a moral value. In the *Constitution of Liberty* he even argues that freedom is the most important value in human life. 'We must show that liberty is not merely one particular value but that it is the source and condition of most moral values' (Hayek 1960: 6). In doing this, Hayek acknowledges his emotional attachment to this value ('the temptation to appeal to emotion is often irresistible'), but he restrains himself, assuming that such sentiments 'can have no place in an attempt at rational persuasion' (ibid.: 6). Later he restates the value of freedom even more forcefully as a moral principle, which should be 'accepted as a value in itself, as a principle that must be respected without our asking whether the consequences in the particular instance will be beneficial' (ibid.: 68). This is a deontological argument, which regards freedom as a right, representing a libertarian position. This position is anti-utilitarian since utility theory evaluates actions only on the basis of their consequences. With this rejection of utilitarianism, Hayek bases his image of economic behaviour upon freedom as an intrinsic human value, not as an instrumental value as in utilitarianism.

Furthermore, Hayek rejects a dichotomous split between positive and negative freedom, implying both interpretations in his use of the word freedom: a freedom *from* as well as a freedom *to* (ibid.: 12).

> Whether he is free or not does not depend on the range of choice but on whether he can expect to shape his course of action in accordance with his present intentions, or whether somebody else has power so to manipulate the conditions as to make him act according to that person's will rather than his own.
>
> (Hayek 1960: 13)

In the negative sense Hayek considers freedom to be the absence of coercion, which he labels as 'evil' (ibid.: 21), a strong moral connotation. He does so, not because coercion would prevent people from satisfying their desires but because coercion devalues them as thinking and *valuing* persons. For Hayek, the individual should be really free to choose what he (or she) values.

This free individual lives in an imperfect world of uncertainty, which adds meaning to freedom, according to Hayek. If our rational capabilities were limitless and we lived in a world of perfect information and certainty there would be no need for liberty, Hayek argues. But in our world:

> liberty is essential in order to leave room for the unforseeable and unpredictable; we want it because we have learned to expect from it the opportunity of realizing many of our aims. It is because every individual knows so little and, in particular, because we rarely know which of us knows best that we trust the independent and competitive efforts of many to induce the emergence of what we shall want when we see it.
>
> (Hayek 1960: 29)

Here Hayek moves from the individual level, where he supports a libertarian position, to the aggregate level, where he argues that freedom contributes to aggregate well-being. Freedom thus is not only valued from an individualistic perspective, but also for everybody else, as contributing to the well-being of society at large. However – and this is critical – Hayek holds that the aggregate beneficial effect of freedom does not arise from design. He rejects functionalism: for Hayek, freedom is an intrinsic value that people try to further in their lives because they believe in it, not because of its consequences or because they are following an overall plan. Aggregate benefits from individual freedom do not arise from design. 'The institutions of freedom, like everything freedom has created, were not established because people foresaw the benefits they would bring' (ibid.: 54). So, in Hayek's view, freedom is not an instrumental value but intentional at the individual level, an intrinsic value. The benefits that the furthering of freedom bring at the aggregate level are not planned; they are the unintended consequences of people's individual commitments to freedom.

Milton Friedman and Rose Friedman

The title gives the message; *Free to Choose* by Rose Friedman and Milton Friedman (1980) appeared two decades later than Hayek's work. Their message arises in the context of the USA: an immigrant country since the early seventeenth century. The Friedmans root their view of freedom squarely in this history, quoting the first lines of the poem by Emma Lazarus inscribed at the foot of the Statue of Liberty (Friedman and Friedman 1980: 35):

Give me your tired, your poor,
Your huddled masses yearning to breathe free,
The wretched refuse of your teeming shore.
Send these, the homeless, tempest-tossed to me:
I lift my lamp beside the golden door.

Free to Choose is rhetorically opposed to the role of the state: the book focuses on negative freedom, which is described as the absence of government interference in markets.[3] The poem is used to depict the US as a place where coercion is absent, attracting millions of immigrants who flee from tyranny and misery. The authors focus on a core element of freedom in an economic sense, namely voluntary exchange. From this perspective, attention is paid also to the price mechanism and efficiency.

Like Hayek, the authors of *Free to Choose* express emotion *vis-à-vis* the virtues of liberty, although less expressively so, disguising a passionate normative claim in modest aesthetic terminology. 'One of the beauties of a free price system is that the prices that bring the information also provide both an incentive to react to the information and the means to do so' (ibid.: 18). Voluntary exchange is deemed a 'beautiful' instrument that is important to efficiency, a statement that can hardly be seen as neutral. Friedman and Friedman argue that voluntary interaction is functional even beyond the market: it brings benefits in a variety of realms in life. 'A society's values, its culture, its social conventions – all these develop in the same way, through voluntary exchange, spontaneous cooperation, the evolution of a complex structure through trial and error, acceptance and rejection' (ibid.: 26). Their defence of liberty rests largely on free exchange, leading to efficient markets, which they would like to see ensured in an economic Bill of Rights (ibid.: 299). Again, no value-neutral policy advice.

The authors extend the moral good that this would bring to society at large. They note, for example, that charity is an expression of voluntary co-operation too. Here, however, they change the wording of 'exchange' for 'co-operation', suggesting that these are substitutes. I will not go into this problematic assumption here, but will address that subject in chapter four. The authors argue in favour of: 'a society that relies primarily on voluntary cooperation to organise both economic and other activity, a society that preserves and expands human freedom, that keeps government in its place, keeping it our servant and not letting it become our master' (ibid.: 37). Again, Friedman and Friedman show their commitment to the moral value of freedom. At the aggregate level and at the individual level the authors stress that freedom enables the achievement of individual ends, which are not necessarily selfish. 'Self-interest is not myopic selfishness. It is whatever it is that interests the participants, whatever they value, whatever goals they pursue' (ibid.: 27). So, it seems that Friedman and Friedman value freedom for its own sake, as a commitment. At the same time, they defend it with instrumental reasons using utilitarian arguments at the individual level, and defend it at the aggregate level with the functionalistic argument that it is beneficial (efficient) for the economy as a whole, arguing 'that reliance on the freedom of people to control their own lives in accordance with their own values is the surest way to achieve the full potential of a great society' (ibid.: 309–10). This shows clearly the methodological inconsistency of the conceptualisation of the value of freedom in neoclassical theory.

When we compare the Hayekian and Friedmanite views on freedom we are not struck by the expected differences so much as by the similarities. Both Hayek and Friedman and Friedman appear highly committed to freedom, even emotionally attached to this moral value. Both positions attach great importance to individuals' free choices of what they value. And both positions recognise the social as well as the individual relevance of freedom.

The influence of these and other economic works upholding the value of freedom should not be underestimated. Alan Peacock (1997) and Jean-François Laslier, Marc Fleurbaey, Nicolas Gravel and Alain Trannoy (1998) have recently listed and discussed the values of freedom in economics. Their descriptions include choice, free exchange, opportunity, individual will, agency, independence, the exercise of one's capacities, intentional action, self-creation, self-determination, awareness, self-esteem, value in the eyes of others, dignity and pride. Many of these values can be found in the works of Hayek and Friedman and Friedman. None has a place in the construct of rationality in neoclassical theory.

There seem to be no fundamental objections in neoclassical economics against the liberalisation of *Rational Economic Man*. However, granting freedom to him confronts us with a new paradox. Since real free economic behaviour cannot occur unless actors relate to each other, they need to come to an agreement on the transactions that they intend to make. They cannot escape social reality, which is imbued with a variety of values.

There is a wide gap between the commitment of most economists to freedom and the deficient, value-neutral notion of rational behaviour that they adhere to; if we are to bridge this gulf, we need to consider values other than freedom alone. In order to persuade others to interact with him, *Rational Economic Man* needs to leave his autonomous position for a while, to engage in the social activity of interaction. There, not individual but social values matter, even to make freedom work. Here we find a second paradox of value in economics:

> *Paradox 2:* Economic explanation requires a conceptualisation of liberal values, such as choice, self-esteem and independence, which are all individual values. But liberal values in turn appear to rely on other types of values, which belong to the social rather than the individual level.

The dissolution of the second paradox can, surprisingly, be found in Hayek's and Friedman and Friedman's texts. They recognise that without certain social values freedom is meaningless. We find two types of these in their texts:

1   public values expressed as norms and rights valid for everyone,
2   interpersonal values that embody responsible relationships between people.

Hayek acknowledges the relevance of rules and norms that support freedom. Friedman and Friedman argue for rights. Each of them brings in yet another type of value into the argument: interpersonal values grounded in responsibility. Hayek presents responsibility as a precondition for freedom without which freedom cannot flourish.

> Liberty not only means that the individual has both the opportunity and the burden of choice; it also means that he must bear the consequences of his actions and will receive praise or blame for them. Liberty and responsibility are inseparable.
>
> (Hayek 1960: 71)

Here we find a recognition of human inter-relatedness that leads us to take the consequences for others into account in our own dealings.[4] Rationality motivated by liberal values thus implies a commitment to other-regarding values.[5] Hayek develops the role of responsibility, clearly aware of the location of responsibility beyond the realms of individual freedom and state authority: it is a different type of value.

> The significance of the concept thus extends far beyond the sphere of coercion, and its greatest importance perhaps lies in its role in guiding man's free decisions. A free society probably demands more than any other that people be guided in their action by a sense of responsibility which extends beyond the duties exacted by the law that general opinion approve of the individuals' being held responsible for both the success and the failure of their endeavours. When men are allowed to act as they see fit, they must also be held responsible for the results of their efforts.
>
> (Hayek 1960: 76)

Like Hayek, Milton and Rose Friedman also argue that at the individual level responsibility is a necessary accompanying value for freedom. 'Freedom is a tenable objective only for responsible individuals' (ibid.: 32). But Friedman and Friedman do not develop the role of responsibility, so we cannot see how it relates to their forceful rejection of the state, nor to their instrumental idea of economic behaviour. They do, however, seem to suggest that responsibility is not an element in a utility function, but rather part of the character of economic actors. What then is this character that apparently contains more ethical commitments than simply a commitment to freedom? What other values do rational economic actors cherish?

Justice in economics

Justice is often regarded as the natural counter-value to freedom. In the economy, it tends to be seen as a correction of unfair side-effects of liberalism. Indeed, at the theoretical level, justice theories are often positioned *vis-à-vis* liberal theories. Economic behaviour that is exclusively rooted in the pursuit of freedom may have negative consequences for others. The negative effects of economic liberalism mentioned in the literature that would require justice are, for example, exploitation of workers, extraction of surplus value in capitalist firms, unequal distribution of gains from international trade by the more powerful trading partner, unequal opportunities for slightly less resourced entrepreneurs in the process of creative destruction, the undeserved destitution of the poor during economic crises, discrimination against women and ethnic minorities, and environmental degradation.

Like freedom, justice has two forms in economics: formal (or procedural) justice and substantive justice. Formal justice embodies the minimum principle of justice: that of equality. It demands that equals should be treated equally and unequals should be treated unequally. This principle is called 'formal' because it does not provide any particular aspects in which equals ought to be treated the same. Nor does it provide criteria for determining which individuals should be considered as equals. Hence, formal justice is constructed as the impartial and consistent application of principles, whether or not the principles themselves are just. Substantive justice, on the other hand, is concerned with what a society perceives as just. It defines what individuals find legitimate and what they can legitimately demand from their government.

In economics justice relates to distribution according to particular principles. Serge-Christophe Kolm (1996) presents an overview of theories of substantive justice as they have been relevant in economics. For distributive justice he mentions a variety of items that could be the object of equality: (access to) productive resources like credit, technology and human capital; income, consumption goods, capacities, basic needs and opportunity (ibid.: 66–7). Other candidates for equality could be added, closer to received welfare theory, such as utility (if interpersonal comparison of utility is allowed) or fundamental preferences. The theoretical construction of justice is through a social contract or original position (or a combination of the two) where a just distribution is agreed among people. Both representations are situations in which individuals jointly decide to accept certain principles that will regulate social and economic life. Here, I present a brief discussion of one well-known theory of justice that is particularly relevant for economics.

John Rawls

John Rawls' *Theory of Justice* (1971) is a substantive theory of justice.[6] He develops a social contract to be agreed in a hypothetical original position, according to what the participants would deem fair. The assumption is that people are free and equal and able to represent their self-interest.[7] The individuals meet without knowing beforehand their place in the society whose rules they are discussing: they negotiate the social contract under a 'veil of ignorance'. This means that they are unaware of their race, sex, place of birth, or wealth. In the initial position, Rawls assumes some basic intuitive ideas of justice are shared among the participants in the social contract 'of society as a fair system of cooperation between free and equal persons' (Rawls 1985: 249). The initial position

33

both expresses reasonable conditions and yields principles which match our considered judgements duly pruned and adjusted. The state of affairs I refer to as reflected equilibrium. It is an equilibrium because at least our principles and judgements coincide; and it is reflective since we know what principles our judgements conform and the premises of their derivation.

(Rawls 1971: 20)

The objects of the deliberations of justice are so called primary goods: a varied collection of means and ends such as rights, liberties, powers, opportunities, income, wealth and self-respect. Fairness, Rawls holds, demands that everyone has a right to these primary goods, irrespective of their social, economic, or cultural position in society. In the *Theory of Justice* the primary goods are to be distributed equally. Other-regarding values are excluded from the negotiation of the social contract since they would complicate matters unnecessarily, according to Rawls. People are assumed to behave exclusively in their own self-interest. Combined with the assumption of formal justice – everyone is equal under the veil of ignorance – this assumption makes for a like-minded companion for *Rational Economic Man*, whom I will call *Fair Economic Man*. He only differs from his companion in a commitment to justice in the otherwise calculative, self-interested and detached character that he brings to the original position.

Rawls argues that, in the original position, people would agree on two principles of justice. The first requires that each person be permitted the maximum amount of liberty compatible with a similar liberty for others. The second principle requires that inequalities in the distribution of primary goods are to be allowed only if they benefit everyone and particularly the least well-off. As a consequence, injustices are inequalities that are not to the benefit of all. This principle allows distributive inequalities as long as they are consistent with equal liberty and fair opportunity. But when the least well-off in society do not benefit from these inequalities, they are no longer allowed.

Rawls' major argument is that his principles are more credible than utilitarianism, where redistribution is not allowed.

In fact, when society is conceived as a system of cooperation to advance the good of its members, it seems quite incredible that some citizens should be expected, on the basis of political principles, to accept lower prospects of life for the sake of others.

(Rawls 1971: 178)

This assumption of utilitarianism is indeed what is implied in neoclassical theory: the poor must suffer in the cause of a Pareto superior utility gain in the aggregate, which may benefit only the rich, or may benefit the rich more than the poor. Rawls thus points to an important deficiency in the neoclassical conceptualisation of freedom: without a substantive form of justice, free market exchange will not occur. The least well-off will simply not accept their situation voluntarily unless there are minimal guarantees that free exchange benefits everyone. So the liberal argument that voluntary exchange needs only freedom is incomplete. Freedom needs justice, either in Rawls' formulation or otherwise. Free exchange that creates large inequalities will simply not be accepted voluntarily by the disadvantaged (unless they have no choice, which shows a lack of freedom as well).

According to Serge-Christophe Kolm (1996) and John Roemer (1996), the values belonging to the moral domain of justice include rights, equality (in distribution), rules, equity, solidarity, fairness, respect and self-respect and various types of entitlements. In today's economics these values are generally depicted as non-economic, and viewed as social or political. However, Rawls' *Theory of Justice* points out that values of justice and of freedom cannot be separated: if you want to have the one, you will need the other too. He thus has shown an important weakness in neoclassical economics and has offered two principles of justice to make freedom work, at least in theory.

But it does not. Rawls' solution is still deficient. His assumption that people come to love and cherish the principles they agree on is not justified in his methodological framework. The conditions that he defined for the social contract to arise deny a responsible attitude from the contractors: the social contract commands self-interest and establishes an abstract rule-based redistribution of primary goods (Bernard Williams 1971). Economists have levelled various critiques against Rawls' theory, particularly on his second principle (or the maximin rule), on his assumptions of the initial position and the veil of ignorance and on his solution to the problem found with the perceived social unacceptability of Pareto Optimality (James Buchanan 1972; John Harsanyi 1975; Daniel Hausman and Michael McPherson 1996; Serge-Christophe Kolm 1996; Deirdre McCloskey 1982; John Roemer 1996; Amartya Sen 1990b, 1992). Due to lack of space here, I will not go into the substantial literature on Rawls but I will focus on the philosophical argument against his solution to the deficiency of liberty, referring to David Gauthier (1977).

Deficiencies of freedom and justice

In a social contract human relationships are considered *as if* they were contractual. It is a similar assumption to that in neoclassical theory where behaviour is explained *as if* performed by *Rational Economic Man*. The theory of the social contract does not assume that social life has historically originated in a contract, nor that it is maintained as a contract. The idea of a contract between *Fair Economic Men* provides a rationale for relationships between persons and between the state and its members, not the cause of those relationships. 'The justification of rights and duties, institutions and practices, is to be found by regarding them as if they were contractual, and showing the rationality of this hypothetical contractual base' (David Gauthier 1977: 135).

As a consequence, Gauthier argues, contract theories understand human beings as separate from and pre-existing to society, which they are assumed to have brought into being. Social contract theories like the *Theory of Justice* assume that the individual is prior to society. But this also implies that individual characteristics for establishing society, such as communication, mutual respect, self-awareness and responsibility are prior to society. Here, we run into the second paradox that was posed earlier in this chapter: freedom cannot do without social values. Why does society need a social contract if in fact the contractors are already social in nature? This paradox is also known as the 'Hobbes Problem' (Deirdre McCloskey 1994a: 147). 'Men who were naturally sociable would not need to contract together in order to form society, and would not rationalize society in contractarian terms' (Gauthier 1977: 138).

Indeed, Rawls implicitly suggests that individuals negotiating a social contract do have social values. They are the capable members of families who represent and negotiate on behalf of their dependants for whose well-being they are assumed to care.[8] As representatives of a household, they must have a notion of what it is to belong to a group, to share with members of a family and to bear responsibility for the 'weak' who cannot – or are not allowed to – negotiate for themselves. The self-interested, patriarchal negotiators are assumed to represent their family's interests responsibly (Annette Baier 1993; Susan Moller Okin 1989; Iris Young 1990; for this argument in economics: Nancy Folbre and Heidi Hartmann 1988; Frances Woolley 2000).[9]

Another methodological problem with Rawls' theory stems from the assumption that, once the contract is established, people will come to cherish, defend and maintain it. The contractors are individualist and self-interested in the original position, but they undergo a fundamental change of identity once the contract is in effect. They turn into committed and emotionally attached human beings, who interact socially and respond to one another. They are prepared to keep to the social contract. But where do these new ethical capabilities come from? They cannot suddenly arise; they must have been there all the time.

> Men's reasons for contracting one with another are supposed to arise out of their pre-social needs in the state of nature. If contractarian ideology is to be effective in rationalising social

relationships, then these needs must be represented, not as only pre-social, but as permanent, so that the reasons for entering the contract will also be reasons for maintaining the society created thereby.

(Gauthier 1977: 139)

It appears, then, that Rawls' social contract would only work when its contractors are committed from the beginning to interpersonal values that express their pre-contractual relationships. Without this type of value, Rawls' main argument against utilitarian economic theories does not hold. His assumption of self-interest cannot explain why those gaining net benefits are prepared to forego their gains voluntarily in favour of the least well-off, since they will only do so when they feel responsible. Rawls persuasively argues that liberty needs to be supplemented by justice for an acceptable economy and society, but his conceptualisation of justice through social contract theory cannot explain why and how people could agree and keep to a contract when they are assumed to be detached, autonomous and self-interested. The explanation of economic behaviour thus requires not only freedom and external constraints of fairness, 'but it also needs internal constraints, the constraints of conscience, and these contradict the requirements of reason. The contractarian principle of rational action undercuts the internal constraints necessary to maintain contractual relationships' (Gauthier 1977: 154). The individuals must share not only a set of fair principles, but also a commitment to develop them before the contract and to keep to them under the contract, even when their interests would be served better by breaking the contract. Without such responsibility, the contract will not succeed in establishing justice. The social contract is not self-sustaining (nor was the free state of nature to which it was intended as a solution).

The society established by the social contract, market society, is from one point of view simply the network of contracts among individual men. But this network is maintained by a legal order which enforces the contracts. The contractual relationships of appropriators must be embedded within a political framework which coerces them into remaining within the market in their actions and relationships. Contractarian ideology represents this framework as itself contractual. But the condition of the market – the condition of the network of contracts – cannot itself be the product of a contract, which would be only part of that network. If the market is not self-sustaining, then it cannot be sustained by a part of itself.

(Gauthier 1977: 155)

Gauthier concludes that both the freedom values of the market and the justice values of the social contract require some pre-existent interpersonal values. As examples of such values he suggests trust, honesty, patriotism and familial feeling. In other words, Gauthier argues that contractors care for each other before they come to an agreement. It is the same argument that feminist economists bring forward time and again against neoclassical, neo-institutional and Marxist schools of economic thought. For example Nancy Folbre (1994: 29) argues that 'individuals are born into social structures that shape their sense of identity and ability to pursue their interests'. However, the interpersonal values of social life have been marginalised in modern economic theory, though not completely excluded from it, as Hayek's and Friedman and Friedman's attention to the role of responsibility indicates. They agree that free individuals can only act freely when at the same time they behave responsibly, that is, when they care about others and others' eventual incapability to satisfy their needs with help of free exchange or distributive rules. For a consistent economic theory and a meaningful concept of rationality, this third category of values needs to be addressed. Because of their interpersonal character, I will call them the values of care.

Care in economics

Care, as a broad category of interpersonal values, has been analysed only recently in philosophy (Annette Baier 1987, 1993, 1995; Peta Bowden 1997; Lorraine Code 1995; Carol Gilligan 1982; Virginia Held 1987, 1995; Feder Kittay and Diana Meyers 1987; Joy Kroeger-Mappes 1994; Mary Jeanne Larrabee 1993; Margaret Olivia Little 1995; Selma Sevenhuijsen 1991, 1998; Joan Tronto 1993). The constituting values of care have been studied since Aristotle's virtue ethics, for example in the Scottish Enlightenment by David Hume (with values such as 'sympathy' and 'affection') and by Adam Smith (focusing on the role of 'sympathy' and 'moral sentiments'). However, since Immanuel Kant's conceptualisation of ethics as contractarian, as rule-based morality in which ethics is understood as moral obligation, values other than those constituting obligations have been neglected in ethics.[10]

Contrary to Kantian moral reasoning, 'care writers reject the assumption – dominant in moral philosophy since the eighteenth century – that we act according to moral axioms and point to a range of everyday ethical experiences that defy such characterisation' (Monique Deveaux 1995: 115). Rather than universal principles prescribing general rules of moral duty and obligation, values of care are developed and sustained in contextually dependent relationships between persons. Care is not an individual and subjective value, as in liberalism, nor public and universal, as in a social contract. Rather, care expresses contextual values developing between concrete persons on the basis of contingent needs arising from human vulnerability. Care involves people's careful responses to these urgent needs, contributing to a closely interwoven network of social relationships. Joan Tronto offers a definition referring to care as a: 'species activity that includes everything that we do to maintain, continue, and repair our "world" so that we can live in it as well as possible' (Tronto 1993: 103 and Berenice Fisher and Joan Tronto 1990: 40). She adds that what is most definitive about care is that it is 'a perspective of taking the other's needs as the starting point for what must be done' (Tronto 1993: 105). This definition of care however, is too broad. Like the notion of utility, it is able to absorb any activity and any end, and therefore loses its meaning. For economics, Tronto's definition of care has hardly any added value over regular definitions of economic activity. It may even include market transactions, as Adam Smith explains with the example of the baker, who bakes his bread to satisfy the needs (or wants, as Smith seems to use these here as if they are identical) of others, but at the same time satisfies his own needs (or wants) in the exchange.

> Give me that which I want, and you shall have this which you want, is the meaning of every such offer; and it is in this manner that we obtain from one another the far greater part of those good offices which we stand in need of.
>
> (Smith, 1776 Book I. II: 26)

So, we should redefine care to make it work as a meaningful concept distinct from free exchange and distributive rules, which may also satisfy people's needs. A definition of care as an undefined satisfaction of people's undefined needs is just too broad. Perhaps I should first concentrate on the practice of caring. This practice contains four steps that can be labelled as caring about, taking care of, care giving and care receiving (Tronto 1993: 106–7). Each of these steps involves a particular value: attentiveness, responsibility, competence and responsiveness (ibid.: 127–37). I suggest the following descriptions of each of these stages for economic practices of care:

- *Attentiveness:* 'caring about'; recognition of urgent and contingent needs of others that cannot be addressed through the other's free exchange, nor through distributive rules.
- *Responsibility:* 'taking care of'; responding to these needs, since they cannot be addressed otherwise. This is our responsibility either because the needs arise from unintended consequences of our personal behaviour or from external effects of our collective behaviour. We have also to respond to those needs that arise not from

human causation but from human vulnerability (to disease, natural disasters and the like), and may equally affect all of us.

- *Competence:* 'care giving'; adequate caring, that is, a careful and skilful response to the need for care.
- *Responsiveness:* 'care receiving'; communication between care giver and care receiver in which both try to overcome discrepancies in the process of caring.

Now, how do we recognise these values of care in economics? How have they been recognised to operate in economic life? To find an answer to these questions I have to go back to David Hume, who studied the social virtues. According to Hume, moral theory is not a matter of obedience to universal law but of cultivating proper character traits. The most important of these traits, or virtues, are those concerning our relations with others, in his view. He argues that it is 'sympathy' rather than 'universal reason' that should form the basis of moral theory. 'Hume's ethics requires us to be able to be rule-followers in some contexts, but do not reduce morality to rule-following. Corrected (sometimes rule-corrected) sympathy, not law-discerning reason, is the fundamental moral capacity' (Annette Baier 1987: 40). This sympathy is not limited to affectionate or loving expressions but may just as well involve revenge or lust; all such interpersonal values derive from sympathy, according to Hume. Virtues may turn into vices. Annette Baier (1993) elaborates Tronto's list, concentrating on trust, responsibility and loyalty. These values are important in their own right: they have intrinsic value, as freedom and justice were viewed earlier as valuable in their own right.

> Contract soon ceases to seem the paradigm source of moral obligation once we attend to parental responsibility, and justice as a virtue of social institutions will come to seem at best only first equal with the virtue, whatever its name, that ensures that each new generation is made appropriately welcome and prepared for their adult lives.
>
> (Baier 1995: 56)

But the recognition and practising of this particular virtue is not at all easy, as Jon Elster has recognised.

> As parents know, one first has to teach children the importance of distributive justice, and then how unimportant it is compared to generosity and compassion. The first task is easy because it only involves going by the book, the second incomparably more difficult.
>
> (Elster 1983: 52)

Moral dilemma

In the ethics of care there is a well-known case that illustrates what a caring commitment is: the Heinz dilemma. Whereas traditional empirical research on moral development has studied only men, Carol Gilligan (1982) has interviewed women and found very different answers to the moral dilemma, rooted in women's different experiences in social life.[11] This study of the Heinz dilemma has led to the literature on the ethics of care. The Heinz dilemma is about a man who considers stealing a drug that he cannot afford to buy in order to save the life of his wife. In a justice morality, derived from Kant, the husband weighs breaking the law against the importance of his cause. In standard moral development psychology the right answer is that Heinz should steal the medicine since a human life is more important than property rights. The answers in Gilligan's research were different. They indicated a different reasoning to one based on property rights or law. The answers indicated that theft could harm the relationship between Heinz and his wife (for example, if he was caught and put in jail and could not, therefore, care for his sick wife any more or be able to steal more drugs when needed). From this contextual ethical reasoning the women interviewed by Gilligan suggested that Heinz should borrow money, seek help, or find another solution. From the perspective of care, the personal relationship between Heinz and his wife was the overriding commitment, not the law or the abstract weighing of property rights versus a human life. The importance of relationships is what distinguishes the ethics of care from the ethics of justice.

In economics we have seen that the relevance of caring commitments was recognised by Amartya Sen (1981), Jon Elster (1983) and Robert Frank (1988). It is with their understanding of such commitments that we may find an initial entry for care into economics, particularly thanks to recent contributions by feminist economists on caring labour (Lee Badgett and Nancy Folbre 1999; Paula England and Nancy Folbre 1999; Nancy Folbre 1994, 1995; Susan Himmelweit 1995, 1999; Julie Nelson 1996). Amartya Sen has provided an example of a caring commitment that neatly parallels the Heinz dilemma. Sen's (1981) case is about Ali, an immigrant shop keeper in London, and a friend of his, Donna. Donna has learnt that some racists are planning to beat up Ali in the evening in a spot he will visit alone. Ali is away during the day and Donna does not know how to warn him. All she knows is that he left a message about his movements at the desk of a business contact, Charles. The police dismiss Donna's story as paranoid fantasy, so the only means of warning Ali is to break into Charles' room to recover the message. She cannot do this without violating Charles' privacy and she knows Charles as a self-centred egoist who will be more disturbed by this than by the beating up of Ali. Now Sen asks us: 'What should Donna do?' (ibid.: 8). Donna cannot find a justification for breaking into Charles' room.

41

Neither in utilitarian thinking nor in justice reasoning can she find a rationale for breaking in. From a justice perspective there is no escape from the moral rule against violation of someone's privacy, particularly since no human life is in danger – only Ali's health and dignity. From a utilitarian perspective, Charles' utility would decrease, and the utility pay-off table provided by Sen indicates that the utility loss for Ali as a consequence of the bashing will be less than the sum total of utility gains by the ten racist attackers. So there are no justifications on the grounds of justice and utilitarianism for Donna to prevent the assault. But as Ali's friend she is committed to helping him. Hence, Sen encourages Donna to follow her 'deeply held and resilient conviction that she must save Ali' (ibid.: 12). In her support, he offers her the notion of commitment to other-regarding values.

Care as responsibility

The example illustrates my argument in chapter one that commitment does not have a place in utilitarian reasoning and is also very different from Kantian rule following. Donna did not act in her friendship with Ali for the sake of utilitarian gain, neither did she follow prescribed moral principles. And the law (through the police) appeared of no help. Instead, she acted *virtuously* as Aristotle would have explained, with David Hume and Adam Smith following him. Interpersonal values are expressed for example in friendship when people act upon their understanding of what it is to be a good friend (Aristotle, *Nicomachean Ethics* Books VIII and IX). In Sen's example, Donna cares for Ali and thereby expresses her friendship to him. Other human bonds than friendship too can invite caring behaviour, including responsibility toward people who may be unknown until the moment of the care giving (for an insightful study on care giving to unknown persons, see Samuel Oliner and Pearl Oliner 1988 who interviewed the helpers of Jews in the Second World War).

Sen's case illustrates that a commitment to caring is other-regarding and not intended to satisfy one's own interests. Rather, a commitment to care involves sympathy (which by no means excludes future benefits to oneself when others might care for oneself!).[12] So, the distinctive issue of care is *not individual or group interest but responsibility toward others*. Care is an interpersonal value in its own right, an intrinsic value just like freedom and justice. Whereas freedom is an individualist value, directed at the self, and justice is a public one directed at everyone equally, care is an interpersonal value between a care giver and a care receiver. However, just like the values of freedom and justice, those of care can turn out to be morally good or bad. There is freedom that benefits some at the cost of others; rules of justice include some and exclude others; care can bring relief or can be patronising. I will go into these issues in later chapters.

Moreover, care can also be given to the natural environment and animals, or to oneself. The distinctive issue is that care be directed at a care receiver, expressing sympathy. That is how care for oneself can be distinguished from freedom values. Care is not an activity of self-fulfilment in competition with others. Rather, it is concerned with one's responsibility toward the community one feels part of. From this perspective, frontal brain damage patients such as Gage and Elliot can be characterised as not taking care of themselves: they became a burden on their family, colleagues and employers. Ultimately they came to depend on care from their relatives.

It is in the commitment to care that we find the ethical capability that rational actors need in order to persuade others to interact with them in economic life, to engage in transactions, or to agree on a contract. It is a commitment to care that both *Rational Economic Man* and *Fair Economic Man* lack so greatly, as shown by the failings of Gage and Elliot to relate to others and to earn their trust. From the basic characteristics of care listed by Tronto, it follows that in every economic transaction actors need to pay some attention to other people's needs: how else could a producer decide what to produce for the market? How else could we distribute resources to the needy? How else would a subsistence farmer decide what crops to plant for her family, and how much of each?

The necessity for responsibility in economic transactions is obvious too. Without responsibility, negative external effects would soon restrain the economic process: no one would care about such effects and the suffering they cause. No one would bother to devise or keep restrictive rules in order to prevent externalities such as destitution and environmental pollution. Moreover, in the absence of responsibility among economic actors, there would be no basis for trust and loyalty to develop between producers and consumers (Robert Putnam 1992). Without these values transactions will not happen, or only at high costs. Without trust, actors cannot persuade each other to interact with them (Francis Fukuyama 1995). And without the emergence of loyalty, the economy would remain a theoretical spot-market without any relations emerging between suppliers and customers, employers and employees, or owners and producers, and no long-term contracts would develop. Risk would become very high, and so would transaction costs. In reality, the economy thrives on actors' mutual trust, their responsible attitudes, their relatedness and loyalty, in short, the 'social capital' that is rooted in their commitment to care about each other. Unfortunately, the caring values that build this social capital have hardly been recognised by men writing on social capital (Gary Becker 1996; Francis Fukuyama 1995; Robert Putnam 1992). They seem unaware that social capital represents the effects of caring behaviour among economic actors, the caring that is essential for the market and the state to function. I will argue that it is only from people's mutual caring that the economy accumulates social capital.

The care economy

Recently, a number of economists have studied the gift of care empirically, trying to value it in economic terms. Time use in unpaid labour is taken as one source of data; a market price of fictive wages or sales of products and services created in unpaid labour time is the other source of data. The result of multiplying these variables suggests a market value (opportunity cost) *as if* unpaid labour was exchanged on the labour market (Marilyn Waring 1988). Estimations of the monetary value of unpaid labour range from 6 per cent to 55 per cent of GNP (Marga Bruyn-Hundt 1996a: 51).[13] Such studies are important because they show the huge opportunity costs of unpaid labour, in terms of lost income for women.

The conceptual fallacy of such exercises lies in the assumption that the value of unpaid labour is analogous to the value of paid labour, that is, measured in market prices. The literature from the ethics of care discussed earlier indicates that this assumption is not justified: values of freedom are different from values of care. The distinguishing feature of unpaid labour is that it is largely a gift (though not completely, since coercion may play a role as well). Diane Elson (1995, 2000) has clarified the unique role of care in the economic process, as a separate sector of the economy. It is thanks to her analysis of the role of the care economy in developing countries that gender analyses increasingly pay attention to the care economy in the developing world (see, for example, a special issue of *World Development* 28(7), 2000). Moreover, most unpaid labour cannot be exchanged on the market since there are no markets available for the personal caring work involved. Nor can public goods substitute for unpaid labour because the sympathy that makes a substantial part of the care giving cannot be offered by the state.

In other words, unpaid caring labour has only an imperfect substitute in paid labour, because of its specific caring characteristics (see also Nancy Folbre 1994). As Susan Himmelweit explains, the meaning of unpaid labour as household production obscures the personal and emotional dimensions of caring labour (Himmelweit 1995, 1999). When care is paid – as it is in caring jobs such as nursing – it is paid less than comparable jobs that do not rely so much on caring motives and activities (Paula England and Nancy Folbre 1999) yet, at the same time, caring labour seems to be highly valued. Therefore, Folbre and England conclude, 'we should be suspicious of any argument that decent pay demeans a noble calling' (England and Folbre 1999: 48). Julie Nelson (1999) also notes this paradox between the high value attributed to caring labour and the low pay in caring jobs. She calls for an end to the fears that decent pay, and even high wages, would reduce the quality of care in the labour market.

Some forms of care giving are partially supplied by the state, including childcare and care for the elderly, the homeless and handicapped. But an analysis of care only in terms of public goods denies the distinctiveness of caring again. Such analyses view care in terms of redistribution by the state (or between women and men) according to rules, and judged in terms of justice (Barbara Bergmann 1986; Jean Gardiner 1997; Antonella Picchio 1992). In these economic studies of caring labour, care is not so much studied in terms of its value as such, but in terms of its distribution. As a consequence, it is only justice that seems to matter, not values of care, gifts, or relationships. Nevertheless, Bergmann, Picchio and Gardiner are right to argue for a state role in care provision, since the state has a responsibility to care for its citizens, to address not only market failures but also needs that arise out of human vulnerability.

The studies dealing with care as a market substitute or as a state task, assume that care is located in the *agora* (free exchange) or the *polis* (distributive rules). But this is too limited: it is the *oikos* (household or community) that needs to be studied for an economic understanding of care.[14] Here we find the chicken-and-egg problem that makes the analysis of care in the economy so difficult: economics has no conceptualisation of care because it does not analyse activities as belonging to a distinct domain of care, while at the same time economics cannot analyse activities located in that domain since it lacks the necessary vocabulary to do so. We can no longer ignore the *oikos* as the location of the furthering of caring values. If one includes not only *agora* and *polis* but also the *oikos*, economics could be regarded as the study of provisioning, as Julie Nelson has phrased it so well (1996: 34).

> An understanding of economics as centrally concerned with provisioning, or providing the necessaries of life, has implications quite different from the idea of economics as centrally concerned with exchange. In the exchange view, the primary distinguishing characteristic of a good is whether or not it can be exchanged on a market, not what human needs or wants it may satisfy or what role it may play in a more global, ecological system. The choice of goods depends only on abstract preferences. This radical conceptual separation of humans from their physical environment implies, among other things, sterility of economics about questions of human welfare. In the provisioning view, on the other hand, there are qualitative differences between different goods and services.
>
> (Julie Nelson 1996: 34)

Thus, recognising provisioning as the central concern for the study of economics, Nelson suggests that economics should be about 'the down-to-earth subject matter of how humans try to meet their needs for goods and services' (Nelson 1996: 36). This subject matter is not very far away from that of Adam Smith, who recognised two objects of the economy:

> first, to provide a plentiful revenue or subsistence for the people, or more properly to enable them to provide such a revenue or subsistence for themselves; and secondly, to supply the state or commonwealth with a revenue sufficient for the public services.
>
> (Adam Smith, 1776 Book IV. Introduction: 428)

Nancy Folbre (1994, 1995) also addresses the lack of attention given to care in economics. She concentrates on caring labour (Badgett and Folbre 1999; Folbre 1995) and on the distribution of the costs of caring (England and Folbre 1999; Folbre 1994). At the same time, her work on caring contributes to a better understanding of care as an economic concept. Folbre, following Joan Tronto, recognises the important commitment underlying caring labour as responsibility. She also asserts a distinctive emotion behind caring labour: affection (Folbre 1995), similar to Smith's sympathy. In a paper with Thomas Weisskopf, Folbre discusses the motives for caring as a mixed bag of altruism, responsibility, intrinsic joy, expectation of an informal quid pro quo, a contracted reward and coercion (Folbre and Weisskopf 1998).

One of Folbre's aims is to develop feminist economic policy advice. For this reason, she provides a helpful outline of the different perspectives that should feature in a discussion on caring policies. There is some distinction between care and free exchange or distributive rules of justice, in terms of altruism and reciprocity (see Folbre 1995: 76–7). In her book on the distribution of the costs of care, Folbre proposes to ground economic theory in the concepts of assets, rules, norms and preferences. These notions should not only help economists to analyse markets, but also states, firms and families, she argues. With this framework, she helps to broaden economic analysis to include the realm of caring values and caring labour. She draws particular attention to the genderedness of care and, in her paper with Lee Badgett, labels women's disproportionate time use in caring labour as 'socially imposed altruism' (Badgett and Folbre 1999: 316). Indeed, it is the genderedness of care that makes its analysis so complex, requiring the disentangling of intrinsic motivation, affection and responsibility on the one hand, from gendered social norms, tradition and labour market segregation on the other.

Exchange, rules and gift

With the distinction of three ethical orientations in economic behaviour and their respective values, I have answered the first and second questions from the introduction of this chapter. Freedom is an important value in economic life, but it requires justice for it to be feasible. Both freedom and justice require the value of care to make them work. Hence, all three values are needed in the economy: freedom, justice and care. From an Aristotelian ontological position, each of these values can be regarded as belonging to a particular domain, between which there is no commensurability and hence no exchange. But how then do these three types of value commitments relate to each other, if they relate at all?

Commitments are not acquired autonomously and subjectively: we learn what is valuable in our childhood, evaluate it in early adulthood and continue to reassess it from time to time. Individuals develop and sustain their commitments to care, justice and freedom in the practices of their daily economic lives.[15] It is in the practising of values that they come to be valued and that actors feel committed to them, learn to deliberate in terms of them, and experience the appropriate forms of interaction belonging to particular value commitments. Therefore, these practices, though located in the economy, can also be characterised as *moral* ones. In these practices, actors develop the ethical capabilities to behave meaningfully (Peta Bowden 1997; Alisdair MacIntyre 1987; Charles Taylor 1992). A practice can be defined as 'an area where there are no clearly defined rules, there are distinctions between different sorts of behaviour such that one sort is considered the appropriate form for one action or context, the other for another action or context' (Taylor 1992: 34). In economic life each type of value is expressed in its own practices. Those of freedom and justice are well known. The practices of freedom deal with exchange, competition and prices, whereas those of justice deal with redistribution, solidarity and rules. But the practices of caring have hardly been analysed in economic terms. Therefore, we need to go deeper into them and explore the characteristics of caring in economic behaviour, characteristics that distinguish care from freedom and justice.

The inter-dependence that is expressed in relationships between actors, and the sympathy that is expressed in these relationships, makes use of a distinct form of interaction and allocation of resources: neither exchange nor distribution but giving. Care operates through gifts between care givers and care receivers. Trust for example is a gift and not an exchange; it has no price. Loyalty is a gift; when bought it becomes a bribe. Responsibility is a gift that carries its own reward; when it is contractual it becomes a duty, an obligation, the subjection to a rule. The same counts for tangible gifts of resources, final goods, or labour time: they are a response to the needs of others. The gift is an unconditional transfer between economic actors; it is free. However, social norms may expect more gifts from some than from others, or at some point a giver may resign from giving because she feels exploited. Just as pure exchange does not exist and there is no such thing as a completely fair distribution (except in textbooks on justice, some people tend to be perceived as more equal than others), there is also no pure gift. Exchange, redistribution and giving exist together in a variety of combinations. They interrelate in such a way that the one cannot do without the other. In fact, every production process of goods and services involves all three allocation mechanisms and all three underlying types of values: freedom, justice and care. Economic processes are necessarily heterogeneous and the goods and services they create can therefore be characterised as composite goods that always include some elements that represent other types of values than the ones they intend to further (see Figure 2.1).

For example, nurses in state hospitals compete for their jobs in a labour market that presumes free exchange. Their salaries come from public resources, representing distributive rules of public expenditures. Finally, the intrinsic motivation for their profession as nurses generally (but not as a contractual obligation) commits them to values of care, urging them to respond carefully to patients' needs with an attentiveness that often goes beyond the requirements implied in their labour contracts. Health budget cuts might force institutions to establish a maximum number of minutes for each nursing activity such as washing and feeding patients. This leaves no contractual time for caring anymore: by contract, nursing is reduced to a sequence of measurable, time-bound technical tasks, but in the daily actions of many nurses care remains as a gift to the patients, beyond the contract, until eventually their intrinsic motivation for caring gets crowded out by too much time pressure, stress and unfair wages.[16]

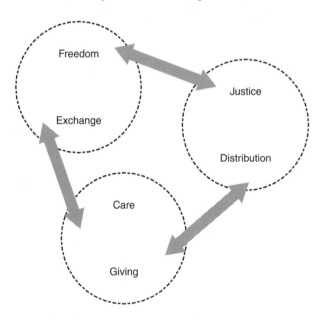

Figure 2.1 The relations between economic value domains

Another example is the financial market. Competition not only features in the financial job market but also in financial transactions. Still, the trade is supposed to conform to rules and laws. Moreover, financial traders express caring values among themselves, refuting the image of the rational fool who is exclusively self-interested. Dealers in financial markets have been observed to give each other relevant information, to bring social relations to the market, and to share jokes and beers (Wayne Baker 1984; Robert Shiller 1989 chapters 1 and 2 and 1995).

With this distinction of care in economic interaction it becomes possible to recognise several aspects of the role of care: as persuasion, as labour effort and as a gift. In each of these instances care appears to make up a substantial part of economic behaviour. McCloskey and Klamer (1995) have estimated that one quarter of GDP involves the gift of talking and listening, that is, persuasion. When we look at time-use data for unpaid labour this gift of care totals from 50 to 175 per cent of paid labour time, with women doing 75 per cent of caring labour (Marga Bruyn-Hundt 1996a; Luisella Goldschmidt-Clermont and Elisabetta Pagnossin-Aligisakis 1995; INSTRAW 1995; Ruth Dixon-Mueller and Richard Anker 1988; UNDP 1995). For the Netherlands the total number of hours put into unpaid labour has been estimated to be 150 per cent of the amount of labour exchanged in labour markets (CBS 1991). The substantive labour-time expression of care has hardly received attention in economics or in the anthropological literature on the gift.[17]

The gift: anthropological perspectives

Anthropologists studied the gift before economists did, as far back as Bronislaw Malinowski (1922), Marcel Mauss (1923) and Claude Lévi-Strauss (1949) (for a valuable collection on the gift, see Aafke Komter 1996). However, many of the studies appear to analyse not gifts but different forms of exchange, such as barter, chains of reciprocity and 'primitive exchange' (Marshall Sahlins 1972). As in modern exchange transactions in markets, some of these transactions described by anthropologists appear to deal with values of freedom and competition rather than with care and responsibility, the values that belong to gift giving. The Potlatch is a case in point. In a Potlatch, Indians in Alaska compete to supply the biggest gift, which contributes to their status and beats the enemy with generosity (sic): when a man fails to reciprocate with an even bigger gift he is defeated (Lévi-Strauss 1949). Lévi-Strauss argues that these 'gifts' imply a moral obligation: 'a right is established in the offering and an obligation in the receiving' (Lévi-Strauss 1949: 22). This interpretation of gifts however, brings them under the category of moral rules, not as an expression of care among actors. Later on Lévi-Strauss designates gifts as 'exchanges' (ibid.: 25).

Sahlins also equates gift and exchange through the notion of reciprocity, following Marcel Mauss who had already used the term 'gift exchange'. Sahlins argues that reciprocity involves a whole range of exchanges, of which the gift is one extreme and negative reciprocity (or appropriation) is the other, while mutual beneficial exchange lies in between. Again, the gift is portrayed as a sub-category of exchange and not as ontologically different from exchange. However, Sahlins confuses his own analysis by stating towards the end of his book *Stone Age Economics* that 'ours is a theory of value in non-exchange, or of non-exchange value' (Sahlins 1972: 277).

David Cheal (1988) locates gifts in modern societies in what he labels 'the moral economy', which he describes as a set of redundant transactions. For him, gifts are luxuries and do not add much to the receiver's well-being. Again, the importance of the gift is denied, and with it the enormous amount of unpaid labour that does contribute, and very basically so, to people's well-being. Contrary to Cheal's assumption the gift of caring labour is not redundant at all in the economy, as the time use figures and discussions on social capital indicate. Chris Gregory justifies his use of the term 'gift exchange' (Gregory 1982: 19) as mutual debts and receipts that create obligations. Again, we see a liberal and Kantian perspective on the gift: the interdependence between actors is portrayed by Gregory in terms of obligations to incur and solve debts, not in terms of a commitment to care. All these anthropological analyses of the gift suggest that gifts are a form of exchange in which the return is implied in the moment of giving: 'gift giving is not free' (James Carrier 1995: 21). As a consequence, the gift is denied as a gift and with it the value of care is denied, though probably the gift of caring labour is the largest gift in the economy.

At the same time however, the anthropological literature on the gift distinguishes itself from conventional economic thought by denying the utilitarian character of gifts. Malinowski argues that the reason why people give is that they value their mutual relationships, not necessarily or exclusively the benefits therefrom. Lévi-Strauss observes that gifts are not necessarily intended to benefit people; rather, they carry their own value. Sahlins (1972: 307) mentions generosity as an intention behind gift giving. Georg Simmel (1908) suggests that the gift expresses trust and loyalty and cannot be instrumental. David Schmidtz (1996: 167) links the motivations that people have in giving to their sense of belonging to a community, though at the same time, rather confusingly, he does not reject a utilitarian explanation.

The gift: economic perspectives

In economics gifts have received some attention too. It will come as no surprise that most economists have done so within their conventional framework of explanation, that is, by explaining gifts both in terms of exchange and in terms of utility maximisation. Kenneth Arrow (1972) is a good example, adding also the idea of a social contract:

> each individual is . . . motivated by purely egoistic satisfaction derived from the goods accruing to him, but there is an implicit social contract such that each performs duties for the other in a way calculated to enhance the satisfaction of all.
>
> (Arrow 1972: 348)

Why a pure egoist would care about 'all' is left unexplained, which starkly illuminates the deficiencies in the rationality concept that Arrow adheres to. Alternatively, Arrow argues that making a gift can increase the giver's utility because it delivers psychological satisfaction (ibid.: 348). His explanation is purely subjective and instrumental: the gift is transformed into a self-interested preference that can be traded off against the satisfaction of other self-interested preferences.

George Akerlof (1982) provides a more subtle explanation of gifts in his influential article on gifts in labour contracts but also fails to distinguish gifts from exchange. He provides an explanation of why workers may work harder even when they do not desire or expect promotion, and why employers may pay above-market wages that are higher than a worker's opportunity costs. Akerlof's explanation rests on two types of values. First, he recognises the operation of the value of justice, which he labels as the norm of a fair day's work. Second, he perceives an expression of care, which he labels as sympathy, developing among workers and between workers and a firm during the close interactions they have with each other. Akerlof rightly perceives this caring as a gift. The gift on the side of the workers is the work effort in excess of the minimum work standard; the gift on the side of the firm is the payment of above market wages. So we expect an explanation of the mutual gifts in terms of sympathy and relationships and the responsibility expressed in these.

Akerlof does not analyse any further the gifts that he perceived, however. Rather, the rest of his argument undermines his recognition of a gift. He unexpectedly turns his analysis around and starts to conceptualise the mutual gifts between employer and employees as exchanges and as utilitarian. He argues that the workers exchange the extra work effort for extra utility, which materialises in above-market wages. The firm exchanges the higher wages for the higher work effort received. The gift has been explained away: reference to it was only used to distinguish contractual work effort and contractual wages from non-contractual extra work effort and non-contractual extra wages. So, in the end Akerlof explains not gifts but non-contractual exchange. Akerlof remarks himself: 'Such giving is a trading relationship – in the sense that if one side of the exchange does not live up to expectations, the other side is also likely to curtail its activities' (Akerlof 1982: 549). In his analysis the difference between exchange and gift has effectively been removed: the gift is explained as extra-contractual exchange.

Kenneth Boulding (1981) did not equate gifts with exchange but confused them with redistribution in his notion of 'grants'. The problem with mixing values of care and justice in this way is that rules and giving, legitimised coercion and responsiveness, and the collective and interpersonal levels are lumped together as if they were the same. In fact Boulding's own example of the difference between tax payment and charity illustrates the problem of categorising care under the label of grants. In his example Boulding shows how distributive rules may be more effective than charity in instances such as tax collection. At the same time his example provides an argument against liberalist and libertarian positions against taxes: he illustrates their legitimacy – stemming from voluntary agreement on the 'coercion' of tax payment – when the rates and procedures of tax collection are agreed upon in a democratic manner.

> If governments were supported by purely voluntary contributions, it is highly likely that they would not be supported very well, and the whole society would suffer from insufficient public goods. It is not the element of threat or coercion alone, therefore, that creates a sense of exploitation but the feeling of illegitimacy. The taxpayer does not necessarily feel that he is exploited by a government that he regards as legitimate. But any taxes collected by a government regarded as illegitimate can be regarded as exploitation.
>
> (Boulding 1981: 84)

Building on these insights of freedom, justice and care, and of exchange, rules and gift, it becomes possible to distinguish ontologically each of these values and their internal allocation mechanisms. My working definition of care in the economy, then, is that care is a gift of goods or services that expresses sympathy for the care receiver and implies mutual sharing and sustaining relationships. Exchange then is a quid pro quo transaction that is concerned with the transactors' dignity and self-fulfilment, implying a competitive relationship to others. Distributive rules are an expression of fairness and imply rights that need to be realised by following agreed rules. Each of these three distinct allocation mechanisms is thus defined in terms of economic actors' experiences of them, at the level of real life. Definitions of economic behaviour that are descriptive of the level of the system are necessarily different: they do not refer to the ethical capabilities implied in the behaviour in each value domain. Therefore, I will use the term 'economic transaction' or 'interaction' to describe the level of the system:

neutral terms that do not imply moral connotations such as sympathy, free choice, or norms.

The definition of economics revisited

Each of the three types of values that operate in the economy implies four ethical capabilities: commitment, emotion, deliberation and interaction. For freedom, commitment is to values such as self-esteem and dignity as Peacock and Laslier, Fleurbaey, Gravel and Trannoy have indicated. For justice, commitment is to values like respect and fairness as Rawls, Kolm and Roemer have pointed out. For care, commitment is to values like trust and sympathy as Gauthier and Baier have suggested. The emotions that belong to each type of values may be indicated as pride in the case of freedom, a sense of rightness for justice, and affection in the case of care, though many other feelings can be attached to each of these values, as they vary between cultures. Deliberation is also different in each case. For freedom, deliberation can be characterised as choice, a deliberate choice and not an algorithm; for justice deliberation is involved in the acceptation of legitimacy of a distributive rule, whereas in the case of caring deliberation is expressed in the responsiveness to a caring need. Finally, each type of values can also be characterised in terms of the particular forms of interaction it requires. As has been discussed above these are exchange, rules and gifts in the respective practices of freedom, justice and care. These forms of interaction are located in the market (*agora*), the state (or other authority) (*polis*) and the care economy (*oikos*). This last notion comprises caring in households as well as caring in a community and voluntary activities in associations and co-operatives.

Because of these multiple dimensions present in each type of values operating in the economy these values can no longer be characterised as singular. Therefore I shall use the notion of *economic value domains*. Each type has its own domain in the economy that I will refer to as follows (without implying a hierarchical order):

1   the economic value domain of freedom,
2   the economic value domain of justice,
3   the economic value domain of care.

Without commitments actors will not be able to interact rationally with each other, as my discussion on *Rational Economic Man* in chapter one has pointed out. Without commitments to the *different* types of values that are shared in the economy and that support each other, the economic process will not be able to function in any reasonable way, as I have argued in the present chapter. In other words, at the micro level rational economic actors have commitments in each value domain. Together with these commitments they have emotions, they deliberate on the basis of their values, and they interact with others in order to further the values they are committed to. Moreover, the commitments of economic actors to the values they cherish are incommensurable: there is no single scale – utilitarian or otherwise – along which the different values that they are committed to can be measured and evaluated. The assumption that actors calculate utilitarian costs and benefits when deciding about buying a new car or having a child is simply not feasible. At the macro level commitments are shared (though also contested) with others who also value freedom, justice and care, rather than ends being subjective and instrumental as neoclassical theory suggests.

Of course the three value domains extend far beyond economic interaction – they have meaning in culture, politics, social life and the like – but I restrict my analysis to their operation in economic life. There the domains have been recognised to exist for a long time (Karl Polanyi 1944, 1968) and to adapt and shift over time. Such changes can be seen for example in the substantial shift of food provisioning from subsistence production in the care economy to production for exchange in the domain of freedom during this century. Or, in a more recent example, we see a change from the distribution of housing in the former USSR from state regulation to the market after the decline of state socialism. Such shifts in economic activity from one domain to another tend to occur endogenously or through policy measures. Often, such changes develop slowly. The value commitments, emotions attached to these commitments, the particular forms of deliberation and of interaction, none of these elements will change overnight (even in what appears to be a sudden change, as in the fall of the Berlin Wall for example).

In the domain of freedom, scarce resources may be allocated through exchange to further individualist values related to the development of one's talents and self-fulfilment (on this type of ends, see for example, Jon Elster (1986) who argues that economic actors seek self-realisation in their activities in the market). Exchange will not further freedom when applied outside this realm, as we can see in cases such as paying taxes or in family home care for an Alzheimer patient. The exercise of individual choice on tax payment or the tax rate to be paid is against the law and can be punished, limiting one's freedom. To assume that an Alzheimer patient can make her free choices on the medical market will most probably not further the patient's freedom but make her even more vulnerable.

In the domain of justice, distributive rules may further public values of solidarity and moral duty (see on this type of ends, among others, Amitai Etzioni 1988), for example in collective bargaining. But distributive rules will not further justice when applied outside this realm, for instance in the allocation of jobs or in subsistence farming.

In the domain of care, scarce resources may be allocated through gifts, for example to further the interpersonal values of parenthood and friend-ship or in unpaid childcare (see on this type of ends, Joan Tronto 1993 and Peta Bowden 1997 among others). But gifts will not further care when applied outside this realm, for example in tenders for road construction (when gifts become bribes) or in the distribution of welfare benefits (when gifts make the welfare system corrupt).

Within each economic value domain, then, values are furthered only when resources are allocated according to the appropriate allocation system for that domain: exchange furthers freedom values, redistribution furthers justice values, while giving furthers caring values (see again Figure 2.1). Within each value domain there is no linear means-ends relationship as assumed in neoclassical economics. Commitment, emotion, deliberation and interaction are mutually related, supporting each other. No constrained maximisation is possible since ends and means are not independent of each other.[18] Rather, the interdependence of the ethical capabilities in each domain suggests that behaviour in a domain is circular: it is a matter of contextual classification (Nelson Goodman 1979) or a matter of tacit conventions and meanings (Mary Douglas 1973), pointing to the working of a 'hermeneutic circle' (Paul Ricoeur 1991: 67, 1992: 179; Charles Taylor 1992: 18).[19] The circle can hardly be broken; subject and object are mutually related. It is a circle analogous to the circular flow in textbook economics, the endless flow of real and monetary variables, which cannot be understood outside the logic of the circular economic process. As a consequence, an explanation of behaviour in each value domain must necessarily involve the social context of a domain. It is through an understanding of the context that behaviour can be inter-preted. Actor (micro level) and context of each value domain (macro level) are mutually implicated.

Finally, I want to stress that the value domains, though operating in society at large, can legitimately be considered as *economic*, in the sense that each domain involves *economic* activity. Each value domain allo-cates scarce resources to contribute to human well-being within its own ethical perspective. The resources are as diverse as physical capital, finance, paid labour, social capital and unpaid labour time. But the resources do not include values. This is important to note since *values are implied in the ends* and in the process by which actors pursue these ends, *not as resources*, as some mistakenly believe. Kenneth Arrow (1972: 355) for example refers to values as resources and Daniel Hausman and Michael McPherson (1996: 220) speak of 'moral resources'. This picture of values involves a conceptual fallacy that turns values into instru-ments, as resources are, rather than perceiving them as defining the ends and the process through which the ends are pursued. But values are not resources. If they were, how scarce would they be? What would be their price? Studies on social capital for example, suggest that values are not scarce in an economic sense at all (Robert Putnam 1992). The scarcity of values may decrease rather than increase with their use. The quantity of trust and truthfulness, if measurable at all, would rather be found to increase when practised intensively within a group of people. And when they are not practised anymore their quantities may diminish, as a friendship falters that is not maintained.

In each economic value domain, then, resources are allocated in the pursuit of valuable ends that are defined in terms of the domain. This relationship between resources and valuable ends is implied in a well-known definition of economics which states that: 'economics is the science which studies human behaviour as a relationship between ends and scarce means which have alternative uses' (Lionel Robbins 1935: 16). Note that this definition, contrary to popular textbook interpretations, does *not* refer to 'endless' wants, but is as simple and human centred as Julie Nelson's definition of economics as the study of human provisioning mentioned earlier. Robbins' definition reflects *not* the alleged endlessness of wants that is nowadays assumed to motivate economic behaviour but the importance of ends for the actors in the economy.

My understanding of the economy as embedded in three value domains thus further specifies Robbins' and Nelson's definitions of economics as the study of provisioning. The ends are understood to be distributed over the three value domains and the allocation of scarce resources is not limited to exchange only, but also includes the allocation mechanisms of the other two domains. My definition of economics thus follows Robbins' definition, which it does not contest or broaden. Nor do I take on his own suggestions to broaden his definition to all kinds of behaviour. Contrary to popular definitions of economics as 'the rational choice approach' to any possible human behaviour (Gary Becker 1991), I restrict my argument to the issue of production under scarcity that furthers economic values. Thus love, fertility, drug abuse, warfare, church membership and Zen-meditation fall outside the study of economics. My intent is to specify Robbins' subject definition of economics, not to broaden it to an approach definition. Therefore, I elaborate on the types of 'ends' as value commitments. For this reason, I divide Robbins' definition of economics into the following three characteristics:

1   the domain of freedom, where scarce means are allocated through exchange to further ends of freedom,
2   the domain of justice, where scarce means are allocated through redistribution to further ends of justice,
3   the domain of care, where scarce means are allocated through giving to further ends of caring.

In this differentiated definition of economics, the values that each domain seeks to further imply the ethical capabilities that are appropriate for each type of values. Figure 2.2 presents an elaboration of the ethical capabilities in each economic value domain of freedom, justice and care. The table is only an illustration. It does not pretend to present values as Truth or as universal moral norms, as some would insist (Sissela Bok 1995). They are not meant as normative, as pointing out good and bad. Rather, they are descriptions of archetypes for economic value categories: the domains in economic life that are shared to some extent by the actors in an economy. In fact, each of these values could be expressed in a variety of ways, positively or negatively, according to dominant moral standards. The value domains refer to the *type* of value that is the end of economic activity; they do not imply any particular normative value to be furthered. I would also point out that the table does not include core economic concepts such as 'rationality', 'voluntarity' and 'efficiency'. These notions apply to every domain and therefore do not appear in the table. Their differentiated role in each domain will be explained in subsequent chapters, particularly in chapter seven.

		Domain of freedom	Domain of justice	Domain of care
Ethical capabilities		Individual values	Public values	Interpersonal values
Commitment	Value	Self-esteem Dignity Self-fulfilment	Respect Fairness Realisation of rights	Trust Sympathy Sustain relationships
	Stock variable	Freedoms	Rights	Social networks
Emotion	Feeling	Pride	Sense of rightness	Affection
	Motivation Perception of others	Autonomy Anonymous	Solidarity Equal/unequal	Responsibility Different
Deliberation	Reward Signal Evaluation Expression	Extrinsic Price Choice Exit	Collective Vote Legitimacy Voice	Intrinsic Relation Responsiveness Loyalty
Interaction	Agency Relation Allocation mechanism	Independent Competitive Exchange	Dependent Rule following Redistribution	Interdependent Sharing Giving
	Location of allocation	Market (*agora*)	State (*polis*)	Care economy (*oikos*)

Figure 2.2 Some characteristics of economic value domains

3

LIBERTÉ, ÉGALITÉ, FRATERNITÉ

> Empirically, we find the main patterns to be, reciprocity, redistribution and exchange. Reciprocity denotes movements between correlative points of symmetrical groupings; redistribution designates appropriational movements toward a centre and out of it again; exchange refers hereto vice-versa movements taking place as between 'hands' under a market system.
>
> (Karl Polanyi 1957: 250)

The three value domains in the history of economic thought

The French Revolution maxim *liberté, égalité, fraternité* comprises the values that are crucial in economic life.[1] The revolutionaries were committed to all three of its elements as if they formed a natural triad.[2] Liberty was called upon in struggles against authoritarian rule. We find appeals to justice against exploitation. And people's 'moral sentiments' for each other were praised as a force against a cold Hobbesian world. But in politics since the revolution, the value of *fraternité* has become marginalised. Liberty and justice still dominate the political discourse. Recently, political scientists and philosophers have tried to reintegrate *fraternité* as communitarianism, or through the role of the family, or the role of friendship (Marilyn Friedman 1989; Alisdair MacIntyre 1987), or as the politics of care (Joan Tronto 1993).

The French revolutionary values neatly parallel the perspective that I have just set out in chapters one and two on the interdependence between freedom, justice and care in the economy. Economics, like politics, pursued only two of these and left out the important dimension of *fraternité*. The French revolutionaries stressed that these values go together in their representation of the good and desirable society. We cannot be free without being just. We cannot be just without caring for one another. An economy, as I have argued, similarly presumes the inclusion of all three values. When freedom, justice and care are indeed all part of the economy, and relate to each other in the sense that we cannot attain one without the others, the question that arises is: how have economists understood these values to operate?

When I started this explorative exercise it seemed to be a breach with history and current practice in economics, a recent addition of the issues of commitment, emotion, deliberation and interaction. Were these indeed new concepts? So I looked for precursors in the hope of finding and learning from continuities. A first survey is discouraging. The conventional history of economic thought recognises freedom and justice as dual values. They are portrayed as if they function as mutually exclusive (Victoria Chick 1995; Sheila Dow 1985, 1990). In this duality care does not appear. It seems that it never became part of economic thought when we follow the canon. But the canon may be misleading.[3] It 'lends unity to the construction of a tradition of thought from the early "founding fathers" to present-day wisdom' (Vivienne Brown 1993: 73). From a different standpoint however, different paths can be traced from the discipline's founding fathers – and mothers. For example, Vivienne Brown (1993, 1994a) recognises the presence of *fraternité* in Adam Smith's writings.[4] Today, Smith is presented in terms of *liberté* only. But there was another Adam Smith who was concerned with *égalité* and *fraternité* as well.

The dualistically structured canon of the history of economic thought thus appears unhelpful for my enquiry: it denies the value of care and it denies a relationship between freedom and justice. But it is not impossible to find a different reading that may bring out a different perspective. 'None of this should stop anyone from looking for a synthesis, and good luck to him – or more likely, her' (Chick 1995: 40). I will not go for a synthesis but I do want to explore to what extent the French revolutionary triad appears in the history of economic thought. If it does, it might help me to conceptualise the value domain of care more explicitly in economics today and to recognise the relationships between freedom, justice and care as they have been perceived before. Of course, this endeavour can only be tentative and incomplete. But before I can embark on such an adventurous journey through the history of economic thought, I need to have a map of the area. At the outset the three value domains are vague at best. As suggested by the work of Brown, Adam Smith appears to be a good starting point to map out the three territories.

Prudence, justice and benevolence

In his *Theory of Moral Sentiments*, Adam Smith argues that people value the following three virtues: prudence, justice (sometimes referred to as propriety) and benevolence (sometimes referred to as beneficence).

> Concern for our happiness recommends to us the virtue of prudence; concern for that of other people, the virtues of justice and beneficence; of which, the one retains us from hurting, the other prompts us to promote that happiness.
>
> (Smith 1759 Part VI. II, Conclusion: 262)

Together, these three virtues represent commitments to each of the three economic value domains that I have distinguished (see also Figure 2.1). Prudence relates to the individual and the ends of the self, reflecting a concern with self-command ('temperance' in the language of Smith). It is therefore something different from mere self-interest (Amartya Sen 1987: 22) and relates to other individual virtues, such as courage (Deirdre McCloskey 1996). It is the virtue that Smith found in commercial society, enabling people to interact freely with each other in mutually beneficial exchanges. It is a virtue of freedom. Smith's concern with prudence particularly features in the *Wealth of Nations* (1776), but justice also features prominently in Smith's account. Justice urges us to respect other people's rights and freedoms, constraining our freedom to do as we like. It receives particular attention in Smith's *Lectures on Jurisprudence* (1766). The third virtue that Smith mentions is that of benevolence. This relates to personal relationship and to sympathy, the 'moral sentiments', embedded in the domain of care. Benevolence, together with temperance, is the subject of the *Theory of Moral Sentiments*. I agree with the argument made by McCloskey (1996) that Smith includes also hope and love here, summarising them under the headings of moral sentiments or benevolence.

Importantly, Smith adds to his three virtues that they are not only deemed most important by many people, but that they are necessary *and* sufficient to describe the rest of the virtues. In other words, he summarises the seven classical virtues of prudence, courage, temperance, justice, hope, love and benevolence into three:

> If virtue, therefore, does not consist in propriety, it must consist either in prudence or benevolence. Besides these three, it is scarce possible to imagine that any other account can be given of the nature of virtue.
>
> (Smith 1759 Part VII, II: 267)[5]

We find a similar triad in David Hume who labelled the virtues: 'real factions . . . from interest, from principle, and from affection' (Hume 1741 Essay VIII: 59).[6]

Smith's concern with self-interest on the one hand and with justice and benevolence on the other has puzzled many economists, as 'das Adam Smith Problem'. But Charles Bazerman (1993), Vivienne Brown (1994b),

Athol Fitzgibbons (1995) and Deirdre McCloskey (1996) have pointed out that Smith's various works have been written in different stylistic forms and with different rhetorical strategies, valuing freedom, justice and benevolence as values in themselves, as commitments, and not as a means to increase one's self-interest. They argue that Smith's texts need not be inconsistent, only different. Brown argues that the different values exposed in the *Wealth of Nations* and the *Theory of Moral Sentiments* are parallel: different but both necessary for a well functioning economy. They can be understood as together representing the viability of commercial society, where prudence needs to be constrained by justice and fed by benevolence. Fitzgibbons not only shows that Smith has an integrated system of values underlying all his works, but also suggests why such a system is needed:

> Smith's innovation was not to praise self-love and let the devil take the hindmost: he believed that a Stoic range of motives, some emanating from a high virtue and some from base self-love, would best advance the interests of the individual and the social body.
>
> (Fitzgibbons 1995: 21)

McCloskey (1996) holds even more forcefully that without the Smithian virtues economists pursue vice rather than the good. One of the intermediating mechanisms between the different virtues that Smith recognised can be found in his idea of the *impartial spectator* who represents the virtuous act of self-command for the benefit of others. The *impartial spectator* helps actors to be prudent as well as just and benevolent. Another link in Smith's value system could be seen in the idea of sympathy as feeling with a particular other.[7] Like the *impartial spectator*, the notion of sympathy contradicts a central concern with self-interest that is generally attributed to Smith's position. Re-reading his works from a standpoint that acknowledges the virtues that he proposes to operate in the economy highlights the misunderstanding involved in the Adam Smith Problem: Smith recognised three different types of values operating in economic life, values that are not instruments to self-interest but rather contributors to the flourishing of a good, commercial society that he perceived emerging.

It is hard to find similar accounts of the three value domains after Smith and Hume. With the decreasing impact of the Scottish Enlightenment of which these two authors were important representatives, attention shifted to a dichotomous interpretation of liberty and justice. For another account mapping out the three value domains I had to make a jump through time to an economic anthropologist who worked during the first half of the twentieth century. Interestingly, his account is not a philosophical or methodological one, but an empirical approach that appears to confirm Smith's triad of core virtues.

Exchange, redistribution and reciprocity

Karl Polanyi (1944, 1957, 1968) studied a wide variety of economies. From these observations he held that every economy consists of a combination of three types of economic interaction, to be distinguished by their particular human relationships. He labelled them exchange, redistribution and reciprocity, located in the subsequent realms of the market, authority and gift giving. The emphasis in Polanyi's categories is on human interaction which he linked to the virtues distinguished by Smith. The exchange in markets is – not uncritically – connected to liberty (Polanyi 1944: 252, 258). Redistribution involves social norms and rules controlled by a central authority, whereas reciprocity represents a community's cultural beliefs and traditions that relate them to each other (see Figures 2.1 and 2.2 for a clarification of the relationships between value commitments and interaction in each economic value domain). It is important to note, however, that Polanyi's use of the term 'reciprocity' is potentially confusing. In economics reciprocity is closely related to exchange, whereas Polanyi explicitly disconnects the two.

Contrary to economists' beliefs, Polanyi argued that an economy flourishes not only because of the single domain of the market, but more importantly 'by the two principles of behaviour not primarily associated with economics: reciprocity and redistribution' (ibid.: 47). In his *Essays* (Polanyi 1968: xiv) an informative table points to the underlying human values for the domains of reciprocity (such as friendship and kinship) and redistribution (political or religious affiliation). He failed to recognise values for market exchange, probably because he defined values socially, not individually. Polanyi took a rather negative view of the market, which he saw as destructive of values, creating no values in itself. Despite this misconception of the market as value-neutral, or even as morally bad, Polanyi was the first to point out a relationship between value commitments and interaction in the economy.

Exchange system, threat system and integrative system

In an elaboration of Polanyi's tripartite economic system, Kenneth Boulding (1970, 1981, 1985) conceptualises the three types of interaction as sub-systems of the greater economic system. He calls them exchange, threat and integration. Each sub-system is defined and localised within its own realm: exchange in the market, threat or rule setting in the state, and integrative relationships in family life, religion, social groups and organisations, according to Boulding. Like Smith and Polanyi, Boulding argues that each realm performs a necessary role in the economy.

> The social system can be divided into three large, overlapping, and interpenetrating systems, which are distinguished by different modes of interaction of human beings, usually assisted by various artefacts, each of which has a certain rationale of its own that is also part of the human learning process. These three systems I have called the *threat system*, the *exchange system*, and the *integrative system*. All actual human institutions and relationships involve mixtures of all three in varying proportions.
>
> (Boulding 1985: 83, emphasis in original)

With the elaboration of Polanyi's work, Boulding supplies a map of the three territories with landmarks that provide information about each domain's infrastructure. But we need more than just a map: we also need a travel guide that tells us something about the people that inhabit the territories of freedom, justice and care. What are their emotions and what is their way of deliberation?

Exit, voice and loyalty

These notions, which I have included in Figure 2.2, refer to the book *Exit, Voice, and Loyalty* by Albert Hirschman (1970).[8] The notion of exit is rooted in the value domain of freedom. It refers to choice, including the option to change one's choices when circumstances change. Hirschman describes exit as an impersonal and autonomous individual act. It implies desertion from a relationship, with the accompanying emotions of such breaking up. For example, consumers may decide to buy from a different producer when the quality of a product deteriorates: they exit from the earlier option. Voice is a different strategy, in that consumers may raise their voice and collectively demand improvements or press for product safety laws rather than leaving the producer in favour of another (see also Margaret Reid 1942; and later Mancur Olson 1975). Therefore, Hirschman labels voice as political, driven by feelings of fairness.[9] Loyalty, then, appears to be a precondition for this to happen: only with at least a minimum amount of consumer loyalty to a particular producer will consumers choose the voice option rather than the exit one. They need to feel some attachment to the product or producer to be loyal. Though important, consumer behaviour is only one example in Hirschman's book.

Although concentrating on exit and voice, Hirschman supplies his readers with a theory of loyalty. He pictures loyalty as conditional for voice: customers, workers and other actors need to have a certain level of loyalty before they will opt for voice rather than exit. 'Thus loyalty, far from being irrational, can serve the socially useful purpose of preventing deterioration from becoming cumulative, as it so often does when there is no barrier to exit' (Hirschman 1970: 79). This is a functionalist argument for loyalty. Loyalty however, also has value in itself. It contributes to emotional attachment to a certain organisation, person, or group of people and their identity. The attachment will generate a more intense work effort or relation, expressing workers' or consumers' commitments. Loyalty may not only help the strategy of voice, as a distinct expression of deliberation, it may also complement voice. Voice is confrontational whereas loyalty is a relational form of expression, which in certain contexts is more appropriate.

> In deciding whether the time has come to leave an organization, members, especially the more influential ones, will sometimes be held back not so much by the moral and material sufferings they would themselves have to go through as a result of exit, but by the anticipation that the organization to which they belong would go from bad to worse if they left.
>
> (Hirschman 1970: 98)

This argument assumes a commitment to care and an emotional attachment to caring. Indeed, Hirschman claims that 'the member continues to *care* about the activity and "output" of the organization' (ibid.: 99, emphasis added).

However important exit, voice and loyalty are in the economy, Hirschman warns that there exists no universal optimal mix between the three types of expression since 'each recovery mechanism is itself subject to the forces of decay which have been evoked here all along' (ibid.: 124).[10]

The authors introduced so far are the most obvious guides for my exploration. Their mapping of the three value domains provides me with an initial, though vague, outline of the territory in terms of commitment, emotion, deliberation and interaction. In the rest of this chapter I will travel through each domain, from ancient times through the eighteenth century into the nineteenth and early twentieth century. However, this voyage would be incomplete if it addressed only one particular group of economists. The diversity of the territory to be explored requires attention to a diverse group of authors, to ensure a thorough understanding of each of the values of freedom, justice and care. Therefore, I will listen not only to the male economists who dominate the canon but equally to what female precursors have to say from their particular standpoints (Sandra Harding 1987). Women economists have been excluded from the canon for far too long (Mary-Ann Dimand, Robert Dimand and Evelyn Forget

1995; Dorothy Lampen Thomson 1973; Michèle Pujol 1992). Their voice may be of particular interest *because* of their exclusion from the dualist canon, bringing in knowledge different from what fits in the dominant representation of the history of economic thought. John Stuart Mill, as one of the very few economists who recognised the flaw of excluding women's voices from economic theory, therefore argued that:

> we may safely assert that the knowledge which men can acquire of women, even as they have been and are without reference to what they might be, is wretchedly imperfect and superficial, and always will be so, until women themselves have told all that they have to tell.
>
> (John Stuart Mill 1869: 153)

An exploration into the value domain of freedom

Epicurus

The voyage into the domain of freedom starts with the Greek moral philosopher Epicurus who wrote on liberty and its virtue of prudence. For Epicurus, the end of human action was happiness. Not self-indulgent pleasure but a quiet state of peace of mind undisturbed by public duties and emotions. 'This pleasure, that is the very centre of our happiness, consists in nothing else than having our mind free from disturbance, and our body free from pain' (*Morals*: 97). The only cares and emotions proper for a man, according to Epicurus, are for his family and for himself.[11]

Epicurus's *Morals* are consequentialist: one chooses a particular action because it brings more pleasure than pain. Therefore, Epicurus holds that we should be prepared to suffer pain in the short run when in the end the pleasures are greater. Among the necessary pains he includes a sober life, without excess of drink, food, or status. Later Jeremy Bentham (1789) declared him to be his spiritual father in his own interpretation of utilitarianism. However, the pleasures that Epicurus mentions are very different from those listed by Bentham.[12] For Bentham, pleasures are related to the senses and social rank, and they do include food, drink and status. With Epicurus, pleasures are defined spiritually, as the good life without feelings of remorse, shame or guilt towards the self or others. The major virtue of Epicurean morality is prudence:

> she discounts the benefit and utility of being freed from ignorance ... [and] likewise she is the source of all the virtues that teach us that life cannot be agreeable, if prudence, honesty and justice do not direct all its motions.
>
> (*Morals*: 99)

Virtues other than prudence, such as honesty and justice, appear to be relevant to the state of peace of mind. Hence, peace of mind does include other virtues besides prudence. The quiet state of rest assumes that we seek to live up to a variety of virtues and that, when we don't act upon them, they can seriously disturb our equilibrium. So Epicurus's idea of freedom includes efforts on behalf of the happiness of others.

> Moreover, the liberty we have of acting as we please, is incompatible with any force that shall tyrannise over us; for which reason we are always guilty when we do ill things, as we are worthy of praise when we suffer ourselves to be guided by the dictates of prudence.
>
> (*Morals*: 101)

Prudence thus appears as an individualist virtue that none the less presumes efforts to fulfil the demands of other-regarding virtues. Without those actions our minds cannot find the rest that defines our happiness. It is here, at the end of Epicurus's treatise on morality, that we see a strong, almost self-evident, relationship established between prudence and the virtues of justice and care. Our liberty demands respect for that of other people, and our choosing requires that we take responsibility for the effects of our actions upon others, or for the consequences of not acting where we should have acted. However, Bentham denied the virtue character of Epicurean utilitarianism when he suggested that individual and independent utility maximisation as the maximisation of pleasure should be foundational for the political sciences.

Adam Smith

Although I have argued that Adam Smith's contribution to the value domains of justice and care has been undervalued in the history of economics, and that his work is mistakenly taken to represent liberalism only, his ideas on freedom are nevertheless important. His position on freedom is even more intriguing against the background of his work on the other values. By addressing his ideas on all three values, I hope to be able to tell a different story from the one delivered in 'das Adam Smith Problem'.

The *Wealth of Nations* (1776) is generally claimed to be the founding text of modern economics, in particular for general equilibrium theory. But the much celebrated 'Invisible Hand' only appears once in the voluminous book, almost incidentally (halfway through Book IV. II on page 456 of the 1981 edition). Smith knew very well that markets are not teleological entities, guided by a heavenly hand. Rather, he perceived economic life as intense human interaction to 'truck, barter, and exchange one thing for another' (Book I. II: 25). The values of this humanly devised market place are liberal, expressing economic actors' virtue of prudence. Prudence guides people's investment choices and their labour efforts, their trades and skills, inducing an efficient resource allocation through a division of labour. The aim is for people 'to enable them to provide [such] a revenue or subsistence for themselves' (Book IV, Introduction: 428). Yet this characterisation of economic behaviour does not rely on utility or profit maximisation, as was Bentham's idea, nor on a self-interested accumulation to satisfy endless needs, as is the modernist idea expressed in economic textbooks of today. Smith's assumption is that liberal markets reward those who work with skill and diligence with a 'liberal reward of labour' (Book IV. VIIb: 565). Where their labour does not earn them a decent living, Smith calls for justice.

> No society can surely be flourishing and happy, of which the greater part of the members are poor and miserable. It is but equity, besides, that they who feed, cloath and lodge the whole body of the people, should have such a share of the produce of their own labour as to be themselves tolerably well fed, cloathed and lodged.
>
> (Smith 1776 Book I. VIII: 96)

According to Smith, not only for individual labourers but also for the economy as a whole, liberty and justice should go hand in hand, the second guaranteeing a decent living when the first fails to provide this. 'The establishment of perfect justice, of perfect liberty, and of perfect equality, is the very simple secret which most effectually secures the highest degree of prosperity to all the three classes' (Smith 1776 Book IV. IX: 669). Thus, Smith regards justice as the wider ethical framework in which liberty is embedded, that is, the ethical and legal context in which freedom is enabled and constrained as well. 'Every man, as long as he does not violate the laws of justice, is left perfectly free to pursue his own interest his own way' (Book IV. IX: 687).

Liberty, as expressed through the virtue of prudence in free exchange, requires moral duty and law but also needs to build on values that are developed in the home, according to Smith. He stresses the education in family life which leads to the reproduction of the ethics of care. Indeed, Smith argues how important the values taught at home are for an efficient labour force. And he is one of the few classical economists to recognise that the production factor of labour is, like that of capital, in fact a produced factor. His argument is not one of moral duty or love, but of economics:

> The children, during the tender years of infancy, are well fed and properly taken care of, and when they are grown up, the value of

their labour greatly over-pays their maintenance. When arrived at maturity, the high price of labour, and the low price of land, enable them to establish themselves in the same manner as their fathers did before them.

(Smith 1776 Book IV. VIIb: 565)

Smith uses a human capital argument, not in the limited sense of formal education and training, but in terms of the investment the care-giving parent puts into her offspring, thereby enabling the reproduction of a healthy, strong and morally well-prepared labour force. Therefore, Smith favours education at home, as was common for daughters in his time, rather than in schools as became the norm for sons.

There are no publick institutions for the education of women, and there is accordingly nothing useless, absurd or fantastical in the common course of their education. They are taught what their parents or guardians judge it necessary or useful for them to learn.

(Smith 1776 Book V. If: 781)

The *Wealth of Nations* thus clearly links freedom to justice and to care, arguing that both these values are necessary for liberty to flourish. There is no contradiction between the three types of values for Smith: they complement each other and do not need to be commensurable as those economists adhering to 'das Adam Smith Problem' believe they should be. For Smith each domain contributes to the economy in its own way, as does the one that most economists have excluded from economics as a 'women's domain'.[13]

It is clear that women's reproductive work, not just in bearing children but also in rearing them in an appropriate environment and in fashioning them into productive workers and loyal citizens, is an essential contribution to the 'wealth of nations'.

(Pujol 1992: 21)

John Stuart Mill and Harriet Taylor

The third exemplary contribution describing the value domain of freedom in economics is not by an individual, but by a writing-couple: John Stuart Mill and Harriet Taylor.[14] Their partnership in writing stimulates a different reading of their texts. In this section I will refer to *On Liberty* and to *Principles of Political Economy* wherein their ideas on freedom are expressed most explicitly.[15]

For Mill and Taylor, liberty was the idea of the free and autonomous individual. Liberty is not utilitarian as Mill made clear, distinguishing

68

himself from an important utilitarian, his father James Mill, follower of Bentham. We recognise an Epicurean influence, for example in the *Principles of Political Economy* where Mill and Taylor reject luxurious consumption as did Epicurus (*Morals:* 52). *On Liberty* describes the value of freedom in opposition to authoritarian control.

> He cannot rightfully be compelled to do or forbear because it will be better for him to do so, because it will make him happier, because in the opinion of others, to do so would be wise or even right. These are good reasons for remonstrating with him, or reasoning with him, or persuading him, or entreating him, but not for compelling him or visiting him with any evil in case he do otherwise.
>
> (Mill 1859: 68)

Mill and Taylor claim that 'over himself, over his own body and mind, the individual is sovereign' (ibid.: 69). Although the masculine pronoun is employed in these quotes, the authors state on various occasions in both books that sovereignty is not to be restricted to the male half of the population. In the *Principles*, they oppose the Factory Acts that restrict women's liberty in the labour market.[16] In the *Subjection of Women*, Mill defends liberty for women in terms of the dignity that it would provide them: 'The power of earning is essential to the dignity of a woman, if she has not independent property' (Mill 1869: 179). No patriarchal protection is needed in their eyes for women who are able to earn an independent livelihood. Here, we see a link with justice: liberties should be distributed equally according to Taylor and Mill, both in public and in private life. In private life, they perceive liberty as the absence of dependence and power.[17]

Liberty is expressed with the help of choice, representing free will. 'The human faculties of perception, judgement, discriminative feeling, mental activity, and even moral preference are exercised only in making a choice' (Mill 1959: 122). Moreover, the deliberation that precedes choice not only draws on commitments and emotions belonging to the domain of liberty, but also involves the other value domains. For Mill and Taylor choice includes the 'rights of others', and this shows a commitment to justice and 'affection' that implies a caring emotion (ibid.: 123). Thus Mill and Taylor guide us to an intersection of roads where the territory of liberty meets the domains of justice and care.

At this crossroads, Mill and Taylor, following Smith, regard justice as a legitimate constraint on liberty. 'The only purpose for which power can be rightfully exercised over any member of a civilized community, against his will, is to prevent harm to others' (ibid.: 68). As was seen with Mill and Taylor's views on women's economic position, justice is more than a mere constraint: justice is valuable in its own right for everyone, so that sovereign individuals are expected to support and cherish it, and help to sustain it.

> There are so many positive acts for the benefit of others which he may rightfully be compelled to perform, such as to give evidence in a court of justice, to bear his fair share in the common defence or in any other joint work necessary to the interest of the society of which he enjoys the protection.
>
> (*On Liberty*: 70)

The argument is phrased in terms of solidarity: the members of a particular community all enjoy its accompanying benefits, and therefore should also share in the costs of upholding the communal framework. Justice thus is not dualistically placed *vis-à-vis* liberty, but appears to be a necessary neighbouring value domain to which liberty is related in various ways.

Liberty, however, does not relate only to solidarity and moral duty. Free individuals are also perceived 'to perform certain acts of individual beneficence, such as saving a fellow creature's life or interposing to protect the defenceless against ill-usage' (ibid: 70). Such benevolent acts are expressed in terms of responsibility since 'he may rightfully be made responsible to society for not doing [them]' (ibid.: 70). Mill and Taylor locate the source of the value of responsibility in what I have called the care economy:

> Every human being has been brought up from infancy at the expense of much labour to some person or persons, and if this labour, or part of it, had not been bestowed, the child would never have attained the age and strength which enabled him to become a labourer in his turn.
>
> (*Principles* 1848 Book I.ii.7: 39)

It is not only the physical capability of workers that is developed in the care economy, but also the ethical capabilities that rational economic actors need in their economic lives. Mill and Taylor label these as the 'fidelity' (ibid.: 139) and 'zeal' of workers, and the 'generosity' of employers (ibid.: 404), which are crucial in the interaction between employer and employee, that is, in a labour relation. Together, these value commitments enable 'security' (ibid.: 113) in a labour relation; in other words they support the intrinsic motivation and, as a consequence, also the productivity of workers. The authors argue that labour productivity is stimulated in secure, long-term work relationships 'where long continuance in the same service, and reciprocal good offices, have produced either personal attachment, or some feeling of common interest' (ibid.: 140). The values of care are thus perceived as a necessary condition for the functioning of the labour market. 'The carefulness, economy, and general trustworthiness of labourers are as important as their intelligence. Friendly relations, and a community of interest and feeling between labourers and employers, are eminently so' (Mill 1848 Book I.xii.3: 187). Moreover, Mill and Taylor perceive another intersection between the domains of freedom and care, again in the labour market. Drawing on women's experiences of carrying out a diversity of tasks in economic life they suggest that the versatility this displays could very well compete with men's specialised labour in industry. They noticed the many different tasks that women tend to carry out in their factory jobs and work at home, and they perceived the ease with which they seem to be able to shift between these tasks.

> Women are in the constant practice of passing quickly from one manual, and still more from one mental operation to another, which therefore rarely costs them either effort or loss of time, while a man's occupation generally consists in working steady for a long time at one thing, or one very limited class of things.
>
> (*Principles* Book I.viii.5: 127–8)

Mill and Taylor praise the flexibility implied in the co-ordination of multiple tasks and recognise an advantage over the physical stress and mental monotony of the specialised factory functions that are mainly performed by men. They suggest that, contrary to received opinion, the combination of different tasks may be more efficient than specialisation in a single one. A division of labour along the lines of specialised functions may not necessarily be more efficient than a flexible combination of different roles.

Finally, Mill and Taylor point out the economy-wide relevance of an important value that is generated and furthered in the domain of care: the value of trust. Trust is not only important in the labour market, they argue, but for all economic interaction. 'The advantage to mankind of being able to trust one another, penetrates into every crevice and cranny of human life: the economical is perhaps the smallest part of it, yet even this is incalculable' (*Principles* Book I.vii.5: 111). The domain of care thus does not just exist alongside the domain of liberty. The domains are interrelated, they interpenetrate each other. The border between them gets blurred while at the same time the two territories remain distinct from each other, each with their own particular characteristics. Mill and Taylor regard the domain of liberty as very important, but they recognise similarly important domains of justice and care that are closely connected to each other.

So far this chapter has explored the domain of liberty, with the help of

Epicurus, Smith and Mill and Taylor, and its relation to the other two territories has been discovered along the road; it is now time to change the perspective to these other domains. The next destination is the domain of justice.

An exploration into the value domain of justice

Plato

A first mapping of the domain of justice can be found in Plato. He expressed his view of the ideal state in the *Republic*. The book sets out a philosophy of public life in the *polis* in which justice is perceived as the pillar for the ideal state.

Equality is an important criterion for the just state, asserting that everyone should obey its rules and respect property rights. Nevertheless, Plato proposes three social classes in society, each with its own tasks (*Republic:* 434). The rules apply to everyone, being just in themselves, designed by the class of wise rulers. The rules also assign different tasks to the different classes, each having a separate role in the state. But justice also matters at the individual level, according to Plato.

> Justice, therefore, we may say, is a principle of this kind; its real concern is not with external actions, but with a man's inward self, his true concern and interest. The just man will not allow the three elements which make up his inward self to trespass on each other's functions or interfere with each other, but, by keeping all three in tune, like the notes of a scale (high, middle, and low, and any others there be), will in the truest sense set his house to rights, attain self-mastery and order, and live on good terms with himself.
>
> (*Republic:* 443d)

Justice here is not only a principle to be followed for the sake of a just state but valuable in its own right, a personal commitment that is part of one's 'inward self'. But emotion is excluded from this self: Plato was afraid that emotion would distract individuals from obeying the rules of justice. The relationship between individuals and the state is pictured as one in which all men and women are 'a link in the unity of the whole' (ibid.: 520). Each has to contribute to the whole, and those with greater capabilities should contribute the most. Socrates, Plato's main character, argues: 'The object of our legislation is not the special welfare of any particular class in our society, but of society as a whole' (ibid.: 519e). The rules therefore prohibit private property, marriage and family life. Children should become public property. On the other hand, all public functions should be open to men and women alike, as to guarantee the most efficient allocation of resources for the just state.

In the *Republic*, all interaction is regulated by the rulers. No freedom is allowed, no caring possible. In fact, the domain of justice has become isolated from the territories of freedom and care. This rule-based society is similar to a social contract, although less democratic than Rawls' one. There is no such thing as collective bargaining before the contract is agreed: it is the class of rulers that designs the principles of justice for all. But the idea of justice is similar to the one proposed in the *Theory of Justice*, suffering from a similar inconsistency: the need for care has been defined away, by Rawls theoretically in the construction of the initial position and by Plato as a rule. Like Rawls however, Plato cannot avoid including some form of care in his analysis, as underlying the attitudes that induce people to agree on rules of justice and to keep to them. That is why in the book's dialogue Socrates asks Glaucon about the organisation of the republic: 'For that shan't we need men who, besides being intelligent and capable, really care for the community?' (ibid.: 412c). When the answer comes in the end, after many discussions between Socrates and others, care appears to be controlled by justice. It has been turned into a rule: 'we compel them to have some care and responsibility for others' (ibid.: 520a). In Plato's *Republic* the value domain of justice not only isolates itself from the other domains, it also declares its hegemony over them.

Karl Marx

The next guide on justice, in the nineteenth century, must undoubtedly be Karl Marx (although today this is not obvious).[18] It is widely acknowledged that Marx presented a radical critique of capitalism. However, what has been recognised only since the 1970s (for example by Allan Wood 1972) is that Marx did not do so on grounds of justice (see for later developments of this argument, among others, Allen Buchanan 1982; Jon Elster 1985; Elliot Pruzan 1988; John Roemer 1982). His critique of capitalism was centred around the notion of exploitation, which is a concept belonging to exchange, not to rules of justice. Exploitation refers to a lack of freedom, not to a lack of justice, though justice may help to prevent exploitation, as I will argue.

Marx did not phrase his critique of capitalism in terms of rights, equality, or any other principle of justice. Rather, he found exploitation to be the negative side-effect inherent in the capitalist mode of production, the necessary and unavoidable consequence of an economy that is exclusively structured around free exchange. His critique thus was aimed at the internal inconsistency of liberalism and its material expression in the capitalist mode of production. One of his objections concerns the utilitarianism behind liberalism, on the ground that it would deny people's humanity.

Marx rejects utilitarianism but does not defend a rights-based image of humanity (Buchanan 1982: 50). Instead, he argues against those socialist utopians who defend equal rights and norms of justice. For Marx, this would not change anything in the exploitative nature of the wage system (Pruzan 1988: 21). He illustrates his objection in an essay on *Value, Price and Profit*:

> To clamour for equal or even equitable retribution on the basis of the wages system is the same as to clamour for freedom on the basis of the slavery system. What you think just or equitable is out of the question. The question is: what is necessary and unavoidable with a given system of production?
>
> (Marx 1855: 80)

His main argument against capitalism is its exploitative nature, consisting of three elements:

- unpaid surplus labour,
- forced labour stemming from the fact that the capitalist owns the means of production,
- the consequence that the product of labour is not controlled by the workers.

Marx's critique employs the language of liberty. For Marx, production should help people to gain freedom: not only the formal freedom of being able to leave a wage labour relation, but particularly what he calls 'real freedom', consisting of the values of autonomy, self-realisation and the ability to choose one's aims. Jon Elster (1985: 205) has characterised this as positive freedom that runs parallel to John Stuart Mill and Harriet Taylor's understanding of the intrinsic value of freedom. So Marx argues against capitalism not because he is against freedom and favours justice instead, but in terms of freedom itself. Moreover, he regards justice as a necessary counter-force against exploitation, but one that cannot change the mechanism of exploitation itself. To him, justice belongs to bourgeois ideology, the superstructure, representing only abstract ideas, without substance for material conditions and basic human values (Buchanan 1982: 50; Elster 1985: 216). Justice would not be forceful enough to resist the capitalist mode of production and accompanying exploitation of wage labour, according to Marx.

However, Marx phrased his critique of exploitation in such normative overtones of moral wrongs and unfairness – as in the accusations of 'robbery' and 'theft' – that it suggests some underlying idea of justice (Elster 1985: 222). Moreover, his argument against exploitation includes a notion of justice: he argues that capitalist profit violates the principles of 'to each

74

according to his contribution', which is a principle of justice, although embedded in the liberal idea of free exchange. Thus Marx's critique of capitalism, even when phrased in terms of constrained freedom, cannot escape some underlying notion of justice.

Marx's thought is claimed to imply two levels of justice. On the one hand there is a social level of justice referred to as either distributive justice (Buchanan 1982), social justice (Pruzan 1988), or a hierarchical theory of justice (Elster 1985). 'Hence, Marx had a hierarchical theory of justice, by which the contribution principle provides a second-best criterion when the needs principle is not yet historically ripe for application' (Elster 1985: 230). On the other hand there is an individual level of justice referred to as the level of rights (Buchanan 1982). Many Marxist interpreters reject the idea that Marx had a theory based on legal rights, but leave the possibility open that he envisioned a type of rights beyond the principled realm of justice. Marx seemed to refer to a communal society that would not need a social contract, society in which human association is regarded as more important than material needs and in which work is satisfying in itself (Buchanan 1982: 51–8, 65). Here we recognise intrinsic motivation, sharing and the importance of relationships: all belonging to the value domain of care. However, Marx did not substantiate his vague references to the role of caring in the post-capitalist society that he envisioned. Therefore, his view of rights also remains unclear. The suggestion that Marx imagined a different category of 'rights' that would be located in the territory of care rather than justice would be sheer speculation.

Nevertheless, what is clear is the relationship that Marx found between justice and freedom. For him freedom is not self-supportive, either historically or logically. His argument is similar to Rawls', though less developed. The exploitation that is the necessary and unavoidable result of an economy that relies only on liberalism demands the counterforce of justice, whatever the exact contents of this justice might be, argues Marx. He recognises that the formal rules of justice, such as private property laws and rules enforcing exchange relationships, are pre-conditional for liberalism to function at all. So, Marx points out, justice is needed to make freedom work, not only in distribution of benefits *afterwards*, to compensate for exploitation, but also in the access to resources *before* the allocation process. Rawls groups these together in the notion of 'primary goods'. It is this insight gained from Marx, that we recognise too in liberal economists such as Smith, Mill and Taylor. Smith argued in the *Wealth of Nations* for an adequate level of subsistence for workers, to be fed, clothed and lodged properly but also to enable them to raise a family:

> Thus far at least seems certain, that, in order to bring up a family, the labour of the husband and wife together must, even in the

lowest species of common labour, be able to earn something more than what is precisely necessary for their own maintenance.
(Smith 1776: Book I. VIII: 85–6)

Justice is called for, according to Smith, when liberty fails to provide workers with a reasonable livelihood. This justice could be organised either in terms of access to resources or in terms of redistribution of benefits, as Amartya Sen argues so clearly with his concept of entitlements.

John Stuart Mill and Harriet Taylor develop their commitment to justice further. They do not regard justice only as enabling liberty or keeping in check the negative and contradictory side effects of liberty. They also value justice for its own sake. In the *Principles* they characterise justice as 'the primary virtue' (Mill 1848 Book I.xi.4: 174) and they defend poor people's land rights (ibid.: 331) and the Poor Laws (ibid.: 754–7). Moreover, Mill and Taylor provide us with some hints to what they envision as social justice, which should not only be grounded in equality as in the socialist discussions of their times. Rather, they follow Marx in their suggestion that justice should go beyond mere equality. Justice should 'now also [be grounded] on sympathetic association; having its root no longer in the instinct of equals for self-protection, but in a cultivated sympathy between them' (ibid.: 174). This is a recognition of the value domain of care and brings out clearly what is missing in social contract theories of justice such as Plato's *Republic* and Rawls' *Theory of Justice*.

Mill and Taylor also, however, fail to develop this idea any further. Their views on justice and care, like Marx's, remain unclear and sometimes contradictory, as in their argument against charity. Charity undermines people's independence and self-esteem, that is, their liberty, they rightly notice. They prefer a more equal distribution of income, which would not undermine but support such independence. This, however, contrasts with their wish for more emphasis on 'sympathy' rather than 'equality' in the public debate of their time. The contradiction between justice and care remains unresolved until the introduction of home economics that tries to develop connecting routes from the domain of justice to the domains of care and freedom.

Margaret Reid

Like Mill and Taylor, Reid developed her ideas on the role of care in the economy from the experiences of women: women's roles as consumers, as supplying unpaid labour in the home and the community, as investing in the next generation of labourers, and as participants in a labour market that treats them on an unequal basis with men in terms of job segregation, lower wages and limited promotion. It is this female epistemology that helped to develop the new field of home economics in the first half of the twentieth century, particularly in Chicago. But at the same time the innovation of developing the values of care into economic analysis received little recognition.

Margaret Reid first developed her ideas outside economics and gradually integrated her work into the economic discipline.[19] But it was not until the second half of the century that home economics came to be recognised as part and parcel of micro economics, an acknowledgement that was affirmed in 1992 with the Nobel Prize awarded to Gary Becker who continued Reid's work. Eventually her work was acknowledged by her former colleagues, but that took fifty years.[20] Her pioneering work on housing studies, the permanent income hypothesis, consumption and unpaid labour influenced generations of students.

Reid shows a commitment to all three value domains in the economy, and they all play a role in what she describes as a 'good market'. In her book *Consumers and the Market* (1942), she develops eight criteria that constitute a good market in her view. One of these criteria is fair prices. She explains these as the level of prices which 'ensure a continuous supply of a particular commodity in the market' (Reid 1942: 115). One way to ensure such fair prices is through the consumer movement voicing its views, as Reid argues. This is the same concern with voice that Hirschman would repeat a few decades later, also in relation to consumption and a consumer movement.

Reid defends fair prices from the perspective of consumer needs, not from the perspective of producers. It is not the idea of self-interest of all parties in the market that drives her idea of fairness, but the needs of the party she is most concerned with. The interests of producers are taken as a necessary constraint on the fairness of prices: if price levels fell too low, there would be no continuous supply anymore. She thus recognises the need for free markets rather than state regulated prices, but at the same time she wants markets to be just. Reid acknowledges the importance of competition in leading to low prices, but also warns her colleagues that competition is only a means and should not be mistaken for an end in itself. Another of her criteria for a good market is that markets should produce socially desirable goods and generate a legitimate income distribution. She asserts that perfect competition does not necessarily bring socially desired production, nor a desirable income distribution (ibid.: 560). Therefore, she introduces a 'guiding principle' for markets that finds a remarkable parallel in Rawls' later developed 'maximin principle'. 'Reduction in productive efficiency and the existence of idle resources should be tolerated only if the major part of any increase in income, either from higher prices or state subsidy, goes to alleviate poverty' (Reid 1942: 578). As with Rawls, Reid's principle of justice is meant to constrain the domain of freedom and to secure people's equal access to basic goods to satisfy their needs.

In *Food for People* (1943) Reid concentrates her analysis on efficiency. Again, her desire is to see people's welfare improve: she argues that economists should try to help this normative aim with as much positive economics as possible. But this does not imply that she accepts value-neutral economic concepts. She creatively redefines efficiency away from maximum production, which she regards 'a very meagre goal' (Reid 1943: 7) to the ethically expressive notion of the absence of waste. She defines waste in four aspects: as unused productive resources, inefficient production methods, production of goods that contribute relatively less to welfare (such as food with poor nutritional capacity) and, in distributive terms, 'waste [that] occurs if rich men are eating to excess while poor men are starving' (ibid.: 9). This pragmatic definition of efficiency requires much interpretation – for example in comparing marginal benefits between different persons – but, unlike Pareto Optimality, it includes the relationship between production and distribution. *Consumers and the Market* and *Food for People* thus develop connections between the domains of freedom and justice in terms of fairness: fair prices, a fair guiding principle of distribution and a reinterpretation of efficiency as the absence of waste.

Reid's book on the *Economics of Household Production* (1934) has a focus on the value domain of care. In her analysis, production in the care economy consists of domestic labour, childcare, community work and subsistence agriculture. Through valuing such production as economic and contributing to well-being, she argues that the economy needs both market production and production in the care economy: they are complementary. Again, she links up with and criticises a received notion in economics: specialisation. While admitting that specialised production for the market brings valuable economies of scale, she suggests that a certain minimum level of agricultural production for the producers' own use is desirable. She underpins this argument for what I shall term 'subsistence production' and other home-based production with three arguments. First, unpaid production is sometimes more efficient than market production because it does not entail what we would call today transaction costs. Second, some goods can never be produced in markets but only within and around the home; these are the ones closely linked with personal relationships, which include moral qualities such as 'companionship, sympathy and interest' (ibid.: 12).[21] Their production for the market would generate less satisfaction, according to Reid, which would imply a waste of resources and hence an inefficiency. The third reason for combining production for exchange with home production in the care economy is that it reduces risks. Reid argues that the risks involved in specialisation in market production in terms of food or income insecurity can be countered by subsistence production. So production for the market, a fair redistribution through state regulation, and subsistence production together with unpaid household labour appear as complementary in the works of Reid. They can only partially be substituted for each other.

Reid thus not only tries to establish connections between the domains of justice and freedom. She also pays serious attention to the value domain of care in the economy, characterised in terms of agricultural subsistence production and unpaid household labour. In this way, she elaborates the tentative ideas of Smith, Marx, Mill and Taylor on what they called social justice, and what all of them characterised in terms of sympathy as Reid does. Rather than envisioning bargains over rights in the domain of justice, she stresses the importance of sympathetic inter-personal relationships that are furthered through caring. What Reid adds to the recognition of values of sympathy by Smith, Marx, Mill and Taylor is, first, the argument of complementary domains as opposed to specialisation in either domain, because the intrinsic values that belong to the production of care cannot be produced through market exchange. Her second addition is the argument of risk minimisation that this complementary production in the domains of freedom and care ensures. The role of the domain of justice remains important though, since it establishes the fairness that is needed in the distribution of resources over the different domains.

In her work, Reid has indicated that what she sees as the 'good econ-omy' necessarily involves the intrinsic valuing of all three domains. Furthermore, she has linked the role of care to conventional economic notions such as efficiency and specialisation. This provides the traveller in the territories of economic value domains with some minimum necessary tools to understand the economics of the domain of care. The road leading to the domain of care begins with signs pointing to the 'good life'.

An exploration into the value domain of care

Aristotle

As I have noted in chapter one, Aristotle wrote on virtue ethics, concen-trating on the contextual idea of what constitutes the good life. He starts from the assumption in his *Politics* that the social and political are primary to the individual: humans are social and political beings, not independent individuals who eventually come to realise that they need to construct and agree on a social contract. Starting from a socialised concept of human being, Aristotle defines in his *Nichomachean Ethics* (*NE*) the end of (economic) life as *eudaimonia*, a pluralist conception of well-being. The valuable ends in human life are chosen for their own sake and they are self-sufficient, Aristotle maintains, not instrumental to a higher goal that would make the ends commensurable: pleasure, utility, or otherwise. The acts involved in pursuing the intrinsically valuable ends should strive for excellence and completeness. They imply that the good life consists of a plurality of incommensurable ends. As a consequence, Aristotle argues, the virtuous person would seek a mean between excess and deficiency of each value, rather than maximise one ultimate, commensurable goal.

Virtue thus involves commitment, but also deliberation. Deliberation is necessarily a voluntary process, thereby involving choice, legitimacy and responsiveness or, taken together: voluntary. 'The virtues are modes of choice or involve choice' (NE: II.5). Virtue cannot be forced, nor is it conditional on a return. It is only through voluntary deliberation that an actor will find the mean between deficiency and excess, not by rule or constrained maximisation (NE: II.9). The mean between deficiency and excess is relative, defined by context and relationships to other people. While seeking it, we try to take into account the possible consequences of our actions, as Aristotle argues; we are responsible to others, since we all form part of the same community. But care alone is insufficient to ensure *eudaimonia* to all; Aristotle argues for various concepts of justice too, as 'the lawful and the fair' (NE: V.1). In exchange, Aristotle interprets justice as appropriate reciprocity, that is, as a mean between benefits for one party and those for another (NE: V.5). In fact, this integration of a justice measure in exchange relations ensures that the gains from trade would be distributed appropriately, that is, according to what in the context of the trade appears as the mean between too great a benefit for one and too little for the other. (This idea can also be found in Mill, 1859, in the argument that the gains from trade should be distributed according to need.) In modernist economics however, trade is perceived as legitimate even when the gains are distributed very unevenly, as in the trade between Europe and Africa while Africa's needs are, relatively speaking, more pressing than Europe's.

In distinguishing virtue from pleasure, Aristotle says that virtue cannot be grounded on pleasure, although the latter may be a by-product of virtuous behaviour (just like usefulness). Thus, modern interpretations of virtues, such as a hedonistic or self-interested interpretation of prudence, are not what Aristotle meant by the term. The good invokes pleasure (NE: X.4) and usefulness (NE: VIII.4) but cannot be equated with them. As an illustration, Aristotle mentions various pleasurable activities that are enhanced when enjoyed by those who perform them; making music is a case in point.

For Aristotle, justice is a virtue, as it is for Smith and Hume. Aristotle understands justice in terms of virtue ethics, as a contextually dependent ethic. His notion of justice seems to precede the idea of social justice to be found in Marx, though he uses the notion of equity to distinguish principles of justice from social justice. The equitable is 'not the legally just, but a correction of legal justice. The reason is that all law is universal but about some things it is not possible to make a universal statement which shall be correct' (NE: V.10).

However, Aristotle does not refer in any way to a domain of care in his description of the virtues, though he puts much emphasis on virtues such as friendship. His study does not point to the *oikos* as an important place where virtue is furthered by the activities in the household economy. This is paradoxical since he does recognise that the virtues need to be learned in one's education at home, and they need to involve responsibility towards others. But he regarded household activities and their actors, slaves and women, as subordinate and hence not the appropriate episte-mological sources for developing his ethics. Despite this, Aristotle can be located in the value domain of care, because his theory of ethics derives from the characteristics of caring, that is, personal relationships, human vulnerability and personal responsibility. This distinguishes Aristotle from ethical theories that have freedom as their sole end on the one hand, and ethical theories that are based on moral principles on the other. Ruth Groenhout (1998) has shown how closely Aristotle's virtue ethics is related to the ethics of care, even though he did not sufficiently recognise the practices of caring by women and slaves.

> Contemporary versions of utilitarian, Kantian, and contract ethics almost universally define the moral reasoner as a disengaged, disembodied, ahistorical self – precisely the conception of moral agency which an ethics of care rejects. . . . In Aristotle's ethics one finds an acknowledgement of the contextual nature of moral reasoning and a recognition of a connection between reason and emotion (rather than an opposition between them).
>
> (Ruth Groenhout 1998: 186)

But, indeed, Aristotle largely neglected the *oikos*, the domain of the care economy, in his virtue ethics. Therefore, we are in need of a more explicit recognition of the values of care. Such a commitment we find with Adam Smith who called these values the moral sentiments.

Adam Smith

Until this point I have discussed Smith's views on freedom in the *Wealth of Nations*, some of his ideas on justice as they appeared in the same book, and the links he made between the territories of freedom and justice and connections from freedom and justice to the values of care. Now it is time to consider his *Theory of Moral Sentiments* (1759) which presents his analysis of what I have named the value domain of care.

Smith's characterisation of this domain is phrased in terms of moral sentiments, sympathy and beneficence. All of these characterisations stress the gift character of caring: it is neither exchange nor redistribution: no return is demanded, no coercion involved. 'Beneficence is always free, it cannot be extorted by force' (Smith 1759 Part II. II.i: 78). Nor are the moral sentiments self-interested. 'Sympathy, however, cannot, in any sense, be regarded as a selfish principle' (ibid. Part VII. III.i: 317). In contrast to assumptions about economic behaviour today, Smith holds that sympathy is not a rare value found only in a small group of altruistic people, but rather, is inherent in human nature.

> How selfish soever man may be supposed, there are evidently some principles in his nature which interest him in the fortune of others, and render their happiness necessary to him, though he derives nothing from it except the pleasure of seeing it.
>
> (Smith 1759 Part I. I.i: 9)

Sympathy is thus understood by Smith as a commitment, more specifically as a commitment to those interpersonal values that sustain relationships between actors; sympathy involves close human interaction. Commitment and interaction also involve emotions. In the *Theory of Moral Sentiments* Smith illustrates sympathy with examples of positive and negative emotions. An example of a positive feeling of sympathy is on sharing the pleasure of art. 'When we have read a book or poem so often that we can no longer find any amusement in reading it by ourselves, we can still take pleasure in reading it to a companion' (ibid. Part I. I.ii: 14). In an example of negative emotions that may accompany sympathy he refers to a mother who imagines and feels the pains of her child that is ill and suffering (ibid. Part I. I.i: 12).

Smith, then, has characterised sympathy as a commitment – not as self-interested or instrumental – and one that involves emotion. Furthermore, he explicitly refers to another ethical capability that I have argued in chapter one is part of rationality: deliberation. Smith acknowledges the ambiguities related to gifts of sympathy but he does not want to qualify them on that ground as economically irrelevant. He merely points out how differently the domain of care operates compared with the other two domains. There is no unambiguous price as in an exchange. Nor is there a rule to be followed. Rather, caring implies the carefulness of responding to someone's needs, depending on contingent circumstances.

> If your benefactor attended you in your sickness, ought you to attend him in his? Or can you fulfil the obligation of gratitude, by making a return of a different kind? If you ought to attend him, how long ought you to attend him? The same time which he attended you, or longer, and how much longer?
>
> (Smith 1759 Part III. VI: 174)

The same sensitivity to the ambiguous moral implications of caring was shown by Amartya Sen in his case of Donna's dilemma. To help deliberation in the ambiguous domain of caring, Smith introduces the figure of the *impartial spectator*, who exemplifies the virtue of sympathy in every person. Its function is to remind us in all our activities of our responsibility to others. Here, we recognise the value of temperance that Smith assumes to be present in rational economic actors (McCloskey 1996). He defines the extent of this responsibility very clearly: we are responsible toward everyone who may be affected by our behaviour. Of course, the range of consequences was much smaller in the eighteenth century than today, so that Smith's 'extreme' example of not having to reckon with the consequences of our behaviour for those living on the moon does not sound so strange to our ears as it must have appeared to the ears of those living in the eighteenth century.[22] The globalised economy of today (even extending into space) implies that our responsibility has to take many more consequences of our behaviour into account than it used to do two centuries ago, consequences both to other people and to nature.

Now, what about the relationship between sympathy and justice? Here, it seems that Smith builds on Aristotle's idea of equity as going beyond justice. For Smith too justice is inadequate for addressing the multiplicity of demands in human life. 'Mere justice is, upon most occasions, but a negative virtue, and only hinders us from hurting our neighbour . . . we may often fulfil all the rules of justice by sitting still and doing nothing' (ibid. Part II. II.i: 82). Although he believed that societies might exist without sympathy, he did not regard these as prosperous.

> All the members of human society stand in need of each others assistance, and are likewise exposed to mutual injuries. Where the necessary assistance is reciprocally afforded from love, from gratitude, from friendship, and esteem, the society flourishes and is happy.
>
> (Smith 1759 Part II. II.ii: 85)[23]

In this last quote Smith suggests an extension of his earlier notion of responsibility (through the *impartial spectator*): people are not only responsible for the consequences for others of their personal and collective behaviour. Beyond this, humans are vulnerable and depend on each other's help, irrespective of any causal relationship between the helper's behaviour in the past and the origin of the receiver's need. So even when others suffer without us being the cause of their suffering, our responsibility as human beings toward our fellows (and maybe also to nature and its creatures) still induces us to respond to others' needs. Here, Smith's idea is very close to the definition of the domain of care that I presented in chapter two as derived from the process of caring that consists of attentiveness, responsibility, competence and responsiveness as described by Joan Tronto.

In the *Theory of Moral Sentiments*, Smith thus develops a substantial analysis of the value domain of care. His view comprehends commitment, emotion, deliberation and interaction: all the ethical capabilities that are needed to describe a value domain. But he ignores the economic practices of caring. His view remains the abstract perspective of a philosopher and economist, a man who spent most of his days in his study, lacking a family life which only features in the examples in his book. It is time to disembark and to explore the domain of care as it is in real life: to experience it through the eyes of someone who practised the activities of the domain every day.

Charlotte Perkins Gilman

Our guide will be Charlotte Perkins Gilman who wrote her books at the end of the nineteenth and beginning of the twentieth centuries. She grounds her analysis of the care economy in the institution of the household, as she argues in *The Home* (Perkins Gilman 1903: 4). It is in the household that she locates the valuable gift of care and where she asserts that caring is predominantly provided by women. In the home, people learn the various virtues from childhood through their parents' care: 'love, sympathy, courtesy, truth, honesty, accuracy, courage, strength, wisdom, justice, humility, self-control, endurance, strength, wisdom, chastity and honour' (Perkins Gilman 1903: 164). Contrary to economists of her time like Marshall and Pigou, she argues in *Women and Economics* that this caring labour in the household 'has a genuine economic value' (Perkins Gilman 1899: 13).

The problem that she signals with the economic value of care is twofold. First, women do not get paid or otherwise compensated for their caring labour and hence the value added that they provide. Second, the idea that the income earned by a husband compensates for the toil of unpaid women's labour presents a false picture of the nature of the economic interaction involved. Perkins Gilman's arguments are diverse. She begins by drawing attention to the lack of a correlation between the amount of unpaid labour supplied and a price in terms of the male income shared with women: there are apparently no meaningful demand and supply curves of caring labour within the home. 'The women who do the most work get the least money, and the women who have the most money do the least work' (ibid.: 14). Moreover, she points out, women without children also receive money from their husbands, hence the redistribution from men's income to women can be no compensation for their work in caring for the next generation. Finally, and like Margaret Reid, she employs an ethical argument, pointing to the ontological differences between exchange and giving. 'Are the cares and duties of the mother, her travail and her love, commodities to be exchanged for bread?' she asks rhetorically, and replies passionately: 'nothing could be more repugnant to human feeling, or more socially and individually injurious, than to make motherhood a trade' (ibid.: 17).

Perkins Gilman incisively points up the gender inequality involved in the under-valuation of women's caring labour. 'She gets her living by getting a husband. He gets his wife, by getting a living' (ibid.: 110). A statement that suggests a more realistic insight into the economics of gender than Pigou's widely known statement that GDP decreases when a man marries his housekeeper.

Charlotte Perkins Gilman is committed to the values of the domain of care, which she describes as a basic human sphere. 'To love and serve one another, to care for one another, to feel for and with one another, – our racial adjective, "human", implies these qualities' (ibid.: 323). But it would be naïve to believe this domain to be always benevolent or sufficient for a satisfactory human life. Perkins Gilman is very well aware of the negative effects of too much reliance on care alone, both for care givers and care receivers. For care givers, she argues that they have other qualities that seek fulfilment too, for example through paid work in the labour market. She stresses that it is not only the wages women want, but also the human values that are furthered by working for a wage in competition with others. She holds that work in the labour market is a natural expression of human energy (ibid.: 116) and the exercise of a human faculty (ibid.: 157) contributing to self-realisation. 'Does the human mother, by her mother-hood, thereby lose control of brain and body, lose power and skill and desire for any other work?' Again, a rhetorical question needs to be answered with a firm *no*. 'We do not' (ibid.: 19). She rejects the idea, popular among male economists, that caring is an exclusive female characteristic, and therefore the natural task for specialisation for women. 'There is no female mind. The brain is not an organ of sex. As well speak of a female liver' (ibid.: 149).

For care receivers also, particularly children, mothers' specialisation in the domain of care has its drawbacks. She illustrates this view effectively with references to newspaper articles reporting cases of bad motherly care, for example: 'Mother and Baby Both Badly Burned'. She quotes from 'Choked in Mother's Arms' to illustrate:

the divine instinct of Maternity giving a two-year-old child half a filbert to eat. It was remarked in the item that the 'desolate couple' had lost two other little ones within two months. It did not state whether the two others were accidentally murdered by a mother's care.

(Perkins Gilman 1903: 244)

Care may not only have negative effects when people specialise in unpaid labour in the home and do not combine this with other activities. Caring labour also needs to be complemented with other activities because some human values can never be furthered in the care economy (just as men suffer deficiencies in their humanness by ignoring caring activities in the home). According to Perkins Gilman, women do 'not bring out our humanness, for all the distinctive lines of human progress lie outside' (Perkins Gilman 1899: 217). The housewife who specialises in caring labour knows no freedom and no justice.

> The housewife is held to her work by duty and love; also by necessity. She cannot 'better herself' by leaving; and indeed, without grave loss and pain, she cannot leave at all. So the housewife struggles on, too busy to complain; and accomplishes, under this threefold bond of duty, love and necessity far more than can be expected of a comparatively free agent.
>
> (Perkins Gilman 1899: 104)

In conclusion, Perkins Gilman argues that the gift of care and free exchange are complementary economic activities. Whereas Margaret Reid came to the same conclusion on the ground of efficiency and risk minimisation, Charlotte Perkins Gilman uses the micro-economic argument that both domains are needed for a fulfilling life. Specialisation in only one domain is excessive, she argues, and brings negative side effects both for the specialising individual herself and for those with whom she interacts. Moreover, men and women both have the capabilities to act in each domain. Finally, she states that the redistribution of activities in both value domains among men and women is a matter of justice.

An initial mapping of the territories

This brief and necessarily sketchy exploration of the history of economic thought has recovered some ideas on the triad of *liberté, égalité, fraternité*. The domains of freedom and justice were found to be described with much rigour. Liberty has long since been recognised as an important value in itself that markets can help to further by expanding choices, furthering dignity and assessing individual autonomy. Justice has been called the primary virtue, not only in political but also in economic life, where justice has been constructed both as constraining freedom – to prevent exploitation – and as supporting it – in assuring equal access to resources and minimum levels of subsistence from wages.

Surprisingly, exploration away from the main roads of the canon also led to some initial insights into the economic value domain of care. The economic role of care has been recognised as sympathy and benevolence, as promoting relationships, as an anti-risk strategy, and particularly as the domain that provides the conditions for the other two domains to function well. Care appears as a complementary value to the values of freedom and justice. And economists, I found, have always had a commitment to all three of these moral values, contrary to what modernist interpretations of our discipline suggest. Smith, Mill and Taylor, Marx, Reid and Perkins Gilman knew very well that free exchange does not function without justice, nor without care.

The overview has indicated a more complex relationship between the three domains: the direction of the links does not appear to go only one way. Justice appears important not only for freedom but for care also, whereas freedom appears relevant for justice and care to function. Mill and Taylor pointed out that freedom also supports justice, in terms of the dignity gained through financial independence that helps to claim equal status. Perkins Gilman argued that freedom supports the domain of care through professional skills that support competent care giving, and justice supports care through a redistribution of caring labour. Thus the overview suggests that the three economic value domains are distinct, in that each of them is important in its own right and organises economic activity in a way that cannot be done in another domain, while at the same time the domains appear to be mutually dependent. None of the authors that I have referred to seems to believe that the economy can function in one value domain only. Even Plato admits that his *Republic* of just rules requires people to care about each other. Likewise, the economists defending justice or care still believe in the importance of freedom. Marx, Reid and Perkins Gilman believe that economic interaction cannot occur without autonomy and competitiveness, on the one hand, and solidarity and rules on the other.

The question that now arises is: how are these domains conceptualised in today's economics? In other words, how can they be integrated in today's economic theory as distinct territories that are at the same time interdependent?

4

BEYOND THE HIGHWAY OF MODERNIST ECONOMICS

> To mistake money for wealth is the same sort of error as to mistake the highway which may be the easiest way of getting to your house or lands, for the house and lands themselves.
>
> (John Stuart Mill 1848 Preliminary Remarks: 6)

The dualism of the highway

Having crossed the territories of freedom, justice and care in the history of economic thought, it is time to move on to present economic thought on these value domains. This chapter therefore will investigate to what extent recent literature on values and economics has addressed the complexities involved in the recognition of the three value domains.

Whereas the history of economic thought shows the acknowledgement by economists of value commitment, the role of emotion, the process of deliberation, and close human interaction in economic behaviour, the modernist development of the discipline has lost sight of the value domains. Instead it has travelled the highway of instrumental values of utilitarianism, it has followed the road signs of disinterestedness, it has used the automatic pilot of constrained maximisation, and its crossroads have been pictured as spot-markets.[1] Awareness of the values of freedom, justice and care somehow got lost along the highway. Nowadays, the discipline adheres to the much criticised idea of value-neutrality.[2]

The highway of neoclassical economics is founded on the Cartesian/Euclidean methodology, as analysed by Sheila Dow (1985, 1990) and Philip Mirowski (1993) among others. The two central features of this methodology are reductionism and dualism, and related to these, a lack of realism. Here I will follow the critique by Dow (1985: 13–14). Reductionism involves the establishment of a set of basic axioms, which are either true by definition or self-evident, and from which theorems are deductively derived. Propositions are broken down into components, such that one set of axioms can be identified from which all theorems are derived. Hence, it is impossible to change only one of the axioms while leaving the rest untouched: slight adaptations are not feasible. Either the whole set of axioms changes or a change in one or two assumptions is so modest that it does not affect the methodology.

Dualism, the other characteristic of Cartesian/Euclidean methodology, is probably even more influential than reductionism since it permeates all aspects of economic analysis. Dualism is the propensity to classify concepts, statements and events according to dualities, as belonging to only one of two all-encompassing categories: 'A' and 'not-A' for example, true or false, logical or illogical, positive or negative, hard or soft, masculine or feminine and so on. Moreover, the dualism in economic methodology implies a hierarchy in which the first element of every pair is preferred over the second. Dow holds that:

> to this day arguments identified as deriving from matter (emotional, normative, opinionated or non-rigorous argument, for example) are conventionally regarded as being almost morally inferior to their opposites.
>
> (Dow 1985: 14)

The dualism that was built into the highway of neoclassical economics has been discussed from various heterodox perspectives. Victoria Chick (1995) uses the dualistic scheme to discuss the position of neoclassical versus Keynesian economics within the discipline; in institutional economics, William Waller (1995) makes the point in explaining the dichotomous relationship between neoclassical and institutional economics; Arjo Klamer (1996) critiques the dualism in cultural economics and visualises it with an image of the square (of supply and demand diagrams) versus the circle (of rhetorical analyses); for feminist economics, Julie Nelson (1993a, 1996) uses the idea of dualism in explaining the exclusion of women and the feminine from conventional economic thought; finally, Ann Jennings (1993) shows how both institutionalism and feminism have been defined as belonging to the other side of the dualism underpinning mainstream economics. With the help of these analyses of dualism in economics I have put together Table 4.1. The table illustrates how economic concepts have been constructed in the methodology of neoclassical economics as dualities: the neoclassical self-perception ('A') versus the neoclassical perception of non-neoclassical theory ('not-A').

The table indicates how fundamental the problem is in today's economics compared with the times of Smith or Mill. Value commitments to freedom, justice and care have no place within economics when one adheres to these dualities. On the one side of the dualism values are perceived as utilitarian ends, instrumental to the higher goal of utility and, because of the properties of a utility function, different ends are commensurable; they are not valued intrinsically. On the other side of the dualism, although values are recognised as ends in themselves they are no longer regarded as economic but

89

Table 4.1 Dualistic reductionism in neoclassical economics

Dimensions	Self-perception of neoclassical economics	Neoclassical perception of non-neoclassical economics
	A	Not-A
Field	Economy	Non-economy
Normative position	Positive science	Normative science
Logic	Deduction	Induction
Methodology	Utilitarianism	Deontology
Analysis	Determinative	Inconclusive
Implied gender	Masculine	Feminine
Motivation	Self-interest	Altruism
Reasoning	Calculated reason	Interpretation
Information channel	Price signals	Emotion
Optimality	Equilibrium	Disequilibrium
Evaluative criterion	Pareto optimality	Equity
Modelling	Robust	Weak
Policy ideal	Laissez-faire	State intervention
Decision making	Constrained maximisation	Coercion

rather as social, cultural, or political values. They will often be characterised as belonging to the category of 'not-A', as not economic, as normative and as lacking robustness (Chick 1995).

As a consequence, attempts to bring values back into economic theory are very difficult. As I argued in chapter two, an understanding of values in economics cannot be provided when the dualistic methodology is followed. Values *are* economic but *not* necessarily instrumental and self-interested. My understanding of value as commitment, following Frank, Elster and Sen, does not fit into the mutually exclusive categories defined by the dominant methodology. Commitment helps to define the ends that we pursue, the way we motivate and signal these ends to others, the ways in which we evaluate them and interact with others in economic life in the shared pursuit of our valuable ends.

In this chapter I will discuss several recent attempts at bringing values back into economics. My purpose is to see whether they are helpful in answering my research question. I will do so from the analysis that I have developed so far in which I distinguish the economic value domains of freedom, justice and care. The question that I now seek to answer is how these value commitments have been placed within the discipline in recent approaches: how do they relate to the dualism that so much characterises the discipline today?

I will begin my discussion with two important Chicago School economists who reject one or more axioms of the neoclassical view of economic behaviour: Gary Becker and Deirdre McCloskey. Then I will shift to the increasingly popular new institutional perspective that brings in values as institutional constraints. Finally, I will discuss two philosophers who suggest analysing values not within but alongside economic analysis.

The utility of values

Gary Becker

In his influential work during the 1970s and 1980s, Gary Becker included human values as ordinary preferences in his theory of rational choice. He did so in particular for family values in the *Treatise of the Family* (Becker 1991). In his *Nobel Lecture* he reported that he had further extended the rational choice approach to include human values in all of social life. 'The rational choice model provides the most promising basis presently available for a unified approach to the analysis of the social world by scholars from different social sciences' (Becker 1993: 403). Becker's work is well-known and widely used, applied, elaborated and criticised. I will not try to summarise his work, nor will I make any attempt at summarising the many extensions and critiques. I will turn immediately to his recent work on values and economics, in particular his 1996 book *Accounting for Tastes*.

In this book Becker acknowledges that values can no longer be treated as exogenous preferences. Moral values are not givens as are preferences for normal goods and services, Becker now argues. Rather, values are formed at the social level and thus cannot be formalised as individual givens. The adaptation of his theoretical framework to include this insight is a fine mediation of an acknowledgement of the social on the one hand, while holding on to the neoclassical axioms on the other. The relaxation of the assumption of exogenous preferences does not affect the rest of the axioms since the endogeneity is limited to moral preferences and is still subject to utility maximisation: to a certain extent, Becker assumes that *Rational Economic Man* can choose his preferences, depending on the expected utility gains they will bring him.

In *Accounting for Tastes*, Becker adheres to the idea of utility as representing the human good people strive for. He

> retains the assumption that individuals behave so as to maximise utility while extending the definition of individual preferences to include personal habits and addictions, peer pressure, parental influences on the tastes of children, advertising, love and sympathy, and other neglected behaviour.
>
> (Becker 1996: 4)[3]

He departs from the conventional construction of utility functions by recognising that a large part of people's choices is not based on given preferences, but is influenced by past experiences and the tastes and behaviour of others. This recognition leads him to make part of the preferences endogenous, whereas other preferences that are concerned with goods and services remain exogenous.

Men and women want respect, recognition, prestige, acceptance, and power from their family, friends, peers, and others. Consumption and other activities have a major social component partly because they take place in public. As a result, people often choose restaurants, neighbourhoods, schools, books to read, political opinions, food or leisure activities with an eye to pleasing peers and others in their social network.

(Becker 1996: 12)

Values such as respect, recognition and prestige belong to what Becker calls stocks of *personal* and *social* capital. These two stocks of capital together form an individual's *human* capital, implying a broader and less formal view of human capital than is commonly understood as levels of education and skills (as it also is in Becker's past work). Personal capital is defined as the stock of past consumption and experiences of an individual, whereas social capital is taken to represent past behaviour by others in the individual's social network. This implies that human capital has not only an indirect effect on future consumption, but also a direct effect on consumption in the present.[4] Thus, utility at time t equals:

$$U_t = u_t (x_t, y_t, z_t, P_t, S_t)$$

where x and y are goods bought on the market, z goods produced in the household, and P and S stand for, respectively, personal and social capital stocks (ibid.: 5).

The inclusion of personal and social capital does not necessarily imply that they have a positive effect on utility. Past consumption of cigarettes may result in disease whereas peer pressure that persuades one to smoke has the same negative effect on future utility. Becker recognises that the following of certain social values may decrease rather than increase one's utility. This effect of endogenous preferences is similar to the effect that commitments may have on one's well-being, as Sen has demonstrated with his example of the man who tried to stop a fight but got hurt in doing so. Though the effects on one's well-being may be similar in both cases, there is an important difference here between Becker and Sen. In Sen's case the commitment leading to lower well-being represents a value that is valued for its own sake, deliberately. It is precisely this value that justifies the risk of personal suffering. In Becker's case, however, the endogenous preferences leading to lower well-being represent a 'wrong' investment in personal and social capital. Therefore, Becker characterises such negative effects on well-being as a misinvestment in one's personal capital or as an irrational choice influenced by the wrong type of social capital. Hence, the endogenous preferences for values are not commitments in Becker's approach. Rather they are means to increase one's utility, just like any other preference in the utility function.

In general, Becker holds that increases in human capital, which are the sum of personal (P_t) and social capital (S_t), will raise rather than lower utility. The idea of endogenous preferences assumes 'that forward-looking persons recognise that their present choices and experiences affect personal capital in the future, and that future capital directly affects future utilities' (ibid.: 7). Furthermore, individuals are assumed to choose their own discount rates on future utilities, ensuring consistency in their preferences over time.

Becker applies his construct of endogenous preferences to various examples of moral values. An important argument that parallels his idea of endogenous preferences is that social influences on one's choices prevent one from free riding. Endogenous preferences result in the internalisation of values. These values increase utility, whereas not satisfying these preferences would imply negative feelings of guilt or shame. *Rational Economic Man* calculates the gains from satisfying an endogenous preference as opposed to the losses in utility resulting from feelings of guilt or shame. As long as this cost/benefit calculation has a positive outcome, the value will be adhered to. Otherwise, one would change one's values through adaptation of one's stock of social capital, for example through changing one's peer group: changing friends, changing job and hence colleagues, or moving to another part of town. Becker therefore argues that people will try to satisfy a value that develops from an endogenous preference only when this contributes to their utility. If not, people will seek to change their endogenous preferences, and when they do not do so Becker describes their choices as irrational. Becker supports his idea with the example of church membership. Whereas Jon Elster, Robert Frank, or Amartya Sen would argue that people go to church either because of their upbringing, a habit, or a sense of deep religious belief, Becker holds that 'people would not attend churches where they acquire norms that lower their utility unless they are compensated with sufficient benefits' (ibid.: 227). So people would only go to church when this contributes to their utility. I do not find his argument plausible.

Becker gives another example that illustrates his utilitarian construction of endogenous preferences, personal and social capital. Assuming that people who love each other share their incomes equally, he suggests that high-earning individuals will marry equally high-earning others. Love thus helps to maximise family income. A marriage is threatened when alternative partners come by who may offer more attractive incomes. Faced with this threat to *Rational Economic Man*'s marriage, Becker points out that marriage not only maximises joint income, but also the well-being of children (assuming that marriage implies having children). Taking as given that divorce lowers children's (future) well-being, Becker argues that parents will keep investing in the marriage, both to prevent the partner from leaving and in order to maximise the well-being of the children. Therefore, he argues, divorce should not be available so easily since it removes the incentive for spouses to 'try harder to maintain their love' (ibid.: 237).[5] Again, it is utility – not only individual utility but also the joint utility of the family, including the children – that explains the adherence to value: in this case the value of love.

Love itself however is misunderstood as a value: the idea that it can be nurtured through incentives that prohibit exit denies the voluntarity involved, the emotion and, in particular, the attraction and responsibility between partners. 'Obviously, the incentive to nurture love is weak when it is easy to divorce since a person who falls out of love can look for a more satisfying second marriage' (ibid.: 237). Becker shows in this quotation that he interprets love as a consumer good that can be exchanged for another when relative prices change, as he did before with children. But this denies the commitment involved in love that he himself admits to be so important. This is inconsistent. Becker tries to adhere to the left-hand side of the dualism of Table 4.1, but at the same time he acknowledges that his explanation of marriage cannot do without an important notion that his methodology denies: commitment. Doesn't marriage require commitment to each other, for better and worse, even when the other's income decreases or children are not born? Or when handsomer alternatives come by? Becker's explanation makes it clear that one should invest in one's love relationship, but he does not clarify how this can be done without a commitment to love, the expression of feelings of love, the responsiveness of love between partners, and the sharing of the bond between partners and between parents and children. How can love be valued without the ethical capabilities that one needs in order to be committed to love and to sustain the bond?

The understanding of people's ends as (partially) endogenous is an important improvement in neoclassical theory (see also Samuel Bowles 1998). It makes the assumption of preference formation consistent with what has been recognised in business schools for a long time: people's preferences are shaped through their social environment and can be influenced through advertising. The way that Becker constructs endogenous preferences, however, does not leave the highway of utility, self-interest, deduction and calculation. He makes endogenous preferences part of constrained maximisation and ends up unable to do justice to human values, as Bowles (1998: 94, Figure 3) has shown in a table on the incompatibility of neoclassically defined behaviour with the recognition of social and moral behaviour. As a consequence, Becker's endogenised *Rational Economic Man* still lacks the ethical capabilities that he needs in order to value the ends that he seeks. He is still stuck with the iron bar through his head, unable to sustain loving relationships with his wife and children, as were Gage and Elliot. The difference with exogenous *Rational Economic Man* is that he is now conscious of this. That does not help him though; he needs to be liberated from his utilitarian mode of evaluation and needs help to see the virtue of commitment. Some help might be found in another creative mind from the Chicago School.

Deirdre McCloskey

McCloskey's integration of values in economics is embedded in the tradition of the discipline. It reflects the landscapes of the value domains as Adam Smith has painted them; it does not strictly follow the highway as does Becker's. As a representative of the old Chicago School, McCloskey grounds her analysis firmly in the history of economic thought and adheres to Smith's commitment to the virtues of prudence, justice and benevolence and the other virtues that he implied in these (love, hope, courage and temperance). McCloskey is much less concerned with deduction, utility maximisation and the ideal of robust modelling that pave the highway of neoclassical economics. Moreover, she rejects the ideal of positivism and the distinct masculine concerns of the dualism on which the utilitarian highway is founded. Her ideas on the integration of values in economic analysis are expressed in many of her works. Here, I will refer to an article (*Bourgeois Virtue*) and a book (*The Vices of Economists. The Virtues of the Bourgeoisie*) that deal with the issue of values most explicitly (McCloskey 1994b, 1996).

McCloskey introduces the notion of bourgeois virtues. These virtues stand for the ones that underlie commercial society and are, in turn, supported by it. They are the virtues of the market, she argues. In Table 4.2 I will reproduce her listing of bourgeois virtues together with others which she argues to belong to other periods of history: the aristocratic (or pagan) virtues and the peasant (or Christian) ones. In today's commercial society, McCloskey argues, the virtues of the market are most relevant, whereas in older days the others were more important.

Table 4.2 The classes and the virtues

Aristocrat/patrician	Peasant/plebeian	Bourgeois/mercantile
Pagan	Christian	Secular
Achilles	St Francis	Benjamin Franklin
Pride of being	Pride of service	Pride of action
Honour	Duty	Integrity
Forthrightness	Candour	Honesty
Loyalty	Solidarity	Trustworthiness
Courage	Fortitude	Enterprise
Wit	Jocularity	Humour
Courtesy	Reverence	Respect
Propriety	Humility	Modesty
Magnanimity	Benevolence	Consideration
Justice	Fairness	Responsibility
Foresight	Wisdom	Prudence
Moderation	Frugality	Thrift
Love	Charity	Affection
Grace	Dignity	Self-possession
Subjective	Objective	Conjective

Source: Deirdre McCloskey, 'Bourgeois Virtue' in *American Scholar* 63 (2), 1994: 179.

McCloskey's main argument is that not only do bourgeois virtues help to bring about commercial society, but they are in turn supported by markets. That is because virtues are necessarily voluntary, as Aristotle set out, and markets function only on a voluntary basis (McCloskey 1994b: 181). When we look down the third column of McCloskey's table, the bourgeois virtues, we find that markets need people to behave in a way that is trustworthy, respectful, responsible, prudent, affectionate and self-possessed, and at the same time markets provide the incentives for people to behave in this manner, she maintains.

So far I find her argument persuasive. These virtues are needed in economic life and at the same time the economy helps to sustain them. But I find her categorisation of the three types of virtues confusing. She does not distinguish between the market and the economy. Are all bourgeois virtues generated and furthered in the market or only some of them, while others are developed in different economic value domains? Moreover, the list of bourgeois virtues is a mixed bag. It includes Smith's virtue of prudence, but not his virtues of justice and benevolence. This suggests a similar categorisation to those that Smith, Hume, and later also Polanyi, Boulding and Hirschman made, as reproduced in my Figure 2.2. In her categorisation, bourgeois virtues appear to be those of the value domain of freedom, located in the market, not including other types of virtues. But this is not plausible in the rest of McCloskey's scheme since she includes in the same category some virtues that the above mentioned economists found to be furthered *outside* the market, *not within* it. For example, she includes in the same column: the 'affection' (as opposed to interest) that Hume found to be furthered outside the market (but nevertheless necessary for the market); the 'trust' that Mill, Polanyi and Hirschman located in caring relationships in the home, in the community, or among consumers or employees but not in a market transaction (though important for market transactions); the 'respect' that Mill and Perkins Gilman found to be supported outside the market (though important for the functioning of markets); and the 'responsibility' that Hayek and Friedman recognised as belonging outside the market but at the same time a precondition for market transactions to happen.

In other words, I do find the general argument that various virtues are needed in the economy persuasive (my own argument runs parallel to McCloskey's in this respect and I owe much to her pioneering work). At the same time, however, I find the categorisation of the virtues that she proposes in Table 4.2 confusing. I will explain this confusion with the help of an example of one particular virtue that both McCloskey and I list.

McCloskey gives the example of respect as a market virtue. She perceives respect in the greetings of American salespersons: 'How can I help you?' (1994b: 181). I agree that the expression of respect is necessary for markets to function. But I doubt, first, whether this example shows respect rather than prudence; second, whether respect is a market value; and, third, whether it is a virtue in this example or an instrumental value.

Market values are furthered through exchange: through market transactions. For example (see again Table 4.2, taken from McCloskey), 'pride of action' is established when one successfully competes for a job; 'enterprise' is stimulated in an industry where market shares are renegotiated; 'self-possession' is furthered (though I prefer the virtue of self-esteem) when one succeeds in earning oneself a decent income or in successfully introducing a new product. 'Respect' however, is of a different kind. When we try to increase the respect that people show us, we have to earn it through our fair treatment of others as human beings, as equals having inalienable rights. In my Figure 2.2, therefore, respect fits in the column of justice values, not of freedom values as in McCloskey's table. Respect is furthered by means of our commitment to justice and not through our skills in the market.

When we try to earn people's respect in the market, it assumes the form of admiration for our higher position, or obedience to our authority, or recognition of our power as consumers to exit the shop. In all these cases respect is no longer a virtue because it loses its voluntarity. Voluntarity is a basic characteristic of virtue as Adam Smith has taught, not instrumentality: 'The idea of the utility of all qualities of this kind, is plainly an after-thought, and not what recommends them to our approbation' (Smith 1759: 20). So, when a virtue is no longer sought voluntarily for its own sake but rather to promote prudence (to increase sales for example), it stops being a virtue. Respect cannot be earned by spending money in shops.[6]

With this subordination of respect to prudence, McCloskey's position on virtues becomes confusing. Is it still the highway that she wants to travel, the highway of commensurable values that are to be maximised in a utility function? Or are there important values outside the highway in the landscape of economic actors' pluralist value commitments? In *The Vices of Economists. The Virtues of the Bourgeoisie*, she argues strongly against the narrow focus of modernist economics on the virtue of prudence, which leads to a very incomplete – even vicious, she claims – economics. I fully agree with her there. So I am puzzled. On the one hand McCloskey rejects reductionism of every virtue to prudence whereas on the other hand her categories are unclear, giving way to the suggestion that it is prudence after all that is the ultimate virtue in economic life.

To conclude, I find McCloskey's work on virtues and economics fascinating and persuasive. A variety of virtues is indeed needed in economic life. Moreover, I think it is courageous to argue for this within the context of the Chicago School; it would probably have been much easier to exit that school and enter into one of the heterodox schools that have left the highway long before. But that would not help to persuade other Chicago School economists, including Becker. However, McCloskey's *Bourgeois Economic (Wo)man* appears a confusing figure, who expresses her commitment to a diversity of values in economic life and at the same time seems to undermine her own commitment by subjecting these values to the single virtue of prudence. Again, the power of the dualistic methodology of mainstream economics appears to be overwhelming. A similar experience can be found in the new institutional economics that tries to shake up yet other neoclassical axioms.

Value as instrumental

New institutional economics

A different but related school in economics also takes values as instrumental, yet does not concentrate on individual behaviour as Becker and McCloskey do but focuses on market processes. The argument of the new institutional economics is evolutionary: institutions represent values and they exist because they are functional in the economic process. They are thought to create a hospitable environment for co-operative, though not necessarily efficient, solutions by minimising transaction costs. A major proponent of new institutionalism, Douglass North (1990, 1991, 1992), defines institutions as 'the humanly devised constraints that shape human interaction' (North 1990: 3). Institutions reflect people's values and are viewed as reducing uncertainty by providing structure to everyday life. In other words: 'institutions define and limit the set of choices of individuals' (North 1990: 4). Institutions are thus are perceived as constraints, parallel to budget and time constraints. They are not thought of as having value in themselves. On the contrary, they are thought of as limitations on individual actors' efforts to realise their valuable ends. In the new institutional economics, values are clearly neither commitments nor ends, but means instead.

The evolutionary idea of institutions suggests that they are always efficient; if not they would not survive. While this idea flourished earlier on, major proponents today have amended this position (for North, see 1990: 7). Institutions do not necessarily generate the most efficient outcome; rather, they are perceived as determining the constraints in the economy where institutions and organisations interact, which may be beneficial for them but at the same time disadvantageous for the economy as a whole. Organisations support institutions that are to their benefit and the resulting institutions support the incentive structure for them to evolve further. The institutions are pictured as the rules of the game while the organisations are portrayed as the players, trying to change the rules to their advantage. Here, power differences come into the analysis. The institutional process does not necessarily result in maximum efficiency.

> Institutions exist to reduce uncertainties involved in human interaction. These uncertainties arise as a consequence of both the complexity of the problems to be solved and the problem-solving

software (to use a computer analogy) possessed by the individual. There is nothing in the above statement that implies that the institutions are efficient.

(North 1990: 25)

The complexity of the problems of economic life and the inadequate human problem-solving software that North refers to can be addressed with the help of Herbert Simon's notion of bounded rationality. According to North, it is the calculative shortcomings of neoclassical rationality that give rise to institutional mediation in economic interaction, with the help either of formal institutions (such as constitutions, laws and property rights) or of informal institutions (for example, taboos, customs and codes of conduct). Institutions are thus a response to bounded rationality and serve the functionalistic goal of co-ordination with minimum transaction costs.[7]

Again, rationality is acknowledged to be deficient but it is claimed that institutions repair the deficiencies. First, institutions are explained as arising out of political interests or organisations' interests (formal and informal institutions respectively) (North 1990: 1, 1991: 97). Then, however, they are functionally explained at the aggregate level as reducing uncertainty, production costs and transaction costs, implying that they make exchange more efficient. This dual explanation reveals an inconsistency: institutions cannot be explained functionally at both levels at the same time. Either they arise because people value them and not because they serve particular interests, or they arise unintentionally, developing in an evolutionary process, serving the economic process in the aggregate. Moreover, North admitted that institutions are not at all necessarily efficient in the aggregate; when reducing transaction costs for some, they may increase them for others.

What if, as North admits, institutions arise that protect the interests of a certain group but at the same time harm economic growth? Or, the other way around, what if they reduce overall costs to the economy but at the same time go against the interests of a powerful group? In both cases, it is interests that North is arguing about, not values. In line with this latter focus, North holds (1991: 109) that institutions and organisations mutually reinforce each other when interests are furthered. Institutions may further the interests of certain organisations, whereas organisations may support an incentive system leading to a particular institutional framework.

Organisations are created with purposive intent in consequence of the opportunity set resulting from the existing set of constraints (institutional ones as well as the traditional ones of economic theory) and in the course of attempts to accomplish their objectives are a major agent of institutional change.

(North 1990: 5)

99

In the new institutional economics, then, interests and relative power – not people's underlying values – determine the creation and evolution of certain institutions that express themselves as constraints. 'The performance of economies is a consequence of the incentive structures put into place; that is, the institutional framework of polity and economy' (Denzau and North 1994: 27). New institutional economics explains how values may be manipulated to serve the interests of a group in imperfect markets, and how this manipulation may reduce this group's transaction costs. Yet the theory does not explain values in economic life, and its functionalistic methodology lacks sufficient explanatory power (see also Jack Vromen 1995).

Instrumental value theory

Another school in institutional economics claims to have a theory that resolves the problem just mentioned: a social value theory or instrumental value theory.[8] In the old institutional economics, going back to Thorstein Veblen, John Commons and Clarence Ayres, the so-called 'instrumental value theory' was developed (Warren Samuels 1995a, 1997; Marc Tool 1977, 1986). Again interests, power and utility are central, although not at the individual but at the social level. According to Marc Tool (1977: 42) a criterion of social value is 'the continuity and instrumental effectiveness of recreating community non-invidiously'. This is meant as a criterion for choosing (Tool 1977: 42, 1986: 8), and as a principle on which end-states are evaluated (Tool 1977: 43). For Warren Samuels (1997: 5), 'instrumental valuation is a process characterised by dialectical cumulative causation and overdetermination, ultimately over whose interest is to count in the social reconstruction of society, polity and economy, which for all parties is the operative of social process' (Samuels 1997: 5).

Here we see a close resemblance to North's view that the economic process can be characterised as a game over interests. An important difference though is that the old institutionalists do not refer to a basic, unequivocal principle such as the minimisation of transaction costs. Instead, they hold that value is social, that it involves a pragmatic and experimental process that includes conscious and unconscious decision making (Samuels 1997: 3). But what is lacking in both theories is the ethical dimension of the good in relation to value.[9] Although the old institutionalists do not reduce values to constraints but see them as part of people's ends, they do not elaborate on the particular values that need to be studied, though Clarence Ayres had distinguished them so well (as liberty, equality and security). Nor is old institutionalism very clear on how values change within the economy.

Oliver Williamson recognises the fallacy of the instrumentalist approach to values, despite being a major contributor to the new institutional theory himself. In his article of 1993 he argues against an instrumental, calculative conceptualisation of one particular human value: *trust*. Contrary to other new institutional economists he seems to take the meaning of trust as intrinsic, as for example in the definition of trust by philosopher Annette Baier:

> To trust is to make oneself or let oneself be more vulnerable than one might have been to harm from others – to give them an opportunity to harm one, in the confidence that they will not take it, because they have no good reason to.
>
> (Baier 1993: 30)

Williamson observes that trust and risk have become almost substitutes in the rational choice approach (Williamson 1993: 463). Like risk, trust then is assumed to be calculable with the help of probability distributions (ibid.: 466). Williamson shows that it is actually the instrumental variable of credibility that is calculated, and *not* the moral value of trust. Trust cannot be calculated but depends on the context of the community one is part of, he argues (ibid.: 475). The risks of commerce vary not only with the characteristics of the transaction but also with the trading context in which they arise. These determine trust in a social way, as cultural, political, regulatory, professional, network and corporate culture types of trust. Whereas the breach of calculative trust, or credibility, can sometimes be efficient, this can never be so for the social types of trust: 'betrayal is demoralising' (ibid.: 482). Williamson refers to the distortion of what he calls 'atmosphere', or the relationships between people, when values such as trust are measured and used as manipulative variables in utilitarian calculations. It 'may well be destructive of atmosphere and lead to a net loss of satisfaction between the parties' (ibid.: 481). Once economists begin to understand the role of trust and other human values, they also would see that these cannot merely be integrated in the existing economic frameworks of utility, market exchange, or cost benefit calculations, since: 'calculativeness will devalue the relation' (ibid.: 484).[10]

I can only agree with and support Williamson's characterisation of trust: it is a value that markets need but that they cannot generate or further through calculation, interest and exchange. It is furthered and nurtured *outside* the market in what I have called the care economy. But from here on, Williamson and I disagree. He maintains that trust is not economic and should not be analysed in economics. In this denial of the economics of trust he moves the value from the left-hand side of the dualism in the dominant economic methodology to the right-hand side of the dualism in Table 4.1: from 'A' that squarely sits within the neoclassical paradigm to 'not-A' that is defined as not economic at all but as moral.

Though he is remarkably to the point in his characterisation of trust as a human value, I find Williamson's position unhelpful in the end. In fact, it denies that there is any sense in trying to conceptualise such values in economic theory, as if values and economics are mutually exclusive. Now that moral values have been shifted back again to the right-hand side of the dualism, where neoclassical economics had located them in the first place, it may be interesting to discuss a view from moral philosophy on this oscillating of moral values between the territory of neoclassical economics and that of morality, the 'A' and 'not-A' sides in dominant economic methodology.

Value as non-economic

The two authors now to be discussed follow Williamson's advice and start their analysis outside the landscape of economics. Amitai Etzioni and Elizabeth Anderson imply, parallel to Williamson on trust, that economics has already been intruding on ethics too much without really understanding what ethics is.[11]

Amitai Etzioni

In his book *The Moral Dimension*, Etzioni (1988) claims to present a middle-ground between neoclassical and Marxist economics. Etzioni's focus is on the paradigmatic distinction between the individual level expressed in neoclassical economics and the social level expressed in Marxism. His synthesis claims to integrate both levels of analysis.

> It sees individuals as able to act rationally and on their own, advancing their self or 'I', but their ability to do so is deeply affected by how well they are anchored within a sound community and sustained by a firm moral and emotive personal underpinning – a community they perceive as theirs, as a 'we', rather than as an imposed, restraining 'they'.
>
> (Etzioni 1988: ix–x)

The connection between 'I' and 'we' is made in terms of individuality and community, where individuals are seen as embedded in the social, which influences the values they seek to follow. 'Individuals and community are both completely essential, and hence have the same fundamental standing . . . the individual and the community make each other and require each other' (ibid.: 9). Etzioni perceives the social level with its social norms in a very different way than Becker and North do. In Etzioni's view, social norms are not subject to rational choice, as in the extended utility function, nor does he conceptualise norms as a set of constraints, as in new institutionalism. Instead, Etzioni asserts that society is us.

After presenting his holistic view of individuals as embedded in and together establishing society, he introduces a sharp distinction between two opposing types of motive on which people are assumed to act: morality and pleasure. The former is located in normative values and the latter in economic rationality. Both, however, are characterised as utilitarian; this is confusing, since Etzioni characterises morality not in a consequentialist manner (as Becker does) but in a Kantian, deontological way. The concept of utility, however, is not a deontological notion. Morally based behaviour is perceived by Etzioni as the following of moral principles of fairness and solidarity. In fact, Etzioni defines moral acts as involving an imperative, a generalisation into moral rules, universality, and as arising from people's intention to adhere to some basic moral principles (ibid.: 41–2). Etzioni's category of moral motives thus largely overlaps with a morality of justice. He explicitly excludes motivations of care, an omission which he justifies by stating that otherwise the category of moral motives would be too large. Besides he adds, displaying a superficial reading of the *Theory of Moral Sentiments*, that many motives from affection could be distributed over the categories of pleasure and morality.

Etzioni portrays pleasure as the rational search for pleasurable consequences, which need not necessarily be self-interested. The substance of such rationality however, is not elaborated, nor the extent to which people's behaviour is motivated by one or the other of the mutually exclusive categories of pleasure and morality. Is it neoclassical economics that he implies here? What is rationality for him, and how is it different from rational choice theory? These are questions that remain unanswered. For example, he puts forward the intriguing suggestion that competition does not arise from impersonal calculation, nor from closely attached social relationships, but that it needs elements of both: individual pleasure calculations and moral imperatives. Without a substantiation of the relationship between the two dualistically placed motives, however, little insight has been gained on the substance of the promised theory.

At the end of his book he repeats his goal of explaining economic behaviour with a new theory lying somewhere in between neoclassical and Marxist economics. But he does not succeed in presenting such a theory. What he does, however, is make it clear that an explanation of economic behaviour needs to pay attention to both sides of the dualism underlying neoclassical theory. It is an important argument. Yet, by sticking to utilitarianism and the dualism in his distinction between the mutually exclusive motives of pleasure and morality, he is not able to provide an alternative to the status quo. Five years later another philosopher addressed the same problem.

Elizabeth Anderson

Anderson (1993) follows a similar line of argument in her book *Value in Ethics and Economics*. She also promises a new theory, which she calls an *expressive theory of value*. In contrast to Etzioni, she does not pretend to develop a synthesis between major economic theories but reproposes an ethical theory of value that is opposed to the economic ones.

Elizabeth Anderson employs a similar dichotomous categorisation of motives to that of Etzioni. One type of motive is labelled, as in Etzioni, pleasure or desire, and according to Anderson only refers to the quantity of a particular good that people want to have, not the quality or the 'why' they want to have it. The other category of motivation is multiple and refers to 'love, admiration, honor, respect, affection, and awe as well' (Anderson 1993: p. xiii). In her category of moral motivation Anderson thus brings in the idea of pluralist value, as opposed to the singular, quantitative motivation she perceives in pleasure. The pluralist values are described in terms of an expressive value theory. Such theories:

> begin not with the external aims or states of affairs a person is to bring about, but with her internal attitudes toward the ends for the sake of which she acts. Expressive theories tell people to adequately express the ways they appropriately value their ends by following norms of attention and response and by governing themselves by norms of action that express these different modes of evaluation. These norms, interpreted in the context of their concrete predicaments, tell people to try to bring about certain states of affairs for certain reasons.
>
> (Anderson 1993: 74)

How these states of affairs are to be brought about in the economy remains unclear, but Anderson seems only concerned with an interpretation of morality that resides outside economic life. The same attitude can be perceived in her definition of rationality. It is defined in terms of the social interaction between people, an interaction that expresses their moral values. 'To be rational is to be suitably responsive to reasons offered by those attempting to reach that point of view' (ibid.: 3). The ethical capability of human interaction is thus found to be an important element in rationality, as I argued in chapter one, but for Anderson rationality is no longer relevant, even partially, as an economic concept.

In her analysis rationality is wholly a moral concept, not economic any more. Defined as such, rationality involves appraisal of different values according to the standards that are appropriate for each, Anderson argues. Thus you can value your grandma in terms of her being sweet or hardworking, but not in kilograms or Dutch guilders, and the other way around for a bag of Granny Smiths. In fact, Anderson acknowledges that values are expressed in different categories that cannot be traded off against one another: the issue of incommensurability. This argument parallels my distinction between different value domains. The important difference though is that Anderson acknowledges incommensurable values only in her category of moral values and not in economic values, whereas in my analysis the *moral* and *economic* go together, representing incommensurabilities between different types of values *in economic behaviour also*.

The problem that now shows up is how Anderson would see economic choices of quantities of the incommensurable moral values. In her distinction between economic value as quantities and moral values as incommensurable valuation of qualities, how are quantity choices made? Do pleasure motives for quantities make the moral values commensurable? If not, how does she explain quantity choices?[12]

I find this inconclusiveness unsatisfactory. Anderson sustains the dualism and only deals with values in terms of the right-hand side of Table 4.1. Values, apparently, have no economic importance for Anderson. This points to the question of whether the distinction between pleasure and moral motives is conceptually adequate. Surprisingly, the dualism is not bridged but continued in Anderson's book, despite her assertion that she rejects the dualistic thinking implied in the discourse on ethics and economics.

The assumption behind Anderson's dualistic conceptualisation of pleasure and morality is that they are opposing and unrelated motives, decision making processes and types of behaviour. The assumption is very strong and, in fact, unhelpful for those economists who are concerned about the ethical dimensions of economic behaviour and of economics itself. The duality implies that few, if any, economic activities involve moral elements. It sustains the belief in a value-free economy. Yet as Mary Douglas and Baron Isherwood (1979) have argued, the transaction in goods and services is strongly embedded in morality and a distinction between higher and lower goods or motives is false.

> Goods that minister to physical needs – food or drink – are no less carriers of meaning than ballet or poetry. Let us put an end to the widespread and misleading distinction between goods that sustain life and health and others that service the mind and heart – spiritual goods.
>
> (Douglas and Isherwood 1979: 49)

The argument presented by these authors is that all goods carry moral meaning, but none by itself. This is not only valid for extreme examples such as blood donation (Richard Titmuss 1970) or the arms race (Martin Navias and Susan Willet 1996; John Tirman 1997). The inter-relatedness of economy and morality is present in every common economic process, such as the daily purchase and sales of human labour on the labour market, the production and pricing of potentially harmful or healing products, or savings and investments.

The dualism between motives as economic and non-economic also implies that little, if any, moral behaviour has economically relevant dimensions. Human activity is located in the world; it is characterised by a multiplicity of motives and forms of human interaction but also takes place in a world that cannot escape scarcity of resources, whether they be material, monetary, time or human energy. People who want to distribute any valuable good according to any moral standard of fairness will be confronted with a limit to the stock of goods to distribute. Their moral motives cannot escape the confrontation with economic dimensions.[13] For the majority of morally embedded decisions, the economic aspect cannot be denied. People who give unpaid personal care to others often want to spend more time with each person or would like to care for more people, but they face time and energy constraints. The time pressure on people's caring responsibilities becomes particularly difficult when some are expected to combine both paid and unpaid work. In caring for others, the time bind is a relevant constraint (Arlie Hochschild 1989, 1997).

In conclusion: Etzioni and Anderson sustain the dualism between economic and moral behaviour, thereby leaving the description and explanation of economic behaviour to the deficient theories of today's economics, while suggesting interesting analyses of value for what they take to be non-economic behaviour, taking place in an ideal world without scarcity or need for provisioning.

The denial of pluralist value commitment in economics

My brief discussion of the works above has pointed out the numerous methodological difficulties involved in an *economic* conceptualisation of *values*. Because of the different perspectives that each of the contributions takes, reading and discussing them with others has helped me to develop my own analysis. Each brings in relevant ideas: Becker's recognition of endogenous preferences; McCloskey's argument for analysing the role of a large variety of virtues that markets need in order to function well; the suggestions about the role of institutions both at individual and aggregate levels of economic behaviour; Etzioni's focus on the mediation between the 'I' and the 'we' levels; and finally, Anderson's idea on pluralist, incommensurable values that receive meaning in human interaction.

The works discussed share a commitment to recognising the role of values in relation to economic behaviour, a commitment that an increasing number of economists and economic philosophers subscribe to (see, for example, James Griffin 1986; Peter Groenewegen 1996; Daniel Hausman and Michael McPherson 1993, 1996; Alan Lewis and Karl-Erik Wärneryd 1994; Jane Mansbridge 1990; Amartya Sen 1987). 'An economics that is engaged actively and self-critically with the moral aspects of its subject matter cannot help but be more interesting, more illuminating, and ultimately more useful than one that tries not to be' (Hausman and McPherson 1993: 723).

However, none of the approaches discussed so far convinced me. The reason is that they still adhere to the dualist methodology underlying neoclassical economics as represented in Table 4.1. The works I have discussed regard values either as utilitarian or as moral obligations; they see values either as singular and located in market exchange or as pluralist and located outside the economy; they regard them either as constraints or as virtues beyond the world of scarcity. The studies that I have discussed mistake the values implied in the landscape of economic interaction for the highway of the left-hand side of Table 4.1, or they prefer to explore different landscapes referred to on the right-hand side of the table, ones defined as lying beyond the economic domain. As a consequence of the dualism adhered to, these studies do not recognise the ontological differences between the economic value domains, nor the complex relationships that economists had recognised in earlier periods, as became clear in chapter three.

My understanding of values as commitments rather than as utilitarian or as moral principles does not follow the dualistic methodology. As I indicated in chapter two, commitment belongs to virtue ethics, a contextual ethics that strives for the good, not regarding it as a universal principle or as subjective preference maximisation. Such an understanding of values in economics as commitments requires a conceptualisation of the ethical capabilities that I found to be related to commitment in chapter one: emotion, deliberation and interaction. Such a conceptualisation does not assume all economic behaviour to be motivated by self-interest, nor all moral behaviour by altruism. It does not assume economic behaviour to reside in a calculation of costs and benefits, or moral behaviour to be sheer feeling and interpretation. Nor does it assume all economic behaviour to be exchange and all moral behaviour to be coercion or love.

But it is no longer possible to proceed in such an abstract manner. What is needed now are some hypotheses about economic actors' behaviour in each value domain and about the combination of activities in different value domains. If actors combine activities in different domains, why do they do so? And when they do, how do they allocate their resources over the market, the state and the care economy? Why not specialise in one domain only, as the division of labour argument would suggest? These questions cannot be addressed with the available economic databases of the OECD, UN or World Bank. There were no data to be found, nor even categories of empirical variables defined. How could one inquire about freedom in economic statistics? Or find the variables of the domain of justice with the help of a survey? How can we measure care? Confronted with these serious constraints on empirical research I was forced to employ an unconventional research method – at least, unconventional in economics. I found an anthropological fieldwork method that is applied to the generation of hypotheses on human behaviour within changing social and moral contexts. Chapter five contains a summary report of this fieldwork that led to some hypotheses on the relationships of the three economic value domains.

5

HYPOTHESES ON ECONOMIC ROLE COMBINATION

> I am supposing that in every society the production of discourse is at once controlled, selected, organised and redistributed according to a certain number of procedures, whose role is to avert its powers and its dangers, to cope with chance events, to evade its ponderous, awesome materiality.
>
> (Michel Foucault 1971: 8)

Economic roles

In the foregoing chapters I have argued that the core values operating in economic life – freedom, justice and care – are commitments that are intrinsically valuable, incommensurable and to an important degree economic, as well as social, cultural and political. Moreover, values in economic life have been recognised to be both moral and economic at the same time. Yet this characterisation remains abstract. Since it is my intention to conceptualise economic behaviour as commitment-based, I need to know more about the value commitments in economic life. I need to identify how they operate in the daily economic practices of exchange, redistribution and care giving. More concretely, I need to find out how the ethical capabilities of rational economic actors enable them to allocate scarce resources in each of the economic value domains, and why they allocate their time and other resources in a particular way over the three domains, rather than specialising in one.

Information on the individual allocation of time and other resources over different value domains can only be gathered from an inquiry into concrete economic practices in each domain. Such inquiry however, turns the economist from a determinate solver of a neatly composed multiple-equation algorithm into an interpreter of the complex and sometimes conflicting signs of economic processes (Vivienne Brown 1994a). An approach to economic behaviour through the interpretation of its context certainly allows a richer understanding of people's motives, ends, values and modes of interaction, when compared to the dominant economic methodology that is founded on abstract dualities and limited by *ceteris paribus* assumptions (Mark Addleson 1995). Although the interpretation of economic practices appears less rigorous, it does establish validity in that it helps to understand behaviour in terms of 'experience-near' concepts (Clifford Geertz 1977: 481). But how can one go about this empirically?

There are basically two ways of undertaking such an inquiry. One would be to set up an experiment, in which economic actors would interact with each other in a context that requires them to take decisions within each subsequent value domain. However, there are two serious problems involved with such a method. First, most experience in experimental economics is in far less complicated settings that often exclude communication between the participants of an experiment. Even then, analysis appears quite difficult. Second, and more important, an experimental setting requires the researcher to set the context and, hence, to pre-determine to a large extent the types of outcomes that will develop. Thus, an experimental setting would be likely to suffer from the subjective bias of the researcher, as happened for example in Rawls' thought experiment on the initial position.

A second method of inquiry into people's daily economic practices in each value domain would be to ask people what they do, how and why. As will be clear, a survey of individual economic practices could easily be far too general or far too detailed. Moreover, a survey may shed light on *what* people do, but is not a very adequate methodological tool to discover *how* and *why* people behave in a particular way. Cross-cultural representativeness would be another problem for this survey method.

In anthropology, I found a technique of inquiry into the different roles in economic life that does not suffer from the problems attached to an experimental setting or a survey. It is the method of focus group discussions (Robert Merton, Marjorie Fiske and Patricia Kendall 1956). Role theory provides a well-known perspective on the practices of social life, helping to understand the complexities and ambiguities involved in people's multiple roles (see for example, Ralf Dahrendorf 1958; Erving Goffman 1959; George Mead 1934; Robert Merton 1949). In economic life I define a role as the set of activities carried out within one economic value domain, though these activities may in fact be carried out through more than one sub-role within each domain. I will regard these sub-roles within one domain together as one role, for example in the case of two paid jobs ('moonlighting') or a variety of different caring responsibilities. Hence I will distinguish three types of roles in economic life: roles in the domain of freedom, roles in the domain of justice, and roles belonging to the domain of care.[1]

The focus group method is particularly aimed at generating hypotheses on the basis of people's different experiences and ideas, or on the 'how and why' of their behaviour. Indeed, it is the diversity in experiences with, and ideas about, economic roles that I want to research in order to find answers to the how and why of economic actors' allocation of resources over different value domains. I engaged in such an experimental empirical research method, following the pioneering work on interviews, group discussions and rhetoric done by others in the economic discipline (Arjo Klamer 1983; Arjo Klamer and David Colander 1990; Arjo Klamer, Deirdre McCloskey and Robert Solow 1988; Deirdre McCloskey 1985).

My first reason for choosing the method of focus group discussions is that the setting of a group interview allows for more context in an inquiry than a survey. The context makes the relationship between economic settings and valuation in economic life explicit (see, for example, Karl Polanyi 1944; Clifford Geertz 1973; Stephen Gudeman 1986; Eric Wolf 1982).[2] Second, I am not looking for time-use figures or other quantitative data; these can only be rough descriptive indicators of the practices in each value domain. Rather, my inquiry into the roles in the different domains concerns actors' commitments and includes questions on motives, ends, forms of interaction, value conflicts and other interpretative dimensions beyond input or output indicators such as time-use data or income. Focus groups bring out a diversity of meanings on a specific issue rather than a set of data on some predefined indicators. Third, a focus group makes it possible to include active participation and diverse representation of the research subjects – economic actors of flesh and blood and their interactions – from the start of the research, rather than controlling the identity of the subjects as happens in experimental settings. The focus group method forces the researcher to embed her analysis at least partially in human practices rather than developing 'as if' concepts in an abstract universe of axioms. In fact, an empirical intermezzo of this form will be more likely to enrich theoretical reasoning, since the focus of the group discussions is on theoretical concepts, like motivation and values, rather than on empirical data.

The choice of focus group interviews therefore follows logically from theoretical analyses of economic rationality. For example, as Hargreaves Heap has noted in his volume on economic rationality about the concept of judgement: 'It is the faculty we use when instrumental calculation can gain no handle on the problem; and we actually respect its use by referring to wisdom rather than knowledge. . . . It is not something that can be reduced to a formula' (Shaun Hargreaves Heap 1989: 159). In his volume however, Hargreaves Heap does not elaborate on this important concept; he does not conceptualise the role that judgement would play in economic rationality. As a response to this major gap in economic theorising about rationality, my focus groups can be regarded as an inquiry into the why and how of economic actor's deliberations.

The technique of a focus group discussion

A focus group discussion is an intensive, non-structured group interview, a discussion really, on a particular topic amongst a small group of persons.

The objective is to generate information from the group interaction. This interaction reveals the attitudes and ideas of the group participants in an open, heuristic process; the objective is *not* the gathering of facts. 'Focus groups are useful when it comes to investigating what participants think, but they excel at uncovering why participants think as they do' (David Morgan 1988: 25). The groups provide a podium for expression, encouraging diversity and interaction among the participants. Therefore, focus group discussions should not be confused with statistical methods of data gathering which require some measure of minimum sample size. Unlike statistical approaches, focus groups do not have to form a representative sample of a population but they should explore attitudes and ideas expressed in the group interaction. For this reason, three to four group discussions are generally enough on one focus, as long as each group brings out as much diversity as possible.[3]

The focus group discussion approach faces two difficulties, compared to more structured and/or quantitative methods of field research. A first difficulty is that the interviewer does not control the answering process as in the case of secondary data sources, surveys and structured interviews. The interviewer has the role of a careful listener, encouraging and respectful, and acts more like a facilitator. The objective is to uncover diversity rather than consensus in order to explore the participants' ideas on the subject rather than the dominant idea. An important obstacle is that economists are not trained in this type of empirical research, which requires a different research attitude (Simel Esim 1997; Irene van Staveren 1997). A second difficulty with focus group discussions is related to the fact that the discussion generates wordings, metaphors, categories and other value-related concepts that derive their meaning from the particular cultural and historical context of the participants in the group. When the interviewer is not familiar with that particular context she faces difficulties in the interpretation of what has been said, how it was said, and why. The method is most often used by anthropologists who are familiar with the local culture and systems of meanings. This poses a problem for economists who are not used to rooting their understanding of an economy explicitly in its cultural and historical context.[4]

After each focus group interview, the reading and re-reading of the transcribed text unveils the categories for analysis, as they were constructed during the process of group discussion. 'Qualitative data is analysed according to the categories of responses found in the data itself' (Judi Aubel 1994: 4). Hence, a focus group is a very open method of inquiry, which makes it particularly appropriate for the generation of hypotheses on a particular subject.

The organisation of my focus groups

I organised four discussions with a total of twenty-eight participants. The group interviews took place between August 1996 and July 1997 in Nairobi

(Kenya), Utrecht (Netherlands), San José (Costa Rica) and Sana'a (Yemen) and are reported in that order. Where the language of the interview was not English, I have translated the texts after transcription (from Dutch and Spanish; the Arabic was translated by two of the group participants during the interview, who were kind enough to function as interpreters for the interviewer as well as for a few participants who felt less confident in their English).[5] I made only minor editorial changes in the transcriptions for reasons of clarity. The names used in this chapter are fictitious, so that I could allow the real participants to speak as openly as they wished. The selection criteria for the four focus groups undertaken in this study were as follows:

Criterion 1: diversity between groups

I tried to incorporate wide geographical and cultural diversity, with locations on each of the four continents of Africa, Asia, the Americas and Europe.[6] On each continent, the selection of individual countries happened in a rather *ad hoc* manner: I chose them because I was invited to go there. I was asked to speak on behalf of the Dutch embassy in Yemen, and for an umbrella NGO that received support from the Dutch embassy in Costa Rica. I went to Kenya to represent a European network of women working on development issues, and I was acquainted with the Dutch umbrella NGO through the Dutch preparations for the UN women's conference of 1995 in which I was involved. It is important to note that, as a consequence, the participants in the group interview may have been influenced by my roles, or their images of my roles, outside the interview as 'the academic', 'the economist', 'the expert', 'the feminist', 'the white woman', 'the mother', or the various other images that I could not prevent from influencing the interview and the effects of which I am not able to measure. The European country is my own. Ethnic differences were largest between groups, though in two groups ethnic diversity was present within the group. Of course, in each group the vocabulary differed too, showing me how biased some of my theoretical notions such as 'autonomy', 'moral duty' and 'interdependence' might have sounded in the ears of the participants had I used these notions in questions of a structured interview.[7]

Criterion 2: homogeneity within groups

Homogeneity was assured through the selection of participants who are aware of the multiple roles in economic life, who recognise their value-laden context, who are able to express economic processes and positions in terms of these, and who themselves carry out a diversity of roles. Within the social, political, cultural and historical context of many countries, though certainly not everywhere in the same way, men generally tend to specialise in the role of paid production and income earning, investing in the necessary capabilities for this role. Furthermore, men also tend to invest in the role of political partic-ipation, that is, in matters of rule setting and distribution in the domain of justice. Women generally carry out these roles too. But apart from these roles they also tend to spend a large number of hours in the unpaid care economy. This is true not only cross-culturally, as became explicit during the UN women's conference of 1995 held in Beijing, but probably also historically, as suggested for example by Louise Tilly and Joan Scott (1978) in a comparative study on women's multiple roles from the pre-industrial period until today in France and England.[8] Women, generally, are more often involved than men in carrying out (more) multiple economic roles: that is, roles in different economic value domains, particularly roles in the domain of care. Time-use data confirm that in a wide diversity of developing and developed countries, women spend more time per day in their combined economic roles than men do (UNDP 1995). As a consequence women are more pressed by lack of time to fulfil their roles than men are (see Table 5.1).

Gender inequality was minimised in the focus groups by selecting female participation only; class difference was relatively small, since most of the participants came from middle class backgrounds.[9] Gender inequality may not have been totally absent, however: the discussions may reflect masculine or feminine meanings derived from the social contexts of the group partici-pants.[10] Logistically, I gathered the participants from national or regional NGOs (non-governmental organisations) working for the improvement of women's economic position. In this selection procedure, I received help from the people who had invited me and who knew most if not all the participants.

Both selection criteria – diversity and homogeneity – led me to choose women as group participants, though I could have run a parallel series of interviews with men to find out differences in the roles between men and women. This, however, is not the subject of my inquiry.

Table 5.1 Time-use in paid and unpaid work for women as a percentage of men

Women's work time compared with men's for selected countries (men's work time = 100%)		
Africa	Kenya – urban	103%
	Kenya – rural	135%
Latin America	Venezuela – urban	106%
	Colombia – urban	112%
Asia	Bangladesh – rural	110%
	Philippines – rural	121%
Europe	Netherlands	109%
	Denmark	98%
Developing countries		113%
Developed countries		106%

Source: UNDP, *Human Development Report 1995*, Oxford: Oxford University Press.

Economic theory has not paid attention to the phenomenon of role combination: it is restricted to the theorem of specialisation in the division of labour. However, John Stuart Mill observed that the combination of different tasks more by women than by men has a rational foundation (Mill 1848 Book I.viii.5: 127–8). He suggested that women's capability to combine tasks rather than to specialise in a single one would prevent the negative mental and physical effects resulting from monotonous tasks and repeated strain. There has, however, hardly been any research on this phenomenon of female task combination and its economic merits. The lack of knowledge seems just as wide as in Mill's days. 'And the present topic is an instance among multitudes, how little the ideas and experience of women have yet counted for, in forming the opinions of mankind' (John Stuart Mill 1848 Book I.viii.5: 128). The focus groups on female role combination that will be reported in this chapter are a response to the gap in knowledge that Mill signalled. The women's voices in my focus group discussions opened up alternative epistemological insights that for over a century-and-a-half have not been allowed in the dualistic methodology of modernist economics (for a similar epistemological argument, see Jack Amariglio 1988: 599).

Nairobi

The only focus group that includes participants from more than one country in the region is the one held in the capital of Kenya. We came together in the garden of a small local hotel, where we had gathered for an NGO meeting between a European network, of which I am a member, and a pan-African network, to which the focus group participants belong. The eight participants have full-time paid jobs in business, with government, or in NGOs. In addition to these positions, they participate in a diversity of activities in the women's movement, in systems of small credits to rural women's groups, in the support of tribal female entrepreneurs, in women's activities in a political party, in support for village-level women's groups or as a pamphleteer.

After our activist's meeting during the previous few days, it seemed natural to start the discussion with a question on how the participants became activists for women's economic rights. Elmira answers from the experience of apartheid in South Africa that:

> we come from a system that has de-humanised us. It leads one to zero decency. If you want to maintain dignity and pride within a nation you need to give them all they need to be in a situation where they control their destiny. They cannot control that destiny if they do not have the resources to do that. And the people who have suffered most are women. They cannot control, they cannot determine their own future. Over half of the unemployed in South Africa are women. Almost half of households are headed by a woman. Women

are impoverished, so what type of children in the next generation will we be bringing up? Whether we like it or not, whoever grows up with women will depend entirely on this woman.

Another participant, Janet from Lesotho, adds similar meanings, stating that it is the lack of independence that she wants to counter. Angélica from Uganda clarifies the rather Western-sounding values expressed by Janet with a story about her own mother's life.

I am the first born of my mother and my father is polygamous. My mother told me she got married to him when she was a young girl. She was a nurse and my father was a medical doctor. So she got into that polygamous situation and at that time she could get on very well because she had that paid job and she would get money. I grew up with my mother first so she paid tuition fees for me. And she separated from my father later on as he got someone else, and that went on and on. So when I grew up my mother had got into another marriage. She had more children and she was living with that second husband of hers. Again, she had to pay fees, she still had that paid job of hers. But that other husband of hers also got someone else. So, after working so hard in that second marriage my mother had to leave and start all over again. I was now grown up. Then slowly I got into an NGO and I realised that I had to analyse what had happened to my mother. Now she didn't have a job any more, she didn't have anywhere to stay actually at that time because she had just been forced out because another partner had come to take her place. So here I was, having to support my mother who didn't have any voice. Actually, she would have had a voice if she had some economic base at that time. Maybe I should have mentioned that eventually her children from the second marriage were actually grabbed from her when they were still very young. So I saw her suffering, she didn't have any money, she didn't have any voice, she was not happy, she was actually very, very frustrated. And I said what could I do for this woman? As I saw this happen to many other women when I started going into the field, I gathered huge testimonies. I became really convinced that these women need help. Because they don't have any little base. And that deprives them of their rights to look after their children, that deprives them of their rights to stay in their homes, that deprives them of their rights to be human beings, to be regarded as people. I think that is the inspiration I have got. That is how I got the push to keep me going.

Mary, from rural Uganda, also tells a personal history to illustrate how she became involved in women's activism.

When I started secondary school I realised that my mother was taken out of school at the age of fifteen so that they could educate my uncle. But we were really suffering at home because my mother was totally a housewife and all she could do was some farming and sell just a little of the food crops. And my father was working in town as a health officer under the city council. I used to walk a total of fourteen miles to the school, the secondary school. So I realised that my father had just a bicycle and it was really difficult for us. And I realised that earlier on my father was really rich but he didn't know how to plan and my mother could not help him to plan and he could not even realise that my mother was a person he could sit with and discuss, not at all. So he used to show me the pictures when he had cars, and women of course, and beautiful houses but at the time I really began to realise who I am and what . . . he had nothing. Following secondary school and high school I went through so many problems. When I reached high school I had to go and stay with my older sister, who was the first born and who was a nurse and she had just started working. So I saw the problems she went through; she had to pay for my school fees in higher secondary and also to maintain herself and also to look after me as a teenager. So I really felt that when I grew up I must find a way of helping women. One, women like my mother in the village, and two, women who have had a certain education level but they had a line of others to look after. So I really obeyed my sister and I started going for a teacher training course and I went to university, but my sister could not go to university because she had to stop somewhere so that I could go on. I realised so many families had to do that; the first born had to suffer a lot, drop out somewhere so that another person can go on.

Both life stories suggest that in modernising Africa women's economic independence is undermined. Women still have the cultural obligation of being financially responsible for their children's education. At the same time, they do not automatically have the means to do so. Mariama from Kenya tells us about her own mother who still has control over resources, particularly land. Her mother managed not only to produce enough subsistence for her own family, but also for others who needed help. This example set by her mother encouraged Mariama to support poor rural women's access to resources. She set up credit groups:

I started to realise that I could empower people and make them self-reliant.

She is very clear about this, she does not want to make people dependent on help, but to empower them to make their own decisions. She tells us that she became very angry when she found out that in the villages where she came, politicians were buying votes through 'gifts'.

> So, I continued to go to the village from time to time and I could see also a negative element of politicians manipulating the people, by giving them handouts and making those people very dependent on them. So they couldn't make decisions on their own. If they came and someone wanted money I would add: 'I am giving it you as a loan and I want to know what you are going to do with it, so that next week you are also giving to another person as a loan' and not that you are just being given a handout.

It was through Mariama's anger that I realised how much she values personal freedom, as decision making, as being able to make choices, and through access to resources. Her emotion made it clear to me why she made so much effort to support these poor village women, visiting them at the weekends after her week's work in town. Moreover, her anger at the village politicians pointed out to me how clear she was on the distinction between politics and economic independence: she was very irritated about the politicians abusing people's lack of alternatives, which she labelled as 'manipulation'. In her eyes these 'handouts' did not contribute at all to the improvement of the poor villager's economic situations; on the contrary, it made things worse, she argued.

Here, I wanted to know more about the meaning of freedom for the participants. Elmira, however, answered with a Friedman-type economic textbook reply:

> What we should have is choices, we should have freedom of choice.

Janet placed this abstract assertion in a context of fragile, gendered understandings in a time when some African women become quite successful, some of them financially stronger than their husbands:

> Women don't want to be economically independent because they want to confront men or be the decision maker in the households. It is not the freedom of choice to rule over men but freedom of choice to be able to also contribute to the financial expenses in the family. In Lesotho that economic independence is so important. Women are 64 per cent heads of households in Lesotho and where you have not economically empowered this woman whose husband is not bringing in money to maintain the family, how does she sustain her family?

Here we see that freedom of choice for women in their roles as income earners is explicitly not defined in terms of rent seeking, that is, seeking power over men. Janet firmly rejects such a suggestion, which is probably used as an argument by some men against women's increasing financial independence. But not everyone in the focus group agrees on the financial emphasis Janet expresses in her view of independence. Together, they come up with a list of resources women should have access to in order to become economically independent, such as education, land and health services. But their independence also depends on what they call a 'mind shift' among men. Elmira explains the problem:

> There has got to be a mind shift, in terms of attitudes, to try to balance the cultural aspects and the norms of society to what is the reality of our society today. Men have to accept women as a partner in the family. In South Africa, men prefer women who can provide for the home, they would marry a woman who is more educated, who is more resourceful, but that woman must know her place. Thirty per cent of South African women are divorced. If you are economically empowered and you earn more than your husband and if you would then want to challenge his position as head of the family this would be arrogance about your achievement. It would cause a lot of dispute. It is a complex issue; her new role in the country causes a crisis for her in the family.

Janet adds:

> You know, women are violent to other women. Because, you see, there is a woman who is causing the problem in the marriage, but there is another woman. There is somebody waiting, there are always more women, and men continue all their lives to move on and move on and they leave their children to be brought up by the women.

This confused me. I was surprised to hear of adverse consequences for women from their increased economic independence. Did not micro-economic bargaining models tell me that a person's position improves with higher bargaining power? (Bina Agarwal 1994; Gary Becker 1991; Marjorie McElroy and Mary Jean Horney 1981; Notburga Ott 1992). Didn't household bargaining models teach me that bargaining power is a function of higher income or, as a threat-point, of higher potential income to be earned outside the co-operative relationship of the household? (Agarwal 1994). In other words, should not these women's position in the household and marriage improve as a consequence of their higher incomes and subsequent greater contributions to the financial resources of the household?

The focus group discussion indicated otherwise. Income maximisation did not seem to be a rational strategy, at least not for these women in their particular cultural and gendered contexts. It would damage their position in the marriage and in the household. The participants point out to me that they seek financial security, rather than income maximisation. Janet explains:

> The economic independence is crucial. I can afford to leave my office and give support in women's issues because I have some security.

Elmira adds that it:

> comes from the level of economic stability you have reached throughout the years. I have reached a level of stability that I could live on one company. [She owns three different companies.] I am here now, the shop goes on without me. So then we can begin to make choices. Once we have a certain level of financial security.

But Anne from Cameroon is not so lucky as to have reached financial security. She is a single woman, self-employed and in a less favourable position.

> I used to do like she says, but, you know, when you feel your position, you have to see the difference. If I close my enterprise for two days because of a funeral or the like, I lose, I cannot afford it.

The participants in the group agree, however, that once you have reached a level of financial security – which requires access to a list of resources they mentioned earlier – you are able to be active for other people's well-being too. Elmira stresses that it is a matter of finding a balance:

> If there are things in society that call my attention I would leave and take my other role. If something happens, for example in my own party, I drop it, I drop everything, and I'll go . . . it is part of me, that is part of my duty. You have to find a balance.

Elmira expresses quite some emotion when she says this. In fact, she adds that:

> These other things, that is my comfort zone. The women's activities, it's my comfort zone.

Back home from Kenya I realised how complex the relations are between the roles these women perform each day. But listening to their stories again on tape I also figured that there were patterns in their stories that would allow me to link their experiences and ideas to the metaphor of economic value domains that I had only just begun to develop at that stage of my research. In fact this first interview helped me to interpret the meaning of my metaphor beyond the level of methodology. But it would become clearer only after the other focus group discussions.

Utrecht

In Utrecht I met with a group belonging to a national umbrella organisation of women working to improve women's economic position. We met in an old building in the city centre where they hold their meetings. The six-person focus group comprised mostly rural or small-town women in their fifties and sixties. They attained adulthood in the conservative nineteen fifties when the Netherlands was almost unique in approaching the ideal of the breadwinner partnered by a homemaking wife.[11] As of the time of the interview only one of the women has a paid job, while one is retired from a paid job and the rest put many hours in demanding unpaid work in organisations such as in the women's bureau of a major national labour union, a large traditional women's organisation, a female farmers' support group, and a national league defending the rights of single women and single mothers living on welfare.

When I ask them why they are so committed to women's economic empowerment, Anneke answers that:

> I think it is very important that women can attain economic independence, to assess their self-esteem, to be independent people.

Yet, this view appears to contrast with her own financial position:

> I share earnings with my partner, well, let's say, my partner has an income and I enjoy it equally, we decide together. So, I don't have an experience of fear or such, I am not afraid that things will change tomorrow, so I feel pretty secure.[12]

Greet came to her activism after a divorce, which threw her into poverty: she has been living on welfare for many years and fights against structures that make women, to a greater degree than men, poor and dependent on the safety net of welfare. Marijke on the other hand, explains how important are the values of the family in which you grow up, to prevent such a lifelong dependence.

> I was raised by a father who said: 'you should learn a profession, to secure your independence from a man'. I thus became a nurse and after my marriage to a farmer I remained at home to care for three children and my father who lived with us. I cared for him until his death. After ten years, we needed to invest in

the farm. The decision was between another pig shed, which would give me an eight-hour job on the farm, or going back to my old profession and looking for a job outside. The interest rate was high in those days and we did not want to take the risk. So I looked for a job in hospitals, but they did not want a part-time nurse (I still had three small children). Finally, I found a job as a nurse in home care.

Joke is also married to a farmer and was a teacher before her marriage.

I could not have a job, I worked on the farm and I had four children, it was very hard work. After we moved to another province, I found that the world around me became very limited; it was difficult to break out because I was tied to the farm and to the family, so I became very depressive, which lasted five years. Then I started to become active in my children's school and I decided to study part-time. Afterwards, I got involved with an NGO of women farmers, which lobbies for a different agricultural policy, with a better distribution of income and better policies for the environment and women's position. I realised: 'here I belong'. I enjoy it very much, I am member of committees and I also became very active in the church. I have done it for five years now. I only worked one and a half years paid, part-time, to do a project for this organisation. I did it because we needed the money very much. But then the accountant [who audited the farm accounts] said to me, 'what is only sixteen thousand guilders on the balance sheet of the company?' At that moment, I became very angry, we had losses that year, and now it was sixteen thousand less. That was something. I just went . . . and I had social security and all . . . now I had to pay for a private health insurance again and so on. I told my husband that the guy would not enter my house again, he wouldn't. He was really offensive.

Joke became upset again at the thought of her unjust treatment by the accountant. He clearly did not value her 'marginal' input to the joint business of the farm, though the waged job reduced the loss on the farm's balance sheet, and provided her with much cheaper health insurance and at least some level of social security. All these financial and security benefits were additional to what the job – though part-time – meant for her: her self-esteem, and her feeling of being useful in addressing what she believed to be a grave social injustice. The accountant did not seem to understand why Joke undertook the effort of having a part-time job alongside the enormous load of work in the farm, the household, the twins who still lived at home, and her voluntary work in the women's movement, the church and farmers' networks. For Joke, however, it was not a matter of trading off costs and benefits, financially, time-wise, or otherwise. It was about the meaningfulness of her activities; meaningful to herself and to the world outside the farm. Specialisation in the farm and the household had made her depressed for five years. She needed the job because it provided her with the necessary fulfilment of capabilities which, when left unused, would otherwise have continued to bother her. The multiple roles, however, brought their own ambiguities.

> There are tensions, for my relationship and the farm. I leave my husband behind, alone with all the farm-work when I am away for meetings. We used to have labourers, but that is impossible today; a farmer's life is very isolated today. And when I am home I have to work hard in the home and the farm, having less time for family members. It creates tensions and it created a conflict in the relationship . . . sometimes we go together to a meeting and then we agree beforehand that I will not take the floor. I am not obeying him, but he says that I make myself too vulnerable when speaking in a room full of men; he wants to protect me. And I think he may be right on that.

The other participants in the group interpret Joke's husband's fears differently however. They agree without much discussion that:

> He feels vulnerable . . .

Irma tells the group her own story, which also expressed her concern with self-esteem.

> My brother was allowed to learn a profession; I was not, I had to wash and iron and I hated it. My father allowed me to finish secondary school, but my mother disagreed and I always resisted their unequal treatment of son and daughter. So I married young. As soon as I was pregnant, I went to study and became a (part-time) teacher of history. I just had to escape, my brains needed a challenge. Always this urge . . . not, however, in the first place for economic independence, but to advance myself, to develop what was in me. It was not so much about an independent income, that was not a priority. Over the years, I learned to see studying and being active as an important means to keep up your self-esteem. When you are only sitting at home, it decreases, I felt it. Economic independence is for me a means to keep up your self-esteem.

This independence thus was not financial; her husband has a good income and she never had a paid job again after the temporary teaching job. Still, Irma holds that studying, activism and voluntary work are satisfying. She is the president of a national countrywomen's organisation with 40,000 members. But she is also the main provider in the home. She cooks, does the shopping and the rest of the housework.

> I cooked for him this morning, otherwise he won't eat.

Another participant had the same experience:

> I was asked: 'what do I get tonight?'

But Marijke reacts:

> I didn't accept this any longer and I think my husband is just as good a cook as I am. So, there is also a process of emancipation within your own family.

After some discussion among the participants, Irma felt that she had to justify the unequally distributed caring tasks at home. She argues that her husband has to follow a medical diet that requires careful cooking. But she also admits that her position involves a risk in case of a divorce: she will have a very unfavourable position in the labour market with her specialisation in unpaid work in and outside the home. Anneke has a similar position.

> Like Irma, I have a husband with a reasonable salary and we have a good relationship, so I am not afraid it will go wrong. But it is very good to have a role in the public sphere. As labour union activists, we have a lot to discuss with the municipal government, we discuss welfare benefits, social security. . . . So, one day, the city elder asks my husband: 'are you the husband of Anneke Janssen?' This was great fun! I felt very independent, I thought, yes, I do important things, which do not necessarily depend on monetary payment. [This gender-reversed anecdote of not being 'the wife of' for once was followed by loud laughs from the other focus group participants.]

Still the role of these women's unpaid work remains unclear: is it caring work, arising from a commitment to care? Is it activism for equal rights arising from a commitment to justice? Or is it self-fulfilment through competition on 'a labour market for unpaid jobs'? Further inquiry makes things even more confusing. Anneke has expressed several times how much she is committed to independence and equality, while at the same time we found during the discussion that she had never had a paid job; she always depended on the income earned by her husband, and stayed at home as a full-time mother with her children. It was not surprising then, that one of the other participants in the discussion asked her how she can hold both commitments, which seem quite contradictory. Anneke tells the group that:

> when I was 46, all three kids left home and I completely turned around. I started higher education and entered a different world. I enjoy life much more now than when I was at home with the kids. It was nice, I was really the mother, sitting at home with apple-pie. But I only learned to know myself after my forty-sixth. It was late, but I love it.

Lini asks further: 'Anneke, if you had the choice, would you have done it differently then?' Anneke replies:

> I find it difficult to answer, since the situation was so different. There was nobody to take care of the children. No, nevertheless, I enjoyed it, the children and all . . .

In Anneke's case, then, there was a historical rupture created by the independence of her children, which helped her to take on different roles. Marijke however, managed to perform different roles simultaneously, including a paid job outside the home:

> I started paid work again when my children were still very small. Because the school was fifteen kilometres away from the farm, the children stayed at school all day, till four. [In the Netherlands, many schools send children home for lunch.] So I was in the luxury position of having the time to do voluntary work, a paid job and to study. Because I was studying for six years, I had to hand over many household tasks. My children had to help in the housework and my husband also shared; he does the shopping and knows more about it than I do. But, of course, you need to get along well with each other. The family needs to agree with your choices: that is very important. Only when this works well within the home, will the other things outside the home work too. When at work, I always felt that I could leave my home behind without worrying.

What these varied experiences and views suggest is that for this group of Dutch women the different roles are regarded as very important, but also as conflicting. Moreover, the division of roles is not always clear, particularly because of the important expectation that this generation of Dutch women would concentrate on care within the household. It seems that where a career in the paid labour market is not feasible these women find satisfaction in a career outside the home where they employ their skills and education in a parallel, competitive, but unpaid labour 'market'. They combine a commitment to the social ends represented in their unpaid jobs and to the personal satisfaction of these jobs for their own self-esteem.

Sana'a

All the six Yemeni participants in the focus group come from Sana'a, the capital of Yemen. The women are dedicated Muslims, well educated, most of them young, some married, one divorced and one soon to be married. Although most of the women had learned a bit of English, only two (Fatima and Antelaq) felt confident enough to speak it and they translated back and forth, into Arabic for the other women and into English for me. We met in the lobby of my hotel, where earlier that day the women had gathered at a conference in which I participated. This focus group may have suffered a bit from being too closely interconnected (some participants appeared to be related, others work for the same NGO, either paid or unpaid), which only became apparent during the interview. During the focus group discussion I could not sense the constraints of these factors because of my very limited knowledge of Yemeni culture and my complete lack of understanding of Arabic, but it is important to be aware of these possible constraints when interpreting the interview.

The activism of the participants in the focus group discussion in Sana'a was explained as follows. Fatima told the group:

> I became interested in activities with women. I am now involved in raising awareness in different areas. We feel that women in our country need awareness, about a range of things. On nutrition, on health, on religion . . . also. I love my country, I love also the women in my country, I want to help to increase their level of well-being, you know, to have an idea about health and about her legal rights given to her by our religion [under Shari'a law].

Aisha answers from her experience in the labour market:

> After I graduated I was a teacher for one year, because you have to be a teacher for one year after graduation. Then I was employed by the government where I had a lot of time – I didn't have much work there – I had time for working with women in the voluntary organisation and women's activities, as well as in another NGO for women. It is a good experience to work with an NGO, because I feel that I am learning. Work in the NGOs is better than for the government because you can give more to the women. You work with people in poverty. And we work with the returnees, coming

back from Saudi Arabia [as a consequence of the Gulf war]. We also work with people called Akhdam [apparently a low 'caste' in Yemen], we can help them.

Yasmina has a similar story which contrasts work for the state, which does not seem to be very challenging or to have much impact on social problems, to (voluntary) work for NGOs.

I am also working for the government and as a volunteer in two NGOs which work with women. After working seven years for the government I feel that I can't use my expertise . . . not add any special use. . . . When I do the work for the NGOs I really feel it is useful and I feel good about it.

Antelaq switched from her paid job for the state to a paid job in the NGO:

I worked with the government, but now I have a contract with the NGO as a programme officer for women and youth. Even if I had no contract with them, I would still be a member of the NGO.

When I ask about the pay difference between the government and a paid job in these NGOs, Naima says that there is no difference. The other participants confirm this.

Not all the focus group participants are mothers, but those who do have children appear to differ considerably in their circumstances concerning childcare. I wondered how they managed to combine their paid and unpaid work outside the home with the care for their children and other work within the home. Antelaq explains, with some hesitance, how difficult this is. Her reaction shows that it is a sensitive subject:

We have many problems but we have to do this work . . . and sometimes we may not be so careful with our children . . . it is very difficult; sometimes I leave them with my sister and . . . you know . . .

Fatima however reacts self-confidently:

I have three children, one two and a half months old, one of four and a half years old and one of six years old. They are in school and crèche. In the afternoon I do not find any problems [the official paid working day in Yemen is only until around two o'clock]. If I have some activities I can go out and their father stays with the other two, and the baby stays with my mother. In the night I stay with them and do activities with them. That is no problem . . .

126

I asked Antelaq about the father's contribution to childcare for her children. She said:

> No, I am divorced . . . But, you see, sometimes with housewives, they go sometimes to a party or they are sitting or something like that and they leave the children alone.

Again, her answer seems less self-confident, even somewhat defensive, as if she feels she has to justify her work outside the house against the common expectation of the appropriate role of mothers, and particularly divorced mothers, in Yemen. The difference between Antelaq's careful replies and Fatima's firm answer may reflect the different positions they have, in particular the difference between being married and being divorced. After divorce it seems that, at least in the case of Antelaq, no help in childcare is to be expected from the father. Fatima therefore argues how important it is to select the 'right' husband. She says:

> it is important when you marry that the person is helpful and will understand your job and help you.

Her own husband seems to share in some of the caring tasks at home, depending however on his willingness to do so.

> My experience is that I have a lot of things to do at my house. My husband helps. After lunch, maybe he goes and washes the dishes, maybe he will take care of the children and help the children with homework. When I have other things to do, not only the voluntary work, then he often takes care of the children. And sometimes, he helps me in my job also. If I have something to do and I could not do it by myself, he can help me.

Again, Antelaq's situation is different and, as she suggests, not only after her divorce. Now, she is resolute in her point of view. She expresses scepticism about the husband's help in childcare and housework:

> If both men and women work and go home, the man just lies there or reads a newspaper or has a shower or something like that . . . whereas the woman is in the kitchen preparing food, and the children too are the responsibility of the woman.

Antelaq points out an important weakness in Fatima's favourable presentation of a harmonious sharing of tasks between men and women. The weakness is that the sharing rests on the assumption of men's willingness to do so. In the discussion that follows all participants agree that this is crucial and that therefore it is very important for women to find a husband who shares their commitment to women's self-realisation in activities outside the home and who also shares a commitment to participating in childcare and housework. But now came the surprise for me – ignorant as I was about Arabic cultures – in the discussion that followed. Nesrine told me that:

> We can ask the husband when we write up the marriage contract. But if the man asks the woman to stay at home with him and if she agrees to that, she knows it from the beginning. She can't refuse. It is written down.

I wondered whether I had understood what Nesrine was explaining to me, So I asked again: 'Is it written down that she will not stay at home and will have a job?' All participants reply:

> Yes, it is written down in the marriage contract.

Fatima explains a bit further:

> Also, when she has not yet finished her study, she has to write it down in the contract, that she wants to continue her study.

Now it dawns on me that these women, through their fathers, negotiate their marriage contract according to what they have managed to convince their fathers is important for them: studying, leaving the house for their own chosen activities, or earning their own incomes. The marriage contract is unique for each marriage, not standard as in most Western countries, though it has, of course, a set of fixed elements. Antelaq clarifies what this means for women in Yemen, how this institutional arrangement granted to them by Islamic law can help women to keep their independence in activities outside the home and to earn their own incomes. The arrangement may help – though not necessarily so – in strengthening their bargaining position within the home *vis-à-vis* their husband over the distribution of childcare and housework. Agreements on women's economic independence in the marriage contract are no guarantee of a fair distribution but they certainly seem to help, as this focus group discussion suggests. Antelaq says:

> You know, my father, for my sister, before she gets married, he will ask about the marriage contract and require that she will complete her education. Because, if it is not included in the marriage contract, maybe her husband will not allow her to complete her education.

When I ask what can be done when a husband does not allow his wife to work outside the home even when it is agreed in the marriage contract, Fatima answers:

> You can go to court, to the imam. But many women do not know their legal rights, as I told you. Even educated women do not know their rights.

So here the link between these women's own problems in combining their multiple roles and their commitment to educating other women about their rights under Shari'a law becomes clear: the Islamic marriage contract grants women some important rights, which, however, they need to claim in a negotiation with their future husband. Therefore, women should be made aware of these rights. This is a long and difficult process. Nesrine explains that:

> Not only the mother and father have an influence, but also other family members. Even though my father supported me, my brothers made problems . . . even my younger brother; over a woman, they have the last word.

Now, Antelaq tells her own personal story about the difficulty of claiming her rights to education:

> You know, after my secondary education, my father said, 'I think it is enough for you'; I had to stay at home, it was enough, and he said: 'you will not work'. I asked him: 'Please, just one year more'. And I did it, and he forgot. He had a lot of trading and work, and after another three, four years he asked me: 'You are still studying?' And I said: 'Yes father'. It was then very difficult for me. I wanted to go to the university in Sana'a, but how could I ask? I went to him and said: 'Father'; 'Yes,' he said; 'I want to study abroad, at a university outside the country'; so he said: 'Well you may study at the university in Sana'a . . .' And than he took me to the university of Sana'a. And it was good for my sisters, I have fought for them.

Antelaq's story indicates that the struggle is indeed very long. Before a daughter can have her rights written down in the marriage contract, she first has to convince her father about the importance of these rights for her. Only then is the father willing to negotiate these rights with the prospective family-in-law. Being the eldest daughter appeared much harder than being a younger sister, as Antelaq already pointed out earlier, when she gave the example of her youngest sister's marriage contract to be negotiated to her advantage by her father. This long-term and difficult process explains why the participants in the focus group are so concerned with consciousness raising in their NGO activities: it is not that women have no rights; on the contrary, they have them granted by law. Rather it is a matter of learning about and claiming their rights, which depends on their own self-confidence to negotiate first with their fathers and subsequently, through their fathers, with their future husband and family-in-law.

What this focus group discussion pointed out to me was the embeddedness of economic value domains in larger domains. For example, the economic rights to education and access to the labour market were founded in religion and religious law (Shari'a). Without the Quran's granting of these rights to women the struggles of the participants in this group would have been much harder.

San José

The eight Costa Rican women who were part of the focus group discussion in San José are all members of the same national women's network but are diverse in their ethnic backgrounds, activities, fields of work, ages and personal circumstances. Most of them live in the capital, some in the rural areas, and one of the participants belongs to the Atlantic coast black community. They work for NGOs, state-related organisations, as free lancers, or own a small business. Half of them are divorced, most of them have children, except for a lesbian woman and the youngest participant in the group who has just started to live with her boyfriend. From these diverse backgrounds, they have come together as an umbrella women's network, representing the main body of the Costa Rican women's movement. The meeting took place in a small conference room in the city of San José where we had just finished the two-day workshop on macro-economic policy and gender they had asked me to give.

Martina, a black woman from the Atlantic coast area, started her contribution to the group discussion with a personal background on her activism.

> When I was younger, I was involved in the black movement in the north of Costa Rica, the Atlantic zone. There, the most important issue was access to productive resources. Our history as black people in this country made our position very vulnerable. We sought to improve the incomes and social circumstances of our people. It was only when we ran into internal contradictions in the black movement that we as women became slowly aware of our own position as women. We started to recognise internal power relations, we questioned who benefited from our work and what was the distribution of resources over men's and women's interests. In the end, the women left the organisation and started to make their own analysis. We started to work from the perspective of black women and seek alternatives that related to the economic responsibilities, which have

always been women's responsibilities in our case. From our community, throughout history, women have sometimes migrated to other countries in order to provide a living for their families. We realise that we have to work within an economic system which is fundamentally unjust.

Martha is motivated by her rural family history. Also she was concerned about injustices, not only in terms of gender inequality but also in terms of class relations and the role of the church. Martha tells the group:

I was born in a very poor farming family but with a father who was ahead of his time, who treated us very liberally. I was a rebel from the time I was very young. When I was eleven years old, I challenged the church hierarchy. I objected since there were unjust situations. For example, I observed that the priest was much in favour of the big landowners of our area and against small landowners such as my dad and many others. My father always supported me. When I said to my mother: 'I will not go to the mass', she told me that I had to go since I was still too small to mind my own business. My dad said: 'leave her, it is something she can decide for herself'. Accordingly, from the time I was a little girl I always challenged such situations, so that I also came to recognise the distinction which was made between men and women. I used to take decisions like men did. But my school mates ended up in the traditional role of reproduction. My sisters, my mother, my aunts, they are all a bunch of reproducing women, living in a very small world, without many other options, which seemed to me very boring and very unjust. I started to study and study, and at the age of twenty I earned an income which was relatively high compared to others of my age, and in terms of my social background. I guess that this provided me with the liberty of not being dependent on someone, I could manage my own affairs and share with friends. . . . All these possibilities, this little space gives you the economic independence, having a professional career, having some success in your profession, it is what they call empowerment, isn't it? And it was only accidentally that I moved to work on women's issues, like a credit programme for rural women, where I felt I was working in an environment which was not hostile to me.

Elena became a women's activist by accident: only after she was transferred to a job in which she was asked to work with rural women.

When I was asked to work for the women's bureau in the agricultural development institute where I had been working for

131

many years, I thought: 'how strange they ask me, they only deal with household affairs there' and I did not want to work there. I have never been a good seamstress, nor a good cook. I am a psychologist, not a lady for cooking. In the beginning, the women came only for household matters to me, traditional female matters. But when I did a study to find out about their needs in the productive domain, and I started to visit them and talk to them, I found out their problems with access to land rights. But when I reported back this issue to the office, they only said 'why bother?'. So, now I really got into it and from that time I found the work enriching, I started to love this work. I believe strongly in the rural family, the rural women and her daily struggles.

The stories of Martina, Martha and Elena demonstrate that these women developed their commitment to independence and equality only after they experienced the absence of these values in their youth, their family history, or in their daily practices. These commitments were not given preferences but developed socially. Martha's story indicates, as also did the focus group discussion held in Nairobi, that personal economic independence is a precondition for one's activities for justice and in sharing with others. Lili adds another type of commitment, based on her personal experience.

I worked in a private company but it was difficult to compete with men who had no responsibility for children at home. I gave up the business with my husband when we divorced. In fact, he left with the company and I stayed with the children. [Here, the group participants had to laugh.]

Thera is the eldest participant in the group, half illiterate and without formal education, living in a poor quarter of San José. She tells us how her commitment developed and how it developed into some very effective lobbying and policy changes.

I have worked all my life as a domestic worker. And I know all the problems, the violations of their rights as women and as workers. There were laws, but they were ineffective. With some other women we set up a project to realise those rights. I was very afraid of doing this, since I have a little problem with reading, but I thought, let's see what I can do. Thus the organisation of domestic workers was set up. We had to find out many things by ourselves and found out about a particular law which protects labour. So, we looked up the labour laws and found more relevant articles, about working hours, half a day off per week. . . . We

132

found out that we were not treated equally to other workers, so we started our struggle. I have been involved for seven years now. And we had our successes: such as a rise in salary every six months, like every other employee, a big difference from the same level of salary we had for thirty years, at starvation level. Although we have finally succeeded in claiming rights such as for maternity leave and social security, we still have to realise them through the system of social security.

When I ask how she manages to work as a domestic worker, keep up her own household and also lead the domestic workers union, she answers:

It is not easy, because it requires a super-human strength. I get up at five in the morning, preparing the uniform, the breakfast, washing clothes, everything, go to work, come home in the evening at eight. . . . I think it would be very difficult for a man, well, he may do it but only when he develops the same mechanism – but it requires a superhuman strength.

The 'mechanism' that Thera suggests seems to refer to the capabilities that women have developed in combining different tasks at the same time: the capabilities that Mill referred to in his *Principles of Political Economy* when he suggested the efficiency of this multiple task combination compared to the dangers in task specialisation by men. The combination of roles may be efficient, but it is certainly not without tensions, as Lili warns.

I realise that we are developing a whole series of symptoms, such as stress or, as in my case, a chronic disease. This is how we women are really keeping up a rhythm of work in which we put other people's needs over our own priorities. As if we are Joan of Arc, always working for others, or Mother Teresa of Calcutta. These are only descriptions, but I am really talking about my personal experience. My daughter and my son have always taken second place to my work. This is because my work has also been my reason for being, my life in which I have put so much energy. But it is not consistent that I have tried to work so that other women can improve their living conditions while I live my own life in worse conditions.

When I ask about her strategy to cope with this problem, Lili answers:

I am looking for an equilibrium, I have to prioritise and to decide on a division of labour. In the household chores we share, my children also do part of the tasks, some things we leave to a cleaning lady, and other things just don't get done. But I can't leave my activism behind. I can't do everything, I know, but I have to prioritise *within* each activity.

This explanation by Lili shows an interesting point: despite the time pressure on all her roles and her feelings of guilt toward her children she does not opt for specialisation in a single role: apparently, there is no trade-off available. Martina elaborates on this issue of role combination.

I am a mother of two little daughters and an adolescent and I have two jobs. I could, without exaggeration, say that all the work I do in a day amounts to, I guess, not less than fifteen hours. Sometimes one asks: how do we manage? Of course I know: at the cost of our health, we do it at the cost of our happiness, we do it at the cost of ourselves . . .

I am not satisfied with this vague reply, so I ask: why? Martina continues:

It is about having an objective in life, and I want to contribute as much as I can, and what I can't do, I won't do yet. But it was not sacrifice which was my objective in life, say, but making others the objective in my life, including my son and daughters. It is incredible this search for an 'internal equilibrium'. First, there is no recipe for all. And we have to give our greatest support for the things we can contribute most and which we most want. But, this involves a process of years, really, it seems to me it is not that easy.

Martha adds other dimensions to the ambiguities involved: social norms and emotional costs:

Social pressure: from the school teacher, therapist, mother-in-law. . . . My youngest son is 7 years old and it affects him when I am not at home. And the school teacher tells my husband and the therapist, and this reinforces a circle of pressure. When you leave, you know it will affect the child, he does not do his homework, behaves badly and says it is because mom is not there to help him. Then there is the inability of my husband to replace me in this domestic question when I am not there. Unfortunately, he doesn't. First, because he is too busy and second because of the social pressure. Moreover, my husband feels that I have the responsibility of helping him with his business, because of my education, so I have to assist him. Thus I have no time left, and when I don't help him, he says it is lack of solidarity. But, on the other hand, it is not a lack of solidarity when I can't do certain things because of the time I have to spend on helping the children. . . . So building consciousness also within the home is hard work which includes much trouble, much emotional cost . . .

When I ask about bargaining with her husband over the distribution of the caring tasks at home and in particular the care for their son, Martha answers firmly:

No, not bargaining, but trying to create consciousness, because let's say, the dream is that the family has a joint task, a collective task to express more solidarity, to share things more. But in order to reach this situation, you have to pass through a process of consciousness raising, with many discussions, many misunderstandings, high emotional costs in . . . discussing.

Thera agrees:

It is an internal struggle, with problems in the home.

Acknowledging the problems with their husbands who are less prepared to share caring tasks at home, Lucila followed a different strategy.

What one can do is to educate our sons, talk with them. For example, I talked a lot with my son, telling him that I hoped he would not follow his father who left him. And I urged him to take care of himself; he learned how to get up and wash himself, to mend his clothes, to iron, he does everything. And even when he was young, he sometimes cooked for me. But, the pressure of the family, the father, the neighbours, was that the boy would grow up as a homosexual, since a man who can cook and . . . moreover, he sews my clothes. My strategy was to seek help and support in a feminist group, in which we talked about our feelings of fear and guilt. Now my son thanks me, he feels independent really, since he does not need a woman to iron for him, to wash or cook for him, nor to give him all the emotional care, since he takes care of himself.

Thera learned to apply this strategy as well toward her son and daughter-in-law.

I ran into troubles with my daughter-in-law when I did not have time to care for her children. I take care of them once in a while, when I want to. So this also makes problems in my relationship with my son, who said to me: 'Mom, how incredible, you are such a bad grandmother'. But when he and his wife came by one day with the smallest child, I told them what I needed to tell them, with much care. I asked my son: 'Well, do you have a mother?' 'Yes', he answered. 'But you seem to want a slave to care for your children. I cared for you until you were grown up; now I have finished my task . . . now it is your responsibility, not mine.'

What these women say about the tensions between their different roles expresses quite some emotional commitment. These emotions are expressed in the metaphors of heroines they use to illustrate the demands on them, and in accounts of their very personal struggles, with victories but also with continuing problems in which they incur emotional and physical costs. Furthermore, their stories demonstrate that bargaining is not necessarily helpful in reducing these costs. On the contrary, when bargaining is employed as a strategy to persuade someone of the important value of caring, it is doomed to fail. Martha and Thera indicated how effective bargaining can be in fighting injustice, particularly in a political process of claiming rights and enforcing laws. They also pointed out, however, as Lucila did, that caring responsibilities cannot be negotiated but can only be developed through a long-term process of consciousness raising and socialisation into a commitment to care.

Shared and contested economic roles

Although the four focus group discussions differ widely from each other, some shared experiences and ideas emerge, though not in terms of conventional categories of economic research or gender studies. Several critical scholars, like Chandra Mohanty (1991), have criticised reductionist explanatory frameworks that analyse women's economic position in developing countries with the help of universal categories of choice, autonomy, exchange and oppression. Such narrow approaches easily depict women in Africa, Latin America and Asia as universal victims of male-dominated culture, economy and religion, from which they should be liberated. In contrast to these deductive categories, my group interviews have generated experiences and ideas in a variety of ways, illustrating the deficiencies in conventional economic and feminist analytical categories.[13]

The experiences exhibited by the group participants in their life histories and discussions indicate that these women, who manage to combine a variety of economic roles, have strong personalities. All of them have been able to supersede the specialisation in traditional female roles that the historical and cultural contexts in which they live expect from them. Also, various participants appeared to have escaped from the lower-class position of the family in which they were born. I repeat these facts to remind the reader that focus group discussions are not and cannot be representative samples. These women by no means represent the average situation of women in their countries. But the views generated in the discussions do contribute to an understanding of economic roles and their combination, because of these women's diverse experiences with role combination. Three hypotheses on economic role combination can be derived from the focus group discussions: the effectiveness of role combination, the lower risks of combining diverse roles and the importance of institutions in the mediation of roles. In the next section, I will briefly discuss each of these hypotheses.

Effectiveness of role combination

The most prevalent view expressed in the focus groups is that specialisation in one role only is ineffective. Specialisation on comparative advantage in a single role and maximisation of benefits belonging to this role (income, rights, companionship, or other goods that Rawls would list as 'primary goods') appeared not to be rational, that is, it did not make sense for the participants in the focus groups. Apparently, a division of labour between roles limits one's capabilities and therefore one's opportunities to address the wide variety of needs and to further the different ends that one has, or that one's dependants have. Therefore, specialisation in only one domain locks out the fulfilment of commitments to values that belong to the other domains.

In the Nairobi group, Elmira and Janet explained that women's specialisation in the market, and their subsequent financial success, undermines their position in the household and marriage: 'her new role in the country causes a crisis for her in the family'. Women's individual control over resources and their firm financial independence is apparently perceived as a threat by the husband to his position. The husband's reaction in turn endangers their caring relationships in the household, particularly with their children. In the San José focus group, women's specialisation in political activism appeared to undermine both their relationships with those for whom they have caring responsibilities, such as their children and their own security of livelihood. Lili expressed these dangers as women's tendency to live up to the image of Joan of Arc, an ideal that is not feasible for most people. Martha pointed out that the fact that she has a higher education than her husband and an independent income does not increase her bargaining power. Instead, her husband demands her help for his own firm, justifying his claim by referring to his wife's training. In the focus group discussion in Utrecht, Joke and Irma were very clear about the dangers of a specialisation in caring roles. They mentioned their own frustration and health problems that emerged when their activities were limited to the domain of care. In

Sana'a, the group participants recognised an additional disadvantage of specialisation in the care economy, which is seclusion, that is, being physically restricted to the household and not allowed to go out without one's husband.

The combination of roles appeared effective, probably because they mutually support one another. In other words, the values supported by activities in one domain seem to support the values in the other domains. But this relationship between roles appeared to be non-instrumental, as the focus group participants stressed. The discussions indicated that it is not only inappropriate but also ineffective to employ the capabilities belonging to one domain to further ends of another. Anne, for example, stated that closing her business every time she had to attend a funeral of a distant relative would not be met with enthusiasm by her customers; it would be silly to expect them to pay for services they did not receive that day. In business it is mutually beneficial exchange that counts, not mercy. In another case, Martha firmly disagreed with my suggestion that she might bargain with her husband over the care for their son. She seemed to be repelled by the thought of it. Bargaining was perceived as an effective strategy in the market and in lobbying for more equitable rules for distribution of resources by the state. In her professional life and her activism she seemed to be good at employing this strategy. But in the domain of care it would not help, she said. The only way to make her husband understand the importance of caring was through a painstaking long-term process of consciousness raising, endless discussions, and trial and error in leaving him some care taking tasks, at great emotional and health costs.

The group discussions suggest that it is through a combination of activities in different value domains that one develops a wide diversity of capabilities, which in turn are needed to achieve diverse valuable ends effectively. Of course, women face time constraints in combining roles, but they do not address this problem through specialisation that might bring economies of scale. Lili explained: 'I can't do everything, I know, but I have to prioritise *within* each activity.' In chapter two, I argued that Charlotte Perkins Gilman made a similar point, when she argued that human beings have different capabilities without which they would not live a full human life, addressing a diversity of valuable ends.

Risk minimisation thanks to role combination

In each focus group there was a recognition of the risks involved in role specialisation in one domain for the furthering of one's ends in general, and even for furthering the same domain's values in the long run. Here, the story of Angélica's mother in rural Uganda was telling. She had given up a paid job in her second marriage to care for her husband and children but was left without any means of support after divorce. Even her children were taken away from her with the argument that she did not have the means to feed and house them and to pay their school fees. In fact Angélica's mother paradoxically lost the relationship with her children because of her specialisation in caring for them and her husband during her second marriage.

In fact, the group discussions indicated that specialisation in one domain increases one's vulnerability to losses inherent in each. Specialisation in the market may lead to income growth and financial independence, but may also lead to unemployment, financial loss, or debt. These risks can be diminished by employing part of one's resources in the domain of justice (tax payments or other forms of public insurance, that entitle one to a livelihood in case of unemployment, illness, or disasters), or part of one's resources in the domain of care (which is not dependent upon market prices or interest rates, but provides a livelihood through sharing of family and community resources). Similarly, specialisation in the domain of justice and the domain of care is risky. Margaret Reid has made this point about risk spreading as well, as an explanation for the observed combination of commercial and subsistence farming in the US before the Second World War. Where the market enables one to reap benefits of exchange, the domains of justice and care provide safety nets against the risk of loss. And where the care economy cherishes relationships, an independent income reduces the risks of dependence on others.

Institutional mediation between roles

The strong commitment of the group participants to a variety of roles appeared to be related to their understanding of the negative side effects of specialisation. This understanding generated another hypothesis: the idea of a necessary balance between roles. Elmira coined the term 'balance' in the Nairobi group, to point out the relationships she seeks among her multiple commitments as an entrepreneur, political activist, single mother and actor in a web of relationships in the women's movement. Lili and Martha mentioned that they try to find an internal equilibrium, or coherence, in their roles, that urges them to confront time pressure not through decreasing the number of roles but by prioritising within each role (they were committed to all of them). Thera added how difficult it is to find this balance, labelling the process as 'finding the right mechanism', which requires the development of capabilities belonging to each role.

Such balance or equilibrium is not found automatically, nor without the help of social structure. From the discussions it appeared how important social context is in helping women to balance their different economic roles. In each interview a different institution appeared to play a central role in the mediation of economic roles. The problems involved in multiple role combination in the past and today have given rise to certain institutions that make the combination possible. Each culture has its own historically developed and culturally embedded institutions, mediating various economic functions such as income earning, childcare and securing access to resources. In various African societies a major institution is seen in the separate but parallel male and female financial responsibilities, both in earning and in expenditure. In the Netherlands, the central institution that emerged after the Second World War is part-time work. In middle class urban Yemen, the marriage contract stands out as a major institution, providing women rights to roles outside the house. Finally, in various contexts in Costa Rica it is the state's legal framework of welfare and family law that is regarded as the most promising institutional setting for helping women in the combined performance of roles.

Separate but parallel responsibilities

In the Nairobi group interview an important point of reference appeared to be the institutional framework of separate but parallel economic roles of men and women. In a review of changing gender relations in sub-Saharan Africa, Els Baerends (1994) assesses the traditional separate economic spheres for women and men. Baerends notes that the separation, unlike that in most western homes, extends far beyond the household as husband and wife also have different kinship networks, stemming from rules of exogamy and uni-linear kinship systems. The separate but parallel responsibilities of husband and wife for providing food and other basic material household needs reveals a rational strategy of risk reduction. 'The fact that husband and wife have different kinship networks provides the family with access to support from very distinct sources which has great importance in times of local scarcity' (Baerends 1994: 14). Indeed, the gender division of labour is not between paid and unpaid work, or work outside the home and inside, but lies in different roles for both men and women within each domain. 'Generally, in subsistence family production, each sex specialises in the production of particular types of goods and services' (Eleanor Fapohunda 1983: 33). Other studies confirm the independent roles in provisioning that women have in many African societies especially in West Africa (Rae Lesser Blumberg 1991; Esther Boserup 1970; Christine Oppong 1983). A consequence of the parallel but separate economic responsibilities of men and women in African societies is that most of the income is not pooled but distributed according to specific, gendered rules over categories of expenditures. These responsibilities and rules help actors to combine roles in different domains of economic life: in the market, in distributive matters and in the care economy.

Part-time work

The Dutch institutional mediation between various spheres appeared to be part-time work, especially for mothers. Hettie Pott-Buter (1993) carried out a historical study of labour force participation of Dutch women in which she found that female labour force participation rates in the Netherlands have been consistently lower than in most European countries over the past century and a half. This was strongly related to the prohibition against married women staying in the civil service, which remained in force until 1957. Soon thereafter these bourgeois family values started to erode and female labour force participation increased to 54 per cent in 1999 (CBS 2000). This however had two significant side-effects: a general withdrawal from the labour force after childbirth and a widespread occurrence of part-time work. Today, half of the women who give birth to their first child leave paid work, and of those continuing their labour-force participation one-fifth stop somewhat later, when the combination of paid work, housework and childcare appears to be too burdensome compared to the marginal monetary returns (Wim Groot and Henriette Maassen van den Brink 1997). These trends were reflected in the experiences shared among the Utrecht focus group participants. OECD data indicate that in the Netherlands, in 1995, 67 per cent of all working women worked part-time (OECD 1996). This high rate cannot be found in any other OECD country. In the US for example, 27 per cent of women work part-time, in Italy 12 per cent and in Germany 34 per cent. In a study for the Dutch Ministry of Social Affairs and Employment, the authors argue that this female strategy of part-time work has become a vicious circle 'of low wages, low labour force participation, increased wage gap and further decrease of labour supply by women' (Groot and Maassen van den Brink 1997: 29). As a consequence, a committee has recommended to the Minister redistributive measures of unpaid labour between women and men, such as a legal right to part-time work as an incentive for men to negotiate a reduced paid working week with their employers, the reduction of fiscal and welfare breadwinner facilities, and a further increase in childcare services (Commissie Toekomstscenario's 1995; Marga Bruyn-Hundt 1996b).

Marriage contract

In Yemen, or at least among urban middle class young women from Sana'a, the marriage contract creates an important opportunity to combine different roles in economic life. After the daughter has persuaded her father about the importance of these roles for her, he negotiates with the future family-in-law for the daughter's liberty to educate herself, to develop her talents, to take part in public life, to spend time outside the home in self-chosen activities and, last but not least, to earn an income of her own. Marriage in Yemen is not considered exclusively in romantic terms, as it often appears in Western societies, but also as a contract in which the bride has the right to insert clauses (John Esposito 1982). The Quran (Surah 2: 282) advises women to formalise the arrangement and to have the marriage contract in written form.[14] This contractual character of marriage and the clauses is also reflected in the fact that the bride herself, not her father or any other male relative, should receive the dowry from her husband (Surah 4: 4). The 1974 Yemeni Family Act of the former socialist oriented South Yemen (People's Democratic Republic of Yemen) was one of the most progressive in the Arab world (though after reunification in 1992 with North Yemen (Yemen Arab Republic) family law was adapted to include more conservative interpretations of Islamic Shari'a). In the Family Act marriage was defined as a contract between a man and a woman with equal rights and duties. According to Nikki Keddie (1991), equality in the marriage contract was propagated by women's organisations, often backed with government support. Women's support for the marriage contract can also be deduced from the common practice whereby, although the formal representatives of bride and groom are male relatives, the informal negotiations are often initiated by female members of both families.

Legal framework

The Costa Rican focus group participants were all engaged in some form of debate, struggle, or lobbying process with the government. Thera was preparing for a parliamentarian debate on the labour law to enforce labour rights for domestic workers. Two others were active in human rights groups in the field of violence against women, demanding better laws from the state. The strategies followed for women's economic empowerment by the representatives of the women's movement in the focus group discussion explicitly aim at the state. 'We have to strive for a national consensus in order to establish state policies for gender equality' (Ana Isabel García Quesada 1996: 101). A major women's NGO with which most of the participants were associated had contributed to a lobby paper for the upcoming parliamentary elections. This women's political agenda 'seeks to integrate political democracy, economic development, equality, and social equity' (Grupo Agenda Política de Mujeres Costarricenses 1997: 7). The demands range from proposals for increasing the scope and level of welfare policies in order to combat the feminisation of poverty (ibid.: 10), and for the calculation and expression of monetary value for women's unpaid labour in the national accounts (ibid.: 11), to changes in the family law that would encourage equal responsibility of men and women for childcare and housework (ibid.: 44). In a volume about the Costa Rican women's movement, compiled by representatives of the movement, the editor characterises the movement as particularly active for justice, striving for an ideal 'which seeks to eliminate every injustice and to proclaim the right of all humankind to happiness' (Editorial Mujeres 1995: 10).

The women's movement in Costa Rica has contributed to developing a relatively strong welfare state compared to other Central Latin American states, and this is illustrated by the parallel involvement of Costa Rican feminists in women's activism and state organisations. According to UN statistics on women's political participation, Costa Rican women have a higher representation than women in other central American countries, including both the country's neighbours, Panama and Nicaragua. Women's share in parliament is twice as high in Costa Rica as in its neighbours (UNDP 2000). In Costa Rica in 1995, 24 per cent of government positions at sub-ministerial level are held by women and 15 per cent of ministerial positions, compared to 11 per cent at sub-ministerial level and 11 per cent at ministerial level in Panama, and 11 per cent and 10 per cent respectively in Nicaragua (UNDP 1997). It is through their relatively strong involvement in politics and decision making on distributive matters in the country that Costa Rican women have activated legal support – in labour, welfare and family law – for their multiple roles in life. With the help of these laws their own role combination becomes more feasible, while in the longer run they may stimulate men's participation in traditional 'women's roles' too.

Three hypotheses

Reflecting on economic behaviour, Amartya Sen (1987) has suggested that in the activities that economic actors carry out, the pursuit of 'what' is related to 'how'. It is precisely this relationship that appears to be confirmed by the participants in the focus group interviews. Certain value commitments imply some emotions and exclude others; they suggest certain types of deliberation and not others; and these in turn imply certain types of interaction rather than others. The implication of a relationship between 'what' and 'how' is, according to Sen, that the variety of activities that economic actors undertake must have some consistency in order to make sense. Instead of simply assuming consistency through principles of transitivity and continuity in a utilitarian approach, Sen argues that our understanding of pluralist economic behaviour requires interpretation because the pluralist values represent discontinuity rather than continuity.

The views expressed in the four focus group discussions indicate how closely the roles are related. Equal access to resources was defined as a precondition for gaining freedom, independence and financial security. This, it was argued, could generate the time necessary to fulfil caring responsibilities, and that fulfilment in turn was defined as comforting and self-rewarding. Relationships thus entertained may help to cushion the hardships suffered in the competitive environment of the market and the struggles in the political arena. Moreover, care was found to be a precondition for one's investment in capabilities for functioning in the market, as illustrated in the story of Mary being supported by the sister who enabled her to study. Thus the 'why' of role combination appeared to be related to effectiveness in realising each domain's value commitments, while minimising risks to one's livelihood.

The discussions demonstrate that the different roles these women perform reflect partially shared experiences and ideas on the combination of economic activities. At the same time the discussions show that the roles are contested as well, between cultures but also within each group. Where for the one unpaid work is predominantly an expression of caring, for the other it may just as well imply a struggle for equal rights, or a satisfaction of one's own independence outside the home. Throughout the shared and contested economic roles, tensions appear. Discontinuities show up in the contested nature of the incommensurable activities. The group participants want to have jobs but worry about caring. They want to care but worry about their access to resources. They want to force political change but they worry about their own independence. The roles appeared to be incommensurable. It is not only that these women face a time constraint. The most difficult struggle appeared to be how to combine the roles in a meaningful way, since no easy trade-offs are possible. A close analysis of the transcribed interviews revealed that the 'how' of role combination was supported by the mediating task of institutions.

In conclusion, the focus group discussions appeared helpful for my analysis of economic value domains. The discussions on the roles that actors carry out in each of these domains have generated new insights, have supported some ideas developed in earlier chapters, and have clarified some of the conceptual issues raised in earlier chapters. With these insights, three hypotheses on economic role combination have been generated, which will be used in the following chapters as an embodiment of the theoretical analysis:

- the effectiveness of role combination,
- risk minimisation with role combination,
- the institutional mediation of a balance.

6

TOWARD AN ARISTOTELIAN ECONOMICS

> Nobody dast blame this man. You don't understand; Willy
> was a salesman. And for a salesman, there is no rock bottom
> to the life. He don't put a bolt to a nut, he don't tell you the
> law or give you medicine. He's a man way out there in the
> blue, riding on a smile and a shoeshine. And when they start
> not smiling back – that's an earthquake. And then you get
> yourself a couple of spots on your hat, and you're finished.
> Nobody dast blame this man. A salesman is opt to dream,
> boy. It comes with the territory.
>
> (Arthur Miller, *Death of a Salesman*: 111)

The capabilities of selling, telling the law and giving medicine

Now that I have analysed economic rationality from the perspective of
ethical capabilities quite substantially, in this chapter I will address the
second research question as formulated in the introduction. This question
was on the consequences of the alternative notion of economic rationality
for economics in general and for some central notions in economics in
particular. This chapter will build on the earlier findings. Thus, I will
employ the definitions of the three economic value domains as developed
in chapter two, and some initial understandings of the relations between
these value domains in the history of economic thought. In particular, I
will draw on Aristotle's ethics as I have summarised these in chapters one
and three. However, since this is a practical ethics that only works within
a context rather than in the abstract, I need to draw on the hypotheses that
arose from the focus interviews reported in chapter five. In this way, I
hope to introduce an Aristotelian perspective on economics that potentially provides a more realistic as well as a more valid explanation of
economic behaviour.

I will begin the Aristotelian analysis in this chapter with a metaphor
that brings out all the necessary elements of an Aristotelian economic

perspective: the theatre play of the *Death of a Salesman*. It serves, I hope, to illustrate the need for a realist and inherently social-based methodology for economics, rather than methodological individualism.

The tragedy of the salesman

The quote cited at the beginning of the chapter is from Arthur Miller's play about an unsuccessful 'economic man'; it comes from a funeral speech by Willy Loman's friend, Charley. He cautions people not to condemn Willy for committing suicide when he lost his job as a salesman. He just was not made for any other occupation. He derived all his esteem, pride and dreams from being a salesman. It was the only field he knew in life.

Willy did not perform one role among others; he *was* a salesman, through and through. To him there was no other role in life, not even at home. The family roles had been divided sharply, his wife Linda taking care of the household and their sons. Willy was a salesman on the road and at home, with his friend Charley and with his sons. As Charley says, he was not the kind of man to live by rules or tell others the law. No, he was riding on a smile and a shoeshine. Nor was he the kind of person to become involved in care giving relations with others, in listening carefully and responding to other people's needs; he would not 'give you medicine'. No, he believed in becoming 'big' in business, maybe even together with 'his boys'.

This, however, does not imply that Willy is a hard, selfish man, a brutal husband, or an uninvolved father. Such an interpretation would be a misunderstanding. On the contrary, Willy loves his wife Linda, his boys Biff and Happy, his friend Charley. He often plays cards with Charley hiding from him the fact that he has financial troubles. He does not want to worry his friend. 'Business is bad, it's murderous. But not for me, of course' (*Death of a Salesman*: 40). To Linda he expresses his devotion after coming back home from travelling: 'I'm telling you, I was sellin' thousands and thousands, but I had to come home' (ibid.: 26). When Linda starts to count the commission he admits that he made at most $200. About one of his sons he says: 'He could be big in no time' (ibid.: 11). When the children were still small Willy used to tell them about his successes. 'I never have to wait in line to see a buyer. "Willy Loman is here!" That's all they have to know, and I go right through' (ibid.: 26).

Willy is getting older, though, and his sales are less successful. When he is finally fired, his young boss, whom he himself named Howard at his birth, advises him to take life easy and to accept help from his sons. In fact they are unemployed themselves and have only seasonal jobs. But Willy still expects them to become successful businessmen soon. 'They're working on a very big deal' he tells Howard (ibid.: 65). Howard sees through his dream and replies: 'This is no time for false pride, Willy' (ibid.). Willy protests that times have changed since the old days.

> In those days there was personality in it, Howard. There was respect, and comradeship, and gratitude in it. Today it's all cut and dried, and there's no chance for bringing friendship to bear – or personality. You see what I mean? They don't know me anymore.
>
> (Death of a Salesman: 63)

Miller's play expresses in Willy's failure the underlying value that guides his life: freedom. The audience gets to see the tragedy of a man who is emotionally attached to a single value commitment. Willy needs the other values, but believes them to be rooted in the same domain as the freedom he dreams of. He refers to the respect he received in the old days, even alluding to friendship. These days people don't smile back anymore; they don't even know him. In his last meeting with Howard, Willy pleads to be kept in the firm on a low salary, just enough to live on. But Howard turns him down. Willy is not profitable anymore. Charley takes pity on his friend.

> Willy, when're you gonna realize that them things don't mean anything? You named him Howard, but you can't sell that. The only thing you got in this world is what you can sell. And the funny thing is that you're a salesman, and you don't know that.
>
> (Death of a Salesman: 76)

Toward the end of the play it becomes clear that Willy's dream confuses different values. He looks for friendship in business relations while at the same time he keeps his real friend Charley at a distance when he needs him most. He expects respect from potential clients but has no problem with betraying his wife with a mistress in Boston. In his dream the marketplace appears as the only stage of life, defining his ends wholly in terms of business success, from talking to his wife to the education of his sons. Finally, Biff finds out about the shallowness of his father's dream. 'And I never got anywhere because you blew me so full of hot air I could never stand taking orders from anybody! That's whose fault it is!' (ibid.: 104). Biff blames Willy for the false image of success he gave him. 'It's goddam time you heard that! I had to be boss big shot in two weeks, and I'm through with it!' (ibid.). But for Willy this insight comes too late, which leads him to his fate. He cannot live with the idea of having failed as a salesman, since it is the only role he has. He believes that specialising in selling will bring him everything he wants. He mistakenly believes that selling opens the door to all other values in life, like respect and friendship. He does not want to accept the relevance of other value domains outside the market. He leaves caring to his wife and justice to his friend, who tries to repair Willy's lost self-respect by offering him a job. Willy rejects the offer, unwilling to say goodbye to his dream. He prefers to die, imagining the crowd of former business partners who would come to his funeral.[1]

Willy was not able to sell without people's smiles. He came to lack the capability of earning the smiles. He didn't look beyond the realm of the market. In his dreams he either did not imagine other realms or else rejected them. At the same time, the play illustrates that trying to develop other values *within* the market is also ineffective. In his specialisation in the territory of selling Willy could not find the care and justice he needed so much when he got older and less successful in his sales. He had not invested in these values because he focused only on selling.

Capability failure of the salesman

Death of a Salesman illustrates the importance of the ethical capabilities that belong to the value domains of justice and care for one's functioning in the domain of freedom. They are in fact necessary for one's functioning in the economy as a whole: in following and contributing to the distributive rules that are needed in the economic process; in being able to experience care from family and friends; and to give care to others who need such care for their own functioning. Willy invested in the capabilities of freedom, but did not invest in the capabilities belonging to the domains of justice and care.

Without a commitment to justice Willy does not understand the value of respect. Without a commitment to care he is no longer able to sustain relationships with his clients. Without the ethical capabilities of emotion, such as experiencing feelings of fairness, he is not able to defend his right to a decent living for himself and his family (for example through a labour union or a law suit against his employer). Without being able to experience affection, a caring emotion, he fails to accept his friend's help (he is too proud to accept the job that Charley offers him). Without the ethical capability to deliberate about values of justice and care, he sees no other option than to exit, literally. Finally, without the ethical capability of human interaction, he does not see how to earn a living in any other way than through selling. He cannot see himself as depending on welfare, nor stand the thought of having to rely for a while on his sons or his brother, the care of family members (see again Figure 2.2 for the expressions of each type of ethical capability: commitment, emotion, deliberation and interaction). In short, Willy the salesman fails economically, socially and personally, just as Gage and Elliot did (see chapter one), despite his huge investment in the ethical capabilities belonging to the domain of freedom.

Willy's tragic failure points to a deficiency inherent in the domain of freedom: the furthering of its values is dependent upon capabilities from other value domains. Willy's friend Charley referred to one of these other capabilities in his funeral speech: the expression of sympathy in people's smiles. When acting on the market, trying to sell, being competitive and contributing to individual feelings of independence and achievement, a salesman – or any other economic actor – cannot do without people's smiles. Without these no exchange transactions will take place. Smiles are an expression of a commitment to caring: an actor's valuing of relationship and trust. Only on the basis of sustained relationships can actors deserve smiles and act on them in any economic transaction, whether it takes place in the market, through the state, or in the care economy. It is only when an actor cares, that is, contributes to the values of the caring domain, that he or she will deserve the smiles that are needed in exchange transactions or in agreeing on distributive rules. The salesman needs people's smiles in order to persuade them to buy from him. But he cannot earn the smiles in the marketplace because relationship, trust and honesty cannot be obtained through the moments of exchange in the market. Exchange *presumes* these caring values in the first place.

Capabilities of justice are also needed in the market. These capabilities involve a commitment to fairness and the acceptance of shared social norms, rules of behaviour and laws. The salesman did not like submitting to laws. He preferred to wave them away. He assumed that he could park his car anywhere without a fine. However, he might not like telling people the law, but he needed at least to understand what laws are and to respect them before he could pull off a 'big deal' in the market place, one that required an understanding of contracts, property rights and anti-trust regulation.

And so the salesman failed. He invested in the ethical capabilities of only one domain, the domain of free exchange. This specialisation resulted in a deficient set of capabilities that led him to his failure.

Meaningful rationality

It is not only the value domain of freedom that has shortcomings. All domains have their deficiencies. Freedom cannot exist without justice, nor without care. But care cannot function without justice and freedom. Nor can justice exist without freedom and care. Therefore, we need to be active in all of the economic value domains to compensate in our roles in one domain for what we are unable to further in another.[2] Economic actors need to invest in the ethical capabilities of *all* value domains. They need to commit themselves to freedom as well as to justice and care. They need to be able to experience the emotions that belong to *each* domain: not only pride, but also a sense of rightness and affection. They cannot do without deliberation either; they need to be able to choose in the domain of freedom, to agree on a legitimate set of rules in the domain of justice, and to respond to each other's needs in the domain of care. Finally, economic actors need the capabilities of human interaction in each value domain. They need to be able to exchange, to agree on and follow distributive rules, and to give. Without these pluralist capabilities, economic actors are not able to function meaningfully in the economy.

Charlotte Perkins Gilman (1899) made exactly this argument. She was the first to recognise at the individual level that the capabilities of economic life are plural, relying on the roles that actors perform in different economic value domains. It is, as she argues, the *plurality* of these values that reflects our humanness, for men and women alike (Perkins Gilman 1903: 292, 315). Activities restricted to income earning deny one's capabilities in caring, leaving economic life incomplete. On the other hand, a life devoted only to caring, as is the case for housewives, says Perkins Gilman, 'does not bring out our humanness' (ibid.: 217) since 'it does not embrace all the virtues' (ibid.: 272). Perkins Gilman thus implies that for a meaningful economic life actors need to develop capabilities in *all* three domains, which she phrases interestingly in terms of *virtues*, following Aristotle, Hume and Smith. This implies that a division of labour in which different groups of people specialise in different domains would not be rational.[3] Here we recognise the idea of a balance between one's roles, or an internal equilibrium, a hypothesis that was generated with the help of focus group discussions in chapter five.

Specialisation on comparative advantage, so central to neoclassical economics, can no longer be regarded as automatically a rational strategy. Such specialisation would leave each group with inadequate capabilities to contribute to the values of the particular domain they are assigned to, as the tragic fate of the salesman illustrates. Trying to compensate for the deficiency of other values outside their own domain is meaningless: it will undermine the values. The salesman who expects to receive special consideration or mercy from his boss when negotiating a new labour contract, as Willy does, is not behaving according to the logic of the relevant domain; he makes a fool of himself. Mercy does not mean anything in the domain of free exchange; as Charley tries to explain to Willy: 'you can't sell that'. Mercy belongs to the domain of care and can only be understood and furthered there. It does not help to keep investing in one domain only, while under-investing in the capabilities that belong to the other value domains, a matter of declining marginal contribution to a domain's values. It is only when actors have multiple capabilities in different value domains that behaviour makes sense and can be considered rational in a meaningful way.

As a consequence, in order to be rational, economic actors need to invest in all the virtues, that is, in *all* ethical capabilities in *each* of the domains. They need to develop value *commitments* to freedom, justice and care with their respective virtues. They need to acquire the capability to experience *emotions* belonging to each of these domains, such as pride (freedom), rightness (justice) and affection (care). They need to develop capabilities to *deliberate*, that is, to make choices (freedom), to agree on a legitimate distribution (justice), and to evaluate in relationship with other people's contingent needs (care). Finally, economic actors need to learn to *interact* with each other, that is, to compete in exchange (freedom), to follow agreed rules (justice), and to share what they are able to give (care). Perkins Gilman's idea on the meaningfulness of combining different types of virtues reflecting different value domains thus implies an alternative notion of rationality. This *meaningful rationality* requires economic actors to be committed to different values that they develop in different and incommensurable domains, each of which requires them to develop capabilities appropriate for that particular value domain.

We therefore need a pluralist notion of capabilities that not only captures the idea of a plurality of incommensurable values but also the idea of the contextual and interpretative character of the virtues that each of these values involve. The only connection that can be found in economic literature of today is the capability theory.

The capability theory, which was developed by Sen, is not concerned with utility, nor with distributive rules for primary goods; rather, it focuses on economic actors' capabilities to function well in life. These capabilities to function are personal: they differ according to the circumstances of every individual. By virtue of their contribution to the good life, they reflect people's values, says Sen (1993a: 32). However, there is only one type of values allowed in Sen's definition of capabilities: the values of freedom (1992: 5; 1993a: 33; 1999: 3, 10). Capabilities are defined exclusively in terms of actors' free choices to live the life that they wish (1993a: 35). It is about their individuality, their autonomy, their choices and their independence: these are all capabilities belonging to the value domain of freedom. In Sen's notion there is no room for the other Smithian virtues: justice and benevolence. Justice is important in Sen's theory, but only as an instrument – as entitlements – to further individual freedom, not as part of the ends themselves.[4] Entitlements bring a rock bottom to life that the territory of selling lacks (as Charley acknowledges over Willy's grave). 'Entitlement is essentially a legal concept, dealing with rules that govern who can have the use of what' (Sen 1990a: 140). Whereas justice values appear only as instrumental in Sen's theory, the values of care do not appear at all. It seems that his work on commitment to non-violence, or to friendship as in Donna's dilemma, is kept out of his capability theory. As a consequence, Sen's theory has no answer to the salesman's questions about why he cannot sell without people's smiles and how to earn those smiles. Sen's notion of capability only involves the capabilities that Willy already possesses in abundance, and that could not help him to solve the problem of losing his job.

Capability theory is indeed helpful in providing a conceptual basis for including the idea of virtues in economics, but in Sen's own elaboration its limitation to the value domain of freedom is unhelpful and unnecessary.[5] Therefore, I suggest expanding his notion of capabilities from the domain of freedom values to include also the value domains of justice and care.[6] Now we need to return to the idea of virtues that appears so central in defining capabilities.

I have argued that actors need to invest in the virtues of each of the domains of care, justice and freedom, without over-investing in one domain and under-investing in the others. Meaningful rationality implies not specialisation but combination. But what then would be the optimum shares of each domain's capabilities? In other words: what is the balance, the internal equilibrium? Utility theory is not of much help in answering this question since the virtues are incommensurable. There is no utility function possible with ends that can be traded-off against each other. Moreover, virtues are not fixed entities like apples or cars but are contextually defined. As Elmira put it in the Nairobi focus group, the hardships of apartheid, bureaucracy and strong competition cannot be compensated for by friendships, but her friends do provide her with comfort, an emotion that helps her to continue her multiple roles. There is no constrained maximisation possible with virtues. A deontological theory of virtues is not helpful either since there are no rules that relate virtues to each other. A criterion such as Rawls' *maximin rule* is meaningless when applied to virtues, since these cannot be measured with a single standard. Each virtue defines its own standard of the good; there is no simple rule or algorithm available (cf. Stuart Hampshire 1983). Courage can only be measured in terms of courage, for example, not in terms of benevolence, and the other way round. Virtues are pluralist, incommensurable and contextually defined, as Smith exemplified in the *Theory of Moral Sentiments*. It is not only economists such as Smith and Perkins Gilman who have recognised this virtue-character of economic behaviour. Keynes also showed his understanding of the plurality and contextuality of important economic variables which cannot be measured and compared with each other with the help of a common standard:

> To say that net output today is greater, but the price-level is lower, than ten years ago or one year ago, is a proposition of a similar character to the statement that Queen Victoria was a better queen but not a happier woman than Queen Elizabeth.
>
> (Keynes 1936: 40)

For a further understanding of virtues as the capabilities that underlie meaningful rationality in economic behaviour I turn again to Aristotle and his theory of virtues.

The Aristotelian mean

The ethical capabilities leading to the virtuous mean

In the *Nichomachean Ethics*, Aristotle refers to the good in life as *eudaimonia*, which encompasses a multitude of virtues. His labels were somewhat differently phrased ('liberality', 'justice' and 'the virtues of social intercourse') but the categories remained more or less the same two millennia later with Adam Smith. For Aristotle, *eudaimonia* includes virtues relating to freedom, such as courage, liberality, patience and pride (*NE:* IV.1–4). It also however involves justice, for Aristotle a major virtue that includes fairness, lawfulness, the application of the principle of equality in distributive justice and the notions of rectificatory justice and political justice (*NE:* V.1–10). And finally, *eudaimonia* includes a third type of virtues, which relate to the economic roles of care.[7] Aristotle mentions virtues that are expressed in personal relationships, such as temperance, friendliness, truthfulness, equitability and the quasi virtue of shame (*NE:* IV.5–9). In Aristotle's ethics virtues appear in each domain, as Adam Smith, David Hume and Charlotte Perkins Gilman understood. I will therefore characterise these as the capabilities that rational economic actors possess in each economic value domain to function well: the ethical capabilities of commitment, emotion, deliberation and interaction in each domain. Only with the help of these are actors' virtues developed, and through these the values of the domain in which these virtues operate are furthered.

Figure 6.1 illustrates the relationship between a value domain, capabilities and virtues. The values of each domain can only be furthered in a virtuous way. For this virtue, actors need to possess a set of capabilities appropriate for a particular value domain. This relationship between capabilities, virtues and a value domain holds for all three domains. Thus, in the value domain of freedom, the capabilities of commitment, emotion, deliberation and interaction help to contribute to the virtues of freedom, such as prudence. As a consequence, the value of freedom is furthered. The same counts for the domain of justice and its virtue of propriety. For the domain of care, Joan Tronto (1995: 13) has argued a similar relationship for the capabilities of caring and caring virtues such as Smith's virtue of benevolence.

Central to Aristotle's *Nicomachean Ethics* is that virtue can only be found by trial and error as a mean between deficiency and excess: virtue depends on deliberation, as I argued in chapter one. It is important to repeat Aristotle's view that virtues are not pre-given, they are not universals, nor subjectively prescribed in individual objective functions. Virtues can only be developed within the social context in which human interaction takes place (*NE:* III.1). We deliberate about them in practice (*NE:* II.1). The way we act in striving towards virtue is just as important

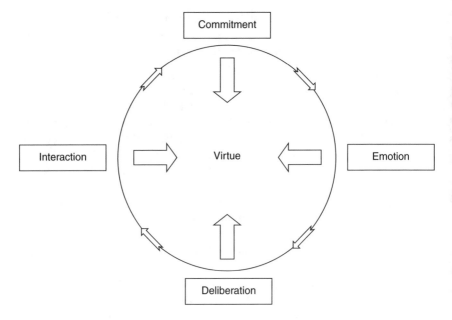

Figure 6.1 The relationship between capabilities and virtues within an economic value domain

as the virtue itself: the process of deliberation is part of virtue (*NE:* II.1). In other words, the 'what' is related to the 'how', as I elaborated in chapter five. These characteristics of virtues make it difficult to define them. Aristotle does not define virtues extensively, nor does he pretend that his examples make up a complete, universal list.[8] Economists may benefit from his advice: 'We must not expect more precision than the subject-matter admits of' (*NE:* I.3). Virtue is not an optimum or a stable equilibrium. Rather, it is a mean between excess and deficiency that can only be deliberated within a domain-specific context, not by following an algorithm.

Willy prospered through his virtues as a salesman but failed in the other virtues. He had over-invested in the value domain of freedom, which led to an excess of virtues of prudence, whereas he had under-invested in the other two domains leaving him with deficient virtues in the domains of justice and care. He failed to find the virtuous mean in each domain. What I have illustrated with the play of *Death of a Salesman* I in fact argued at a more abstract level in chapter two: the value domain of freedom cannot do without justice, and freedom and justice cannot do without care. In the historical exploration of the value domains in chapter three I found that a similar relationship operates the other way around, suggesting that each domain is deficient in itself and needs input from the other two. For an effective furthering of its values each domain relies on values that are furthered in other domains. When actors invest in one domain only, that domain comes to dominate the others and becomes excessive.

These two characteristics – deficiency and excess – are important Aristotelian concepts. In Aristotle's ethics, virtues only develop when one succeeds in deliberating the mean between excess and deficiency, as courage is a mean between being reckless and being a coward (*NE*: III.7). Tronto (1995: 14) argues that for care the mean lies between autonomy and dependence, values that belong to the domains of freedom and justice respectively. This insight indicates that the virtues of one domain can be found with the help of the other two domains: the deficiencies of one domain are diminished with help of the others, while the excesses of a domain are limited by the influence of the others. At the same time, virtues have intrinsic value and cannot be used instrumentally; in Aristotelian ontology, values do not stand in an instrumental relationship to each other but each value is furthered for its own sake. These two features of Aristotle's ontology and ethics now come together as the basic characteristics of what I will call an *Aristotelian economics*. In an Aristotelian economic analysis *value domains are interdependent but not instrumentally related*.

An Aristotelian economics is thus concerned with the contextually determined relationship between the different economic value domains. This relationship is non-instrumental but interdependent: each domain functions on its own terms but at the same time it is a precondition for the functioning of the other domains, without being instrumental. This relationship follows from the deficiencies inherent in each domain and the potential excesses resulting from specialisation in one alone. The mean *within* each domain necessarily implies a balancing *between* the domains. Hence, the relationship between them is endogenous. There are no given thresholds as in mechanistic models of economics. Instead, the thresholds between deficiency and excess are highly contextually defined and can only be found by economic actors in close interaction with each other, through deliberation, guided by their emotional attachment to the domains' values to which they are committed. But this does not imply that we cannot say anything about them. The Aristotelian notions of deficiency and excess are quite powerful for the explanation of the process of balancing that occurs simultaneously within and between the value domains.

Deficiency

When the domain of freedom, justice, or care is deficient it cannot adequately perform its role in the economy. It does not generate the capabilities in economic actors that help them to further the domain's values. And a deficient value domain is not able to feed into the other value domains to diminish their respective deficiencies. A threshold must be achieved for each domain to function well and to be able to feed into the others. So each of the domains with each of their respective locations in the economy (the market, the state and the care economy) needs to function above a minimum level. But the value of this level is indeterminate. The lower threshold is endogenous to the economic process that includes all three value domains. To illustrate the idea of a lower threshold, I will give a few examples on each of the value domains that we recognise to operate in different economic settings.

An example of a deficient domain of freedom is the former USSR, where markets were officially forbidden (though underground barter trade did exist as an indication of the economy's need for free exchange). The very limited domain of freedom not only led to substantial inefficiencies in the USSR economy but also placed a great burden on the other two domains that distributed most of economic activity over the state and the care economy. An example of a deficient domain of justice may be found in the 1990s in Russia, after the shift from a centrally planned to a market economy. The demolition of the former communist state was so profound that any effective system of tax collection, redistribution, entitlements and solidarity has come to be dominated by the excessive freedom of a happy few who control much of the economic system. The volatility of Russia's financial markets has not been dampened by central bank control or other centrally designed rules, nor has it been countered by responsible anti-risk strategies by investors. Russia's new economy is discouraging, suffering from a deficient domain of justice. In southern Italy, the deficient domain seems to be the domain of care. According to Robert Putnam (1992), southern Italy lags significantly behind northern Italy in the accumulation of social capital. These deficient levels of social capital inhibit the proper functioning of government agencies (think of corruption for example) and of the market (income per head is lower in the south compared to the north).

The lower threshold of each domain thus expresses its need for other values that enable the domains to function.

Excess

Against deficiency, Aristotle poses excess. When the domain of care, justice, or freedom becomes dominant, it becomes excessive. It dominates the other value domains and constrains their functioning. Therefore it seems plausible that there exists an upper threshold for each domain as well, though, like the lower threshold, indeterminate. Only by each remaining under this upper threshold can domination of one domain by another be prevented. The influence of other domains is needed to restrict an excessive expansion of one at the cost of the others.

Excesses in the domain of justice may be found in over-regulation and

oppression. Too much bureaucracy may lead to a general feeling of inertia and dependence; it can constrain behaviour too much, as Hayek and
Friedman fear. Excesses in the domain of care may be defined in terms of
sacrifice. Domination is ineffective for the economy as a whole in the same
manner as specialisation in a single role is ineffective at the individual
level. Domination limits the functioning of the other value domains and
thereby also prevents the transfer of positive effects from the dominant
domain to the others. Michael Walzer (1983: 20) has argued that the domination of one sphere in social life over the others goes against what in a
pluralist society with pluralist values is perceived as meaningful. The
spheres that Walzer distinguishes are different from mine but that does
not affect the argument about domination. Walzer's example is that of a
town where employment, housing, shops, services and education are all
provided by a single company. This means that when the market in which
that company operates is depressed, the inhabitants of the town lose their
jobs along with the other economic goods in their lives, such as schooling,
health care and their savings.[9] The risks stemming from domination by a
single domain, and from economic actors' specialisation in one domain
only, are substantial and can seriously destabilise the economy. As with
ecological diversity, a mix of domains in the economy guarantees the
absorption of shocks to the system, ensuring long-term sustainability.

The upper threshold of each domain thus defines the level above which
it will dominate other value domains, constraining their values and, in the
long run, undermining itself since it cannot do without the transfer of
values from other domains.

Virtue is a mean between deficiency and excess. With my interpretation of
deficiency as a lower threshold and of excess as an upper threshold in
each economic value domain I have indicated how the domains relate to
each other. Because of each domain's inherent deficiency and potential
excess they need the transfer of values from each other so that they are
enabled to function above their lower threshold and are constrained to
function below their upper threshold. The mean between deficiency and
excess that develops through the rational behaviour of actors in each
domain, using all their ethical capabilities to further each domain's
values, therefore involves a 'balancing act' between them.

The mean within each domain depends also on the relationship
between the domains: they are interdependent. The deficiency and excess
of one influences the deficiency and excess of the others. Understanding
the distinct domains thus depends on understanding the whole, while
understanding the whole can only emerge from understanding the parts;
recall again the issue of the hermeneutic circle that I explained in chapter
two. The conceptualisation of the mean between excess and deficiency
requires an interpretation of the mutual relationships between the

domains. Theoretically various balances may be possible, as in the well-known phenomenon of multiple equilibria (Judith Mehta 1993).[10] Because of the contextuality of each domain no formula exists for the determination of an equilibrium between freedom, justice and care. There is no universal 'optimal mix' between them (Hirschman 1970: chapter 9). Rather, Hirschman suggests that the balance between exit, voice and loyalty emerges from the particular historical, social and political context in which these three forms of economic interaction are expressed. It is precisely this contextuality that characterises the endogenous relationship between the domains. At the micro level of individual behaviour this contextuality is dealt with by actors' careful deliberation, as became clear in the focus group interviews: actors combine roles as separate responsibilities, not using them instrumentally. At the macro level of value domains the contextuality is resolved through the endogenous process of checks and balances in which each domain seeks a balance *vis-à-vis* the others. But *how* are the effects of each domain's values transferred to the other domains in this balancing process? This necessitates a closer look into the relationships between the domains.

Relationships between domains

Non-instrumental relationships

Here I have argued that the domains are interdependent. But in chapters two, three and four I argued that the domains are separate from each other; each domain has its own logic, its own valued ends, and they are *not* instrumentally linked, as became clear in chapter five. Freedom cannot be furthered through justice or care, as Willy's unsuccessful begging for mercy from his employer illustrates. I will illustrate this important point about the non-instrumental connection between the value domains with the example of labour unions. They function in the domain of justice, but rely also on values of freedom and care *in a non-instrumental manner*.

A labour union generally stands for a fair distribution of income between capital and labour. It will probably be motivated by some form of solidarity among labourers and would generally try to agree on certain rules of distribution in negotiations with employers. If the union does not keep to the perspective belonging to the domain of justice, solidarity will be undermined: if every member of the union is supposed to care about his or her own share of the total wage, members will start to compete with each other instead of building solidarity to increase the total wage sum in an industry compared to net profits. Solidarity does not build on an individualist approach but requires a group perspective in which each deserves equal respect. The same characteristics belonging to the justice domain are reflected in the rhetoric employed by labour unions, which speaks of rights and fairness. Unions generally do not argue in terms of the individual self-fulfilment of workers, nor do they appeal to the employer's sympathy or charity. Such appeals to values of freedom or care are not meaningful in a discourse of wage negotiations.

At the same time the negotiators representing the union and the employers need to possess some capabilities that belong to the domains of care and freedom. They must have a commitment to sustain the relationship between capital and labour in the industry but they should also be prudent about their negotiation strategies; they must feel responsible for reaching an agreement that satisfies both parties but they need to feel free from coercion in their bargaining; they have to deliberate carefully but also be decisive; and finally, both parties at the negotiations need to share the idea of a motivated and productive workforce but at the same time keep their distance from each other so as to represent their different group interests. Only with the capabilities that they have acquired in the domains of care and freedom will the negotiators operating in the domain of justice be able to reach a settlement that is considered fair and agreed upon as legitimate.

Given the three fundamental characteristics of an Aristotelian economics – intrinsically valuable domains, inter-dependence and non-instrumental relationships between value domains – I need to conceptualise a relationship between domains that is non-instrumental. In economics we have such a concept available: the idea of unintended consequences or externalities. In conventional economic theory externalities involve an inter-dependence of utility functions or production functions. For example, positive externalities arise from the geographical concentration of individual production sites, generating location benefits for the whole industry (for example the positive externalities accruing to the firms located in Silicon Valley). Negative externalities arise for example from water pollution by a pulp mill that affects fishing families further down the river. The external effects of the behaviour of individual firms are unintended consequences affecting others.

Generally the concept of externalities is only applied to market transactions affecting production functions or utility. In my analysis externalities occur within each of the value domains. External effects occur not only in markets (in the domain of freedom) but also in the state (in the domain of justice) and in the care economy (in the domain of care). In other words external effects do not only arise in exchange but equally in distribution and giving. Moreover, they do not affect utility or production functions, which are concepts that do not feature in an Aristotelian analysis, but rather concern the values that operate in each domain. The transfer of values between the domains thus occurs through the positive and negative external effects of the functioning of each value domain. *Outside their own domain values are transferred as unintended consequences or externalities to other domains although within their own domain they are furthered intentionally.*

This is a complex matter. It is more complex than the idea of externalities in conventional economic analysis since there the unintended consequences are not intended elsewhere. Micro chips producers do not intend to benefit their competitors when locating in Silicon Valley, nor do pulp mill owners intend to spoil the fishing downstream. It just happens. In the relationships between the value domains that I am concerned with the *transfer* of the benefits or costs to another domain is *unintended*. But the *values* that are transferred along with the potential benefits or costs are definitely *intended* within their *own* domain: they have intrinsic value and are furthered for their own sake in their own domain. It is only their *transfer to other domains* that is unintended, not their furthering in their own domain.

For example, we are aware that the experience of caring for children helps us to develop capabilities of sympathy and sharing that we need in our roles as employees *vis-à-vis* our colleagues, employers and customers, or to negotiate wage levels in my example of labour unions. But suppose we decided to have children with the intention of improving our capabilities in the labour market or to attract more customers. This instrumental act would not be a meaningful transfer of the values of the domain of care to the domain of freedom. It would undermine the caring for our children if it were done instrumentally for purposes that reside outside the domain of care and the children would notice this and feel uncared for. It would also undermine our objective in the labour market since colleagues and customers would notice that such an instrumental caring attitude is not genuine. When we do not really care about the people with whom we interact in the market, but only act *as if* we care about them for the sake of prudence without really understanding what caring is, we do not signal a commitment to care, and this affects our reputation in the market too. This is the same point I made in chapter four when discussing McCloskey's position on the role of respect in the market. People want to be treated with genuine sympathy and we need to be worthy of their smiles in a moral sense, as the salesman found out too late.

Values thus do not arise unintentionally but need to be cherished, to be brought about deliberately and through conscious interaction with others. But outside their own domain they play a role as well, although unintentionally. A similar idea of unintended consequences of values has been brought forward by Jon Elster. He has introduced the notion of 'by-products' to describe the external effects of human values. According to Elster (1983) by-products cannot be created instrumentally. For example, trust cannot be created in exchange. If one tries, trust degenerates into coercion or a bribe, an inappropriateness that Elster characterises as a 'moral fallacy' (Elster 1983: 43). This does not imply, Elster adds, that by-products are always unexpected; we may well expect them to occur because of our experiences of other instances where by-products developed, but he argues that we cannot bring them about instrumentally. Here I agree: values are not instrumental. However, my use of the non-instrumental role of values outside the domain where they are generated differs from Elster's in that I make a distinction between different value domains, which he does not. Without this distinction between types of values, Elster assumes that a value cannot be created at all and is always unintended. This is an unconvincing assumption since a value like trust is generated somewhere; it does not fall from heaven nor is it pre-determined and always there. People pursue values deliberately as representing their ends: people have commitments and act upon them.

With my distinction between different value domains that generate values *intentionally within* their borders but allow an *unintended transfer* of values *to other* domains I am able to fill in the blanks of Elster's unsatisfactory assumption about the origin of the values that underlie his by-products. He cannot explain how these values arise in the first place, before they become by-products that are not instrumental. My distinction between different value domains shows that values arise within their own domain where they are furthered and cherished intentionally, while they are unintended consequences for other domains.

In order to prevent confusion with Elster's point I will not use his notion of by-product (see also Wilfred Dolfsma and Irene van Staveren 1998). I will stay with the notion of externalities as I have extended this notion from its conventional use. Figure 6.2 illustrates the notions of excess and deficiency that help to transfer the external effects to the other domains.

I have identified in each value domain a lower threshold (defining

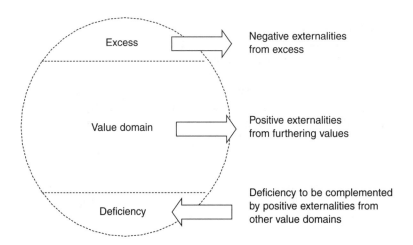

Figure 6.2 Excess and deficiency in value domains

deficiency) and an upper threshold (defining excess). Now I will show how these levels of excess and deficiency help to bring about the unintended transfers of values between the domains.

The upper threshold that characterises excess marks the level where one domain may come to dominate the others. Above this threshold the values of a domain function to excess and as a consequence they will spill over to other domains, as too much caring will spoil a child.[11] Hence, above the upper threshold a value domain will generate negative externalities in the other domains. For example, when the domain of justice becomes dominant it constrains economic actors' freedom and social bonds by over-regulation, and it distorts the economic process with its attempts at control. As a consequence the other domains come under pressure and are pushed toward their lower thresholds of deficiency.

The lower threshold that characterises deficiency marks the level where one domain risks being marginalised *vis-à-vis* the others. Below the lower threshold a value domain is deficient and needs the transfusion of values from other domains. Hence, it will not be able to transfer values to other domains; it does not generate enough for its own functioning. Once above the lower threshold however, a domain will start to generate positive externalities to the other domains. Its values will be transferred unintentionally to support the other domains, contributing to the decrease of these domains' deficiencies. For example, the domain of freedom furthers self-esteem, which is important for justice and care too. Without self-esteem it is very hard to work for solidarity or to give time-consuming attention to others. The domain of care generates social capital that is needed in the market but cannot be brought about intentionally there, as Francis Fukuyama recognised.

> The social capital needed . . . cannot be acquired, as in the case of other forms of human capital, through a rational investment decision. That is, an individual can decide to 'invest' in conventional human capital like a college education, or training to become a machinist or computer programmer, simply by going to the appropriate school. Acquisition of social capital, by contrast, requires habituation to the moral norms of a community and, in its context, the acquisition of virtues like loyalty, honesty, and dependability.
>
> (Fukuyama 1995: 26–7)

Nor, he argues, can the values of care be created in the domain of justice, although social capital is needed there too to resolve the deficiency of justice values.

> A strong and stable family structure and durable social institutions cannot be legislated into existence the way a government can create

a central bank or an army. A thriving civil society depends on a people's habits, customs, and ethics – attributes that can be shaped only indirectly through conscious political action and must otherwise be nourished through an increased awareness and respect for culture.

(Fukuyama 1995: 5)

The dynamic relationship between the three economic value domains is an endogenous one that fills the gaps of deficiency and prevents the danger of excess, resulting in a dynamic but unstable balance between the domains. The balance only occurs at a mean between deficiency and excess, as Aristotle argued for the virtues. In this Aristotelian move towards the mean, positive externalities are stimulated and negative ones are discouraged, because each domain's values are furthered best when a domain functions below excess and above deficiency: exactly the position that also helps to further the values of other domains.

This balancing of each domain *vis-à-vis* the others reflects Boulding's idea of the economy as an open system that does not behave according to the laws of mechanical physics but instead challenges these laws by bringing in the indeterminacy of the social level and interdepen dent human behaviour.[12] Both types of feedback – positive and negative – are needed in an open system. Only together can they provide the checks and balances for a social system as an economy. In my analysis the balancing act implies preventing over-investment and domination of one domain and of under-investment and marginalisation of another. The balance can only develop through careful deliberation by the actors who perform their pluralist economic roles in each of the domains. It is through their intentional contributions to each domain's valuable ends that the domains relate to each other.

The externalities of freedom, justice and care

The externalities from each value domain vary from case to case. By way of example I have named in Table 6.1 a few of the positive and negative externalities that may be transferred between the domains.

The positive externalities arising above the lower threshold of deficiency in the domain of freedom are transferred to the domains of justice and care, for example as self-esteem for building solidarity. As such these external effects from the domain of freedom help to diminish the deficiencies in the other domains. The positive externalities arising above the level of deficiency in the domain of justice are transferred to the domains of care and freedom, respect being an example. The positive externalities arising above the level of deficiency in the domain of care are transferred to the domains of justice and freedom, for instance as trust. This role of trust is acknowledged in institutional economics by

Table 6.1 Externalities spilling over from each value domain

	Domain of freedom	Domain of justice	Domain of care
Positive externalities	Self-esteem	Respect	Trust
	Competence	Social norms	Networks
	Freedoms	Entitlements	Social capital
Negative externalities	Exploitation	Oppression	Sacrifice
	Uncertainty	Inertia of old rules	Absorption
	Volatility	Bureaucracy	Lack of progress

Williamson, who however, like Elster, does not know where to locate the generation of this value.

The negative externalities that arise in each value domain occur when the values of a domain are in excess. Negative externalities from the domain of freedom may lead to great uncertainty, as Walzer demonstrated in his case study of a firm that provides most of the primary goods in town. Negative externalities from the domain of justice may lead to an extended bureaucracy, as was the case in the former USSR. Finally, negative externalities from the domain of care may result in sacrifice, as Boulding recognised in 'the sacrifice trap' in people's giving to others (Kenneth Boulding 1981: 124).

A discussion of the externalities that are transferred between the value domains can also start from the perspective of the deficiencies that they help to resolve. I will give some examples from this perspective of the deficiencies of each value domain where I rely on the insights that were gathered in chapter three from the history of economic thought.

The domain of freedom needs a labour force that has been brought up with care and that possesses the capabilities of trustworthiness, zeal and loyalty (Mill 1848; Smith 1776). These capabilities cannot be generated through exchange, but they appear to be a condition for smooth and enduring exchange relationships. Furthermore, it was acknowledged that freedom presumes another caring value: responsibility (Friedman and Friedman 1980: 32; Hayek 1960: 71; Mill 1848, 1859). When free economic actors do not act responsibly *vis-à-vis* other participants in the economy they unnecessarily limit the liberties of these others. All these caring capabilities that are transferred to market interactions can be summed up in the notion of social capital, compensating for the deficiency of freedom values. As well as care, the domain of freedom also needs justice, shown in qualities such as equal respect for other people's rights and minimum entitlements for everyone (Sen 1993a; Smith 1776 Book I.viii; Mill 1848, 1859). Without such respect or minimum entitlements economic actors may be forced to engage in 'desperate exchanges' which may do them and society at large more harm than good.

Similarly, the domain of justice needs freedom, a sense of independence and dignity in economic actors, essential for earning other
people's respect and being treated equally (Mill 1869). Mill and Taylor
gave the example of equality between men and women in economic life,
which does not occur merely by rule but requires women's extended
activities in the domain of freedom before their equal position on paper
is taken seriously. Furthermore, for justice to operate effectively its
principles need to be agreed on voluntarily, preferably by a majority.
The domain of freedom is also in need of care. Without an underlying
sense of loyalty, shared commitment and interdependence, it is difficult
to establish a voice and consequent social norms and legal rules in the
economic process (Hirschman 1970; Marx 1867; Smith 1759). It becomes
ever more difficult and costly to enforce and control these rules without
loyalty and responsibility.

The domain of care similarly needs the other domains to resolve its
deficiencies. Care needs freedom to be able to give time and goods and
services to others without compensation (Smith 1759). Without a realm of
freedom care cannot flourish. Care is a gift motivated by benevolence,
which is necessarily free (Smith 1759). At the same time, care needs the
acceptance of some norm of equality in the distribution of caring tasks
(Perkins Gilman 1903). If not, an unequal distribution of care giving may
result in conflict over caring tasks among (potential) care givers and in
bad caring for care receivers. Furthermore, a certain level of solidarity is
needed for those caring activities that can only be produced efficiently on
a larger scale, for example through farmers' co-operatives (Perkins
Gilman 1903) or through consumer co-operatives (Pigou 1929).

The interdependence between the three economic value domains also
suggests that for the economy as a whole combination is more meaningful than specialisation as I have already argued for the individual level.
But how about efficiency?

Meaningful efficiency

Each economic value domain allocates scarce resources to further its
values. Each of them does so through the location and form of interaction
that is appropriate to their respective values: the giving of care, the following of distributive rules and market exchange. What is particularly
economic about these domains is not only that they require actors to
behave rationally in each domain but also that the valuable ends need to
be furthered as efficiently as possible. The value domains are not placed
in the *Pantheon* where the Gods do not face scarcity of means and where
time is eternal. In the three domains of the economy resources are scarce
– time, labour effort, material resources and capital – and thus must be

employed with minimum waste (Reid 1934). But how are they employed most efficiently? And how can we assess efficiency?

Neoclassical economics assumes that it is always the market that allocates resources most efficiently, but this theorem rests on some very restrictive axioms. Pareto Optimality assumes completely free markets and the absence of positive and negative externalities. Moreover the axiom assumes the absence of market failures and ignores the need for public supply of merit goods. Finally, the neoclassical notion of efficiency ignores the existence of trade-offs between the market and the care economy. Because of the strong assumptions implied in the notion of Pareto Optimality, the evaluative force of efficiency in conventional economics loses much of its meaning, as Margaret Reid recognised. Therefore, I suggest going back to her interpretation of efficiency as the minimisation of waste (Reid 1934: 199, 1943: 8–9). I will show that this common-sense notion of efficiency is applicable to each domain in the economy and not only to the market. Moreover, my Aristotelian analysis indicates that efficiency requires economic activity to occur in *each* domain, because of interdependence. The existence of trade-offs between domains (substitution) and positive externalities (complementarity) indicates that efficiency requires a mix of activity in each domain rather than specialisation in one domain.

I will illustrate this with examples for each value domain. The examples are no more than illustrations; they are not case studies. Each of them requires further research. Nevertheless they illustrate the need for a balance between the value domains in the economy indicating that specialisation of activity in one domain results not only in inappropriate functioning and a disappointing contribution to actors' valuable ends, but also leads to inefficiency. First I will indicate that the domain that relies on free exchange is not necessarily efficient without the other two domains. The two sections that follow will illustrate the potential efficiency of the domains of justice and care.

The inefficiency of freedom

The privatisation of public sector activities is generally assumed to lead to greater efficiency than supply by the state as soon as market failures are resolved through private ownership, cost recovery measures and measures that stimulate competitiveness. There are successful examples of the privatisation of telecom companies, bus companies and other public sector businesses, but not every sector appears to operate more efficiently after privatisation. Notable exceptions seem to occur in the sector of health care, with disappointing effects reported in the developed world as well as in developing countries.

Various case studies from developing countries show that cost-recovery fees in privatised health care systems result in a lower demand for privatised health care services with a subsequent increase in malnutrition and health problems, particularly for women and children (Diane Elson and Barbara Evers 1998). In the long run this can undermine the productivity of the next generation in the labour market. In the short run, the drain of capable doctors and nurses from the public health care system to private clinics, in combination with cuts in hospital budgets, causes longer waiting lists and queues in clinics. As a consequence women, who tend to bear the main responsibility for the family's health care in a gendered division of roles, have less time available for productive activities. Moreover, because of a substitution effect following a price increase for health care services, women will provide substitute care at home. Again, this is time-consuming and leaves less time available for other activities. A farmer in Zambia has illustrated the inefficiencies incurred when poor households cannot afford to pay market prices for basic health care services. She reported that she lost the whole planting season because she had to care for her husband who was staying in a hospital in town, far away from their farm. The trade-off between market and care suggests that privatised heath care services may shift costs between sectors and from the short term to the long term rather than reduce costs: a false efficiency.

In the Netherlands the recent reforms in health care are subject to serious political and academic debate (Leo Boon 1998). The recent privatisation of home care has not led to a decrease in waiting lists, nor has the quality of care increased or labour shortages diminished (Dinny de Bakker, Cordula Wagner and Emmy Sluijs, 1996; Martijn Nieuwhof 1998; Ziekenfondsraad 1998). On the contrary, the newly introduced competitiveness in the sector has driven down caring time per activity and time pressure on nurses has increased. As a consequence, sick leave in the home care sector is very high and the labour supply is increasingly lagging behind demand for nurses (in the southern provinces of the Netherlands, nurses have been hired from Belgium to fill the gap). At the same time, family care givers remain over-burdened because of an increasing demand for their unpaid care giving (Agnes van Swaay 1997).

An evaluation study in the United States of the home care industry in North Carolina indicates that private, for-profit providers of home care are in fact less efficient than non-profit and public care providers in the area. 'Given the available evidence, we conclude that non-profit and public group homes in North Carolina are superior in efficiency and service related to for-profit group homes' (William Van Lear and Lynette Fowler 1997: 1047). The authors' explanation is that:

we believe that the motive force driving nonprofits – namely human service – compels administrators and client caretakers to perform quality service. Though job turnover is high in this industry, turnover is primarily due to the rigors of the work and low pay.

Many of those who staff group homes are degreed health care professionals who genuinely care for the clients and are fulfilled by performing a public service.

(Van Lear and Fowler 1997: 1047–8)

Here we see reference to intrinsic motivation. The authors also suggest that the lower efficiency of for-profit home care providers can be explained by the fact that in the non-profit sector:

concerns about stockprices are not a distraction for management. Since nonprofits do not pay out dividends and profit maximisation is of no concern, nonprofits can charge less for their services and/or allocate more funding to client services. . . . Executives of nonprofits are accountable to state funding agencies, relatives of clients, and a community board. We think these pressures imply a greater assurance of quality of care in nonprofit operations.

(Van Lear and Fowler 1997: 1048)

It seems that the intrinsic motivation of caring gets crowded out in the competitive process in the home care market, with consequent inefficiencies both in the short and in the long term for the industry, patients and ultimately also for unpaid family care givers. Hence, for an effective organisation of the health care sector the value of care needs to be recognised and furthered rather than crowded out. The market however, is unable to do this. The state can contribute to the values of care by allocating sufficient resources to public health care services, stimulating health care workers' motivation not only through fair wages but also through a work environment that enables them to care well (good quality equipment and sufficient time per patient to respond to their caring needs). Ultimately, however, efficiency in health care predominantly depends on the domain of care. Health care services supplied by the market and the state are only complementary to the care provided by oneself, relatives, family, neighbours and other unpaid providers in the care economy. Without the sympathy, responsibility, responsiveness, and the positive gifts of time and energy produced in the care economy, private and public health care provisioning will remain largely ineffective. Moreover, the positive external effects transferred from the domain of care to the market and the state are crucial for competent care giving by workers in private and public hospitals and home care organisations. These positive effects only occur when the care economy in turn is supported by health care policies and not marginalised or exploited by them.

This example suggests that the market does not necessarily lead to efficiency. The next example shows that distributive rules by the state may increase rather than limit efficiency.

The efficiency of justice

A more equal distribution of resources by means of distributive measures by the state has long been defined as inefficient. However, recent evaluation studies by believers in the neoclassical paradigm of the growth success of new industrialised countries in Asia show that a fair distribution of resources in these countries has in fact stimulated GDP growth (Robert Barro 1991; Nancy Birdsall, David Ross and Richard Sabot 1995; see also UNDP 1995, 1996, 1997; Sen 1998).[13] 'Other things being equal, economies with lower inequality near the start of the period 1960–85 grew faster' (Birdsall, Ross and Sabot 1995: 503).

Even in neoclassical economics, then, through the new growth theory, there is a growing recognition that a more equal access to education, health care services and credit stimulates efficiency, and even higher wages for the poor increases their so-called 'X-efficiency' (George Akerlof 1982; Birdsall, Ross and Sabot 1995; Harvey Leibenstein 1976). In the case of East Asia cross-section regressions suggest that:

> low inequality can stimulate growth in four ways: by inducing large increases in the savings and investments of the poor; by contributing to political and macroeconomic stability; by increasing the X-efficiency of low-income workers; and, with higher rural incomes, by increasing market demand for domestic producers.
>
> (Birdsall, Ross and Sabot 1995: 497)

Again, intrinsic motivation in the labour market seems to play a role through the motivation arising from the fairness of wages as Akerlof has argued already.

Not only distribution in favour of the poor, but also redistribution of resources from men to women can have substantial impacts on efficiency. The explanation resides in decreasing marginal benefits from investment: where there is discrimination against women, additional investments in resources for men will generate fewer benefits than when the same amount of resources is invested in female producers. A comparative study of East Asia and sub-Saharan Africa points out that the unequal access to education and employment for women in sub-Saharan Africa has slowed down growth in the region by 0.8 percentage points per capita per year in the period 1960–92 (World Bank 1998: 17). Since growth was only 0.7 per cent over this period a redistribution in access from men to women would have doubled per capita growth over this period.

This example has indicated that the domain of justice may contribute to (narrowly defined) efficiency, rather than limit it, where the values of justice are furthered. However, the domain of care plays a role too. Political stability relies on the trust people have in government; X-efficiency is not only stimulated by fair wages but also by various elements of intrinsic motivation that are rooted in caring relationships among employees and between employees and their employers: the 'zeal' and 'honesty' that Mill and Taylor recognised in an efficient workforce.

The next example will show a field in which the domain of care may be the most efficient: in the case of blood donation, markets fail and regulation is costly and counter-productive, and caring appears to be the most efficient form of allocation.

The efficiency of care

Giving is the dominant form of interaction in the domain of care, which can be more effective than exchange under competition or rule setting, as has been suggested for example by Michael Argyle (1991) from experimental settings. According to Argyle caring may be more efficient because of the following five characteristics: intrinsic motivation, close coordination, mutual help, communication and a balanced division of labour (Argyle 1991: 127). Moreover, economic behaviour motivated by caring will diminish the free riding and rent seeking that arise in the domains of freedom and justice. The example here concerns the gift of blood. Donor blood can be characterised as a personal good. Its bodily source is personal. Sometimes supplier and receiver know each other or are related to each other. More often blood is given to unknown others, but the transaction is still personal. The activity generally takes place in a friendly environment with personal attention. And although the receiver is unknown, he or she is not imagined to be disinterested or anonymous, but a person in need who is assumed to be grateful for our responsibility. (If donors had the image of recipients of their blood feeding it to their dogs for example, they would probably be less inclined to continue their gift; giving assumes some real need and involves some sacrifice to support the gift's value, a sacrifice which should somehow be proportionate.)

Richard Titmuss' study of 1970 lists some characteristics of the gift character of blood donation, such as sometimes physically painful consequences to the donor, the absence of personal and predictable penalties for not giving, the absence of certainty of a reciprocal gift in future and the general rejection of such regulated reciprocity by donors, the absence of an obligation on recipients of transfusions to donate blood in future, the impossibility of fully screening blood for its quality (serum hepatitis and today also HIV), the perishability of blood whereby the giver has no power to determine whether it is used or wasted, and the vital importance of blood to the receiver (Titmuss 1970: 74). The donor who supplies her blood as a free gift acts voluntarily, without legal sanction and without the benefits of payment or other types of reciprocity.[14] Titmuss also distinguished other categories of blood donors, ranging from those who exchange their blood for a market price to those who act out of a morally or legally backed obligation. In the United States much (but not all) collection of blood is organised through exchange. People sell their blood for a market price and compare the benefits to activities with different returns. In England, the allocation of donor blood is through gift. In surveys donors motivate their gifts in terms of responsibility, their acknowledgement of and response to people's need for donor blood. But they are not idealistic altruists as the standard neoclassical dualism on motivation suggests for motivations other than self-interest (see Table 4.1). The donors who gave their blood as a gift did not see themselves as sacrificing but as, in a sense, contributing to a value for a community in which this value is shared with others; the act involves some sacrifice but can in no way be reduced to this alone (ibid.: 238).

What follows from Titmuss' study is that individual donor gifts are meaningful rational acts, appropriately placed within the value domain of care. Titmuss refers to donors' meaningful behaviour in the care economy, referring to the voluntarity in giving and the social context in which they perceive giving as the right thing to do. 'Choice cannot be abstracted from its social context, its values and disvalues, and measured in "value free" forms' (ibid.: 243). In terms of efficiency, Titmuss found that the market allocation system for blood in the United States proved less efficient than the gift allocation system of England.

> In terms of economic efficiency [the commercialised blood market] is highly wasteful of blood; shortages, chronic and acute, characterise the demand and supply position and make illusory the concept of equilibrium. It is administratively inefficient and results in more bureaucratisation and much greater administrative, accounting and computer overheads. In terms of price per unit of blood to the patient (or consumer) it is a system which is five to fifteen times more costly than the voluntary system in Britain. And, finally, in terms of quality, commercial markets are much more likely to distribute contaminated blood; the risks for the patients of disease and death are substantially greater.
>
> (Titmuss 1970: 246)

The examples above are only indicative. More empirical research is required focusing on the Aristotelian ideas brought forward in this chapter: ethical capabilities, substitution and complementarity between domains, and the positive and negative externalities occurring between the domains. The examples suggest that different types of activities and the values that are expressed in them are produced more efficiently in one value domain than in another, while at the same time values from other domains are needed as well. This implies that efficiency can no longer be regarded as axiomatic as in Pareto Optimality. Rather, efficiency becomes meaningful when productive activities take place in their appropriate value domain where the underlying values are furthered best with minimum waste of resources. Efficiency thus is a contextual issue, not one of rules or an algorithm. Efficient resource allocation depends on an endogenous balance between the three value domains and is highly contextual. Such Aristotelian evaluation of productive activity leads to the notion of *meaningful efficiency*.

Meaningful balancing

Meaningful efficiency thus implies that production is placed within the value domain to which it contributes best, without excess and deficiency, while at the same time minimising waste compared to production in a different domain. Since the underlying values of freedom, justice and care are always contested and therefore changing, there is no fixed distribution of activities over the three domains, as Hirschman has explained: there exists no rule for an optimal mix. Moreover, the interdependence between the three domains and the contextuality of each domain's deficiency and excess indicate that efficiency is a contextual issue. Efficiency is established in the balancing process between the domains with the help of the positive and negative externalities that are transferred between them. Understanding this balancing process for a particular economy may provide not only insights into the level of efficiency at which an economy operates but may equally well provide suggestions for policy measures to increase this efficiency by encouraging shifts in activities between value domains.

An example can be found in Keynes' recognition of private virtues and public vices in savings (see also an example in Boulding 1985: 105–6). Keynes' solution of the problem of high savings causing insufficient aggregate demand and leading towards lower investment and employment levels, possibly leading to a crisis, was to keep consumption levels up with help of government expenditure. From the perspective of the three value domains a more valuable and efficient strategy might be proposed, involving a redistribution of time from the domain of freedom (income earning, which is largely saved) to the domain of care (unpaid labour). With such a policy people would reduce their hours of paid work (in Keynes' day, part-time work was not as widely accepted as it is today) and receive lower incomes as a consequence. Since the propensity to save varies positively with income, saving in the economy will go down, absolutely and in proportion to GDP, even when more people work for pay than before and the total hours worked in the economy as a whole remain the same. Production, consumption and employment levels will remain above the level where a negative spiral toward a crisis would set in, while at the same time people have more time available for production in the care economy. So, where Keynes' strategy to counter negative effects from the market focused on the value domain of justice, I might suggest concentrating on the domain of care instead, inducing a shift from monetary savings to time savings. Higher public debt and higher interest rates would be avoided, while the positive externalities of an increased activity in the domain of care (social capital) can be reaped in the domains of freedom and justice.

In conclusion, the present chapter has indicated that meaningful rationality implies a contextual and deliberated combination of economic roles in each domain, whereas meaningful efficiency implies a contextual and endogenously related combination of economic activity in each value domain. In both cases the combination involves delicate balancing. At the micro level, balancing involves a careful deliberation of one's roles. At the macro level, it implies an endogenous process of positive and negative feedback through external effects between the three value domains.

In this chapter economic rationality has been characterised as meaningful rationality, involving the four ethical capabilities listed in chapter one. This was suggested as a possible alternative to the dominant picture of rationality that is struck with an iron bar through the head. Meaningful rationality was interpreted in an Aristotelian way, as a mean between deficiency and excess. Also, drawing on the hypotheses derived in chapter five, meaningful rationality was found to involve role combination in a non-instrumental way. This characterisation of rationality subsequently served to develop a tentative conceptual framework for economic analysis from an Aristotelian perspective. In this conceptual framework, Aristotelian ethics was linked with common economic concepts, and this changed their meaning substantially. Five main economic concepts were analysed from an Aristotelian perspective:

- *externalities* from each economic value domain spilling over to the other domains,
- *efficiency* resulting from this non-instrumental relationship between value domains,
- *complementarity* between economic value domains,
- partial *substitution* between economic value domains,
- economic *equilibrium* as meaningful balancing between the domains.

The next chapter will elaborate on this last issue: that is, on how a balance between economic value domains is found, disturbed and re-found.

7

INSTITUTIONAL MEDIATION BETWEEN VALUE DOMAINS

> The growth and mutations of the institutional fabric are an outcome of the conduct of the individual members of the group, since it is out of the experience of the individuals, through the habituation of the individuals, that institutions arise; and it is in this same experience that these institutions act to direct and define the aims and end of conduct.
>
> (Thorstein Veblen 1919: 243)

The mediating role of institutions

The non-instrumental relationship between the three economic value domains of care, justice and freedom was explained in chapter six using the concept of externalities. The positive and negative external effects of behaviour in one domain that are transferred as unintended consequences to other domains relate incommensurable values to each other. The external effects establish non-instrumental relationships between the domains.

Within each domain, however, the problem of incommensurability remains since after the transfer of external effects each domain receives values that are distinct from its own type. The domain of freedom incorporates values that originate in the domains of justice and care, the domain of justice incorporates values that originate in the domains of freedom and care, and the domain of care incorporates values that originate in the domains of freedom and justice. As we saw in the focus group interviews reported in chapter five, the incommensurability of these three types of values causes conflicts between them that are expressed in the complexities and ambiguities involved in the combination of different roles. These conflicts are not new but have existed for a long time. Moreover, they are not merely individual experiences but are widely shared among actors who perform similar economic roles. For actors to behave rationally, they need somehow to find solutions to the incommensurability of their multiple commitments in the roles that they perform. These solutions would also help to overcome the emotional ambiguities that conflicting values

174

generate. They would provide shortcuts for deliberating such conflicts and could be shared with others who face similar complexity and uncertainty arising from the incommensurability of the values they adhere to.

As a reaction to these complex demands on their rationality, actors develop routines that are partially shared with others but also come to be contested. These routines gain social and historical meaning and can be recognised as institutions. Institutions help to mediate the incommensurability that arises from the externalities occurring between the value domains. This understanding of institutions is significantly different from the view taken in new institutional economics and instrumental value theory that I discussed in chapter four. There, institutions were pictured as instruments to maximise actors' interests and as a solution for actors' bounded rationality. Seen thus they do not represent values as the ends actors pursue, but are regarded as means to further ends, or as constraints when institutions do not happen to further the interests of a particular group. I will argue in this chapter that the role of institutions is not that of a means but an expression of different, incommensurable valuable ends. Institutions provide routines for behaviour to deal with this incommensurability and the ambiguities arising from multiple value commitments.

Institutions help economic actors to mediate different commitments, to distinguish different emotions, to deliberate over different values at the same time, and to interact with each other on these shared values. In the focus group interviews some of the institutions that help to mediate the ambiguities involved in the simultaneous commitment to different types of values were mentioned.

In the Nairobi focus group discussion, the major institution mediating economic roles was the cultural norm of parallel but separate responsibilities of men and women in households. In various sub-Saharan African countries both women and men are active in market exchange, in distributive schemes, and in personal networks where information, resources and goods are shared. Within these realms however, men and women tend to have separate responsibilities which for example show in the separate, non-pooled income and expenditure flows in many sub-Saharan African households.

In the Utrecht group discussion, the relevant institution mediating economic territories appeared to be part-time work. Part-time jobs of from twelve to thirty-six hours per week enable people to combine activities in the realms of freedom, such as income earning, with caring responsibilities for children and others, and with active political participation. The institution of part-time work in the Netherlands however, only functions well for women, not for men. This perpetuates the situation of women's lower income levels, their weak position in the labour market and their slightly lower levels of leisure time compared with Dutch men. Therefore, proposals for institutional adaptations are being discussed in the Netherlands to make the institution of part-time work more efficient and more just (that is, justice from a feminist standpoint; Sandra Harding 1995).

In the Sana'a discussion, the relevant institution that emerged was the marriage contract. Only an agreement between the bride's and the groom's family on the bride's freedoms, rights and responsibilities in her economic life can enable her to escape a full-time confinement to care giving only. The contract ensures the father a (psychological but sometimes also material) return on his investment in the bride's education while enabling the bride to earn an independent income, sharing financial responsibility for the household with the groom. Many women in Yemen, however, do not negotiate such a contract for various reasons, even though the Quran encourages them to do so.

Finally, the San José focus group discussion brought up not just one institution but a whole domain of institutions: of family law, social welfare and labour law pertaining to the domain of justice, democratically agreed by parliament. The group members expected most help in their role combination from a reform of family law and labour market regulation, together with the enforcement of existing social laws and other legal measures to expand and strengthen the Costa Rican welfare state, in particular to ameliorate women's marginalised economic position. Thus, the dominant institutions in Costa Rica that mediate women's economic roles take legal forms such as labour laws.

As the focus group interviews suggest, institutions mediate different values that are expressed in the different roles that actors perform. As such, institutions not only mediate incommensurable commitments but also help to overcome the emotional ambiguities that they generate. For example, the institution of part-time work in the Netherlands helps women to overcome their feelings of guilt towards their children because of their less than full-time mothering: they can work when the children are at school and be with their children after school hours. At the same time, the wide acceptance of women's part-time labour contracts in the Netherlands helps them to enjoy the freedom of earning their own income while legitimising achievements that are lower than those of their full-time colleagues.

Thus the Aristotelian mediation of incommensurable values and value domains in an economy requires institutions to resolve the ambiguities and conflicts that arise from the non-instrumental connection between different values in each domain. How do institutions perform this mediating role? What are the characteristics?

An Aristotelian understanding of institutions

Today there are many characterisations of institutions, of which instrumental characterisations seem most popular. For my understanding of institutions, however, I need a different description of them, distinct from characterisations that fit the dualism of conventional economic methodology. Both sides of the dualism of neutrality versus morality are unhelpful, as I argued in chapter four. The identification of institutions as instruments for utility maximisation, or as constraints similar to time and budget constraints, denies the values that actors seek to pursue in their interaction. On the other side of the dualism, the identification of institutions as moral imperatives that are self-reinforcing, persistent and self-legitimising (cf. Hodgson 1998: 179) denies their endogenous role in the economy.

The understanding of the role of institutions that I am seeking is not new. In fact, the mediating role of institutions as expressing the values that actors pursue has already been recognised by economists of the old-institutional school such as Thorstein Veblen, John Commons and Charlotte Perkins Gilman.[1] For my characterisation of institutions I found four basic elements in the literature that describe the role of institutions in the economy and express their value relatedness. These four characteristics set the framework for an Aristotelian understanding of institutions as mediating the incommensurability implied in the non-instrumental relationships between the three value domains of care, justice and freedom.[2]

Characteristic 1: reducing complexity and uncertainty

The early institutional economists recognise the complexity of economic life and the ambiguities involved in multiple value commitments by actors. They also recognise the social, cultural and political context in which economic actors pursue these multiple and incommensurable valuable ends. The uncertainty that follows from complex social interaction generates routines. These become institutionalised and help actors to hold different commitments at the same time. As such, institutions develop from complexity and uncertainty but simultaneously help actors to hold on to their multiple commitments that cause the complexities and uncertainties. Alongside formal institutions that directly guide behaviour such as laws, contracts and organisations, institutions also reflect intangible links between values. These intangible institutions, such as discrimination towards minorities or neighbourly help, guide human behaviour more indirectly, leaving ample space for deliberation. In the words of Mark Granovetter (1985), behaviour is neither under-socialised or completely autonomous, nor over-socialised or completely determined. The guiding role of institutions as mediating different values is thus located at the meso level of the economy, mediating shared values that guide the interaction between actors and reduce complexity and uncertainty within this interaction. Institutions therefore are endogenous to the economic process, at least in the medium and long run.

Characteristic 2: path dependence

Institutional economics regards behavioural change as dependent on history. This perception of a historical embeddedness of institutional change is characterised as path dependence. Hence, the process of change is not entirely reversible. Once a particular routine has been accepted it is not easy to change it: behaviour tends to follow directions that were taken earlier on; in other words, institutions induce behavioural inertia. Or in emotional terms, people become habituated to certain routines and become emotionally attached to their accustomed pattern of behaviour. Contingent behaviour, changing constantly, brings emotional instability and feelings of insecurity. Path dependence on the other hand provides relative stability through formal and informal institutions; these generally do not change overnight. The routines dampen the strong behavioural fluctuations that may arise in the case of purely individual utility maximisation. As a consequence, once a habit comes to be challenged and rejected aggregate behaviour may change considerably, even when the initial change is small. What are perceived as small institutional changes at time X_t may later appear to have been big changes in retrospect, at time X_{t+1}. For example, large changes in demand may occur when a company starts to use only a small amount of genetically manipulated soya beans in the production of baby food.[3]

Characteristic 3: endogenous change

Institutional economics concerns itself with dynamics, not with comparative statistics. Also, institutionalists generally regard change as involving a transformation of structures, not only as an outside shock to a structure. Change in the economic process arises from transformations of the values underlying institutions and therefore is endogenous. The most often mentioned examples are transformations caused by the accumulation of knowledge through learning, or by an increase in technology through creativity. These transformations induce changes in the relationships between variables in the economic process, changing parameter values at particular thresholds. The passing of a threshold may initiate a new institution. For example, the elitist norm of leisure, as described by Veblen (1899), came about when various social and economic parameters coincided to make possible the idleness of the upper classes.

Here, the economy is viewed as an open and moving system without determinate stable equilibrium solutions. Means and ends, causes and effects, are often unstable and difficult to distinguish: 'institutionalists have been holistic. . . . Pursuit of the mechanics of price determination trivialises what the economy is all about, and excludes considerations of social control and social change and all that they entail' (Samuels 1995b: 575).

John Commons (1961: 120) introduced the notion of a 'managed equilibrium' to distinguish the institutional understanding of mediation of incommensurable values towards a contextually defined mean from the neoclassical idea of equilibrium as a Newtonian law of motion toward stability. The process of institutional change is not mechanistic and algorithmic but historical and social. It is the careful deliberation of individual actors that is involved in balancing between different value commitments rather than the mechanics of an algorithm, a deliberation that is expressed in the endogenous feedbacks between the value domains.

Characteristic 4: meso level of interaction

The assumption of methodological individualism that characterises neoclassical theory is rejected by institutional economists. The level of analysis is at the intermediate, not the individual, level, and behaviour is not seen as centrally determined by an authority. This position implies that economic processes cannot be explained in terms of the aggregation of purely individual actions. Rather, institutionalists regard interaction in the economy as a complex and highly interdependent phenomenon, which calls for a holistic explanation of economic phenomena. Therefore the level of analysis is the meso level of interaction between actors mediated by institutions, rather than a completely autonomous individual level. As a consequence the aggregation of partial economic analyses becomes impossible in institutional analysis, since parts cannot be considered independently from the whole. Instead, understanding and explanation focuses on the institutional arrangements that mediate economic actors' interactions.

The four characteristics of institutions that I have briefly introduced help to explain how institutions perform their Aristotelian, mediating role in each value domain. They are able to do so because they address all the ethical capabilities that actors need for meaningful rational interaction. Institutions address the issue of commitment in their mediation of different intrinsic values that help to reduce the complexity and uncertainty involved in the incommensurability of different value commitments; they address the role of emotions by providing routines that deal with feelings of ambiguity over the combination of different commitments; they address the difficulty involved in deliberation over incommensurable values through their endogeneity, which allows for evolution in response to changing circumstances; and finally, they address the issue of interdependent interaction between economic actors by generating shared routines that operate at the social level rather than as subjective habits of individuals.

Institutions thus understood are helpful in explaining how ambiguities and conflicts between values are mediated between the domains. Bearing in mind the positive and negative externalities mentioned in chapter six, we can now distinguish two types of mediation: one arising from positive and the other from negative externalities. As a consequence I distinguish two forms of mediation attached to institutions: enabling mediation, that is, the expression of positive external effects from one value domain to another, and constraining mediation, that is, the expression of negative external effects arising between value domains.[4] I will now provide a short discussion of these two functions of institutional mediation in each value domain. Figure 7.1 provides an illustration.

The enabling function of institutions

The positive externalities occurring between different value domains help the receiving domain to function above its level of deficiency, as I have argued earlier. In this way, institutions enable the receiving value domain to function well. This counts for each of the three domains. In the following sections, I will provide some examples for each of them.

Institutions of freedom as enabling

The economic value domain of freedom provides a liberal institutional environment that rewards people's individuality, competitive achievements and

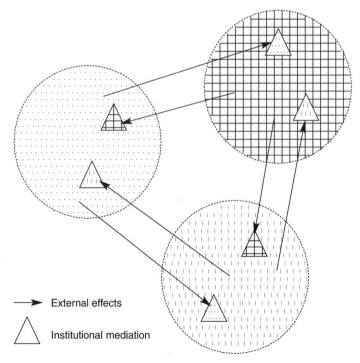

→ External effects

△ Institutional mediation

Figure 7.1 The mediating role of institutions within each value domain

180

independence. The institutions of freedom are market institutions: they enable markets to function free from disturbing forces. Some of these liberal institutions however, are also important for the flourishing of the domain of justice. As Mill and Taylor have noticed, the justice values of rights and respect do not automatically develop from the granting of rights in contracts and conventions. People's achievements in the domain of freedom help to enforce rights and to develop respect, through liberal institutions such as individual property rights and the freedom to buy and sell property. Without the institutionalisation of these freedoms, paper rights in the domain of justice remain ineffective. Thus within the domain of justice institutions such as property rights and contractual obligations mediate the freedom values that arise there.

Other liberal institutions appear to be important for the functioning of the domain of care. As Adam Smith recognised the values of care can only flourish on the basis of voluntarity: benevolence is a gift, not an exchange or coercion.[5] The functioning of the domain of care thus implies the availability of an institutional mediation between care and freedom. Care giving thus requires, for its furthering as a human value, that it can operate on the basis of freedom, of voluntarity. Hence, the domain of freedom should provide relevant institutions which nurture such freedom. The symbolic character of such an institution is very important; ideally we would envisage one which challenges the symbolic connection of femininity to caring and suggests ways to connect care symbolically with masculinity as well, or indeed with humanity in general without such gender symbolism, if that were possible.

Institutions of justice as enabling

The economic value domain of justice provides a rule-based institutional environment. Its values are expressed by institutions such as tax and labour laws, central bank regulations and social policies. Outside the sphere of the state, institutions of justice arise in the form of rights-based organisations such as labour unions. For the functioning of the domain of freedom, rule-based institutions appear indispensable. The market can only serve freedom, and contribute to freedom for everyone (pursuing Bentham's 'greatest happiness for the greatest number'), when it functions on the basis of rights, which may be expressed through the institutionalisation of entitlements such as the minimum wage as Smith, Mill and Taylor have argued, or entitlements to food as Sen has argued in the case of developing countries. Without these entitlements, free exchange is meaningless for those who have nothing to exchange – no capital, no productive labour, nor any other assets – or who can sell only at a price below subsistence level. Moreover, an effective arrangement of entitlements would enable them to develop activities in the domain of freedom and to provide for themselves through exchange processes in the marketplace. Thus entitlements provide an institutional mediation between justice values and freedom values in the domain of freedom.

Other rule-based institutions rooted in the domain of justice may help to further values of care. An important element of justice is equality, as I argued in chapter two. Equality has a symbolic connotation that permeates many discussions on distribution. Institutions that encourage equality in the distribution of care giving would spread the burden of the gift of goods and services, as suggested by Perkins Gilman, thereby increasing the total of marginal contributions rather than retaining a very unequal distribution of care giving. Implicit distributive rules thus mediate between values of justice and values of care in care giving.

Institutions of care as enabling

The economic value domain of care provides an institutional environment thriving on the quantity and quality of inter-personal relationships. The institutions are generally informal and intangible, although they may be supported by formal and material institutions, such as laws on paid parental leave and care-leave clauses in labour contracts. The institutions of care are crucial for the functioning of the domain of freedom, since they provide the trust and social skills necessary to persuade parties in the market to engage in a mutual beneficial exchange. Other institutions of care are embodied in the parental practices of educating the next generation of workers. These institutional practices provide the future labour market with a well educated, socialised and encultured labour force, possessing the capabilities of trustworthiness, zeal and loyalty, as was recognised by Smith, Mill and Taylor, Perkins Gilman and Reid. Moreover, Hayek and Friedman and Friedman acknowledged the importance of responsibility in interactions in the domain of freedom. When free economic actors do not act responsibly toward each other, they unnecessarily limit each other's liberties. Thus the furthering of liberal values requires an institutional mediation between freedom and care as expressed in free actors' responsibility.

To the domain of justice, care delivers the crucial inter-personal values that support any system of justice. Without an underlying sense of loyalty, acceptance of responsibility and the shared idea of inter-dependence, it is very difficult to express a common voice, to build solidarity, or to agree on shared rules in the economic process, as Smith, Marx and Hirschman recognised. It becomes ever more difficult and costly to enforce and monitor these rules without the institutionalisation of economic actors' loyalty and responsibility.

The institutional mediation between values in each domain enables actors to hold on to their multiple commitments by following the routines that these institutions provide. As such, institutions generate a set of feedbacks between value domains, connecting the domains in an endless circular flow. The enabling institutions that resolve value conflicts in each domain are potentially self-reinforcing. But this process runs the risk of exploding: a system with only positive feedbacks and no negative feedbacks to balance the system is impossible in a world of scarcity. There is no escape from the scarcity of resources: the economy is not located in the Pantheon. Self-reinforced growth bears the risk of excess. The economy can become 'overheated'. There is therefore also a need for negative feedbacks, which are indeed provided in the economic system, through constraining mediation.

The constraining function of institutions

When activities in each value domain expand, the domain may function to excess. For example, in the domain of justice rules become too detailed and too all-encompassing; thereby, they might no longer respond to people's feelings of justice but instead frustrate those feelings. In the domain of care, excess may lead to paternalism or maternalism (or, at the household level, a 'benevolent dictator' as the supposedly careful household head is called by Naila Kabeer 1994). This pa/maternalism undermines responsiveness in the process of caring, which may result in bad care. Excessive care giving has negative feedbacks. By an extreme appeal to sharing, it discourages entrepreneurship in the domain of freedom and constrains the domain of justice since care does not accept rule-defined needs. In the domain of freedom, excess may result in high risk undertakings and strong market volatility, leading to so much instability that people's sense of freedom and autonomy is severely undermined. This risk is visible for example in financial markets. Too much freedom has negative externalities to the domain of care, undermining risk-spreading strategies in the care economy. Excess in the domain of freedom also has a negative impact on the domain of justice since it often leads to increased inequalities.

The excess functioning of a domain, whether it is the domain of freedom, justice, or care, occurs in the other domains as a constraint.

Institutions of freedom as constraining

The domain of freedom provides a set of constraints to the domains of justice and care. Liberal constraints on the domain of justice can be found for example in anti-trust laws constraining industry's solidarity among companies. Another institutional constraint on justice, rooted in the domain of freedom, is the freedom of labour to move to its most advantageous location, as was expressed so forcefully in Emma Lazarus' poem on liberty quoted by Friedman and Friedman. Liberal institutions constraining the domain of justice can also be found in the extent of the informal sector in many developing countries where local small-scale forms of trade challenge government influence and regulation of local economic activity. The liberal institutions constraining the influence of the domain of justice prevent an excess of regulation and subsequent domination by distributive rules. Over-regulation not only induces inefficiency but may also fail to further values of equality and fairness since too many categories of equality may be created and too many rules may be established as exceptions to previous ones .

Liberal constraints on the domain of care can be found in the belief in liberal values such as autonomy and independence. The accompanying institutions of exit options provide a constraint on the care economy. Only with the availability of exit options – which must be meaningful ones – are care givers able to prevent exploitation. The exit options function as counter-forces against the 'sacrifice trap' inherent in the caring values of inter-dependence and responsibility, as Mill and Taylor, Perkins Gilman and Boulding have recognised.

Institutions of justice as constraining

Too many rules in the economy do not only undermine values of justice, such as fairness and equality. A multitude of rules generally involves sub-sets of rules which are exceptions to more general rules making some people more equal than others. Over-regulation also constrains values of freedom and values of care. The institutionalisation of too many rules often tends to constrain free exchange and people's sense of autonomy. Actors feel limited by rules and experience them as constraints.

An accumulation of rules may constrain the domain of care. Where more and more social relationships are regulated, people have fewer and fewer incentives to care about one another, since the rules are supposed to do away with such needs. An expanding domain of rule setting and an accompanying expansion of the state may reduce rather than enhance people's mutual care. The domain of justice puts a constraint on freedom through institutions such as the minimum wage, social welfare benefits, maximum price guidelines, and taxes and subsidies. In all these forms, justice puts a necessary constraint on liberty, as formulated by Mill and Taylor and by Marx (though he did not trust the force of these constraints). Reid formulated such constraints as 'guiding principles' for what she called 'a good market'. In the domain of justice, insti-tutional mediation that constrains the domain of care takes the form of the distributive principle that discourages specialisation in the latter domain. Examples of this include welfare reform regulations which require single mothers to seek paid work, or tax reforms which abolish breadwinner facilities and thus remove the fiscal premium on the traditional gender role distribu-tion. An excess of care giving by a particular group is thus prevented by the constraints evolving from institutions that enforce some rule of equality.

Institutions of care as constraining

The domain of care constrains the domain of freedom in agricultural produc-tion and consumer organisations by institutional mediation through co-oper-atives, as Reid has suggested. Another institution rooted in the domain of care and limiting the extent of the domain of freedom is loyalty, which inhibits economic actors from immediately using their exit option in the market. Marketing strategies are very aware of the power of loyalty and make clever use of this human value. Furthermore, the domain of freedom is constrained by caring values such as sharing and risk-aversion, which may lead producers to assign part of what they produce to their household's consumption rather than to the market. This still happens in agriculture in many countries, particularly when agricultural prices are highly volatile.[6]

Caring institutions can also constrain activity in the domain of justice. Personal networks can become very influential, particularly when they consist of a small number of economically influential people or when they manage to mobilise large numbers of people, as the environmental movement does in some countries (think for example of the influence of Greenpeace on the policy of Shell). Such intrinsically motivated networks that are committed to specific social or environmental goals are sometimes able to frustrate state regulation and to change institutions so that they support their ideals, whether these be laudable or not.

Thus, when institutions operate near the level of excess of each value domain, they constrain its expansion and so prevent it from going into excess. At the same time they will constrain other domains, through negative feedback between value domains. This constraining institutional mediation provides so called 'blocked exchanges' (Michael Walzer 1983). Though Walzer's categories are different from mine, the idea of preventing domination of one domain by another is similar. In my analysis of three inter-dependent economic value domains, however, the constraining role of institutions results in a circular flow of negative feedbacks, which mutually constrains all three domains. When this is combined with the circle of positive feedbacks by the enabling role of institutions *within* each domain, the institutional arrangements of an economic process help the economy and its actors to mediate incommensurable values, keeping the domains in an Aristotelian sense between deficiency and excess. In other words the institutions help to mediate the checks and balances that keep the economy in balance (cf. Marc Tool 1979).

This exposition, though illustrated with examples, is very abstract. Therefore, I have sought a case study to illustrate the process of institutional mediation of values.

A case study of balancing

It was difficult to find a suitable case study that would show the role of institutional mediation for all three domains. The case study should not only provide information on activity in all three domains but also on the mediation of these domains. An important starting point can be found in a few historical overviews of the role of caring labour in the US and Europe by Nancy Folbre (1994) and in the UK by Jean Gardiner (1997), but these provide too little quantitative or quantifiable data for the construction of a model. Phillip Anthony O'Hara (1995) builds his argument for the inter-relatedness of different value domains on some quantitative data, although in a very general sense. Comparing higher and lower growth figures in the US over the past decades he suggests a causal relationship between activi-ties in the care economy and the performance of the market. Iulie Aslaksen, Olav Bjerkholt, Charlotte Koren and Stig-Olof Olsson (1997) also focus on the relationship between activity in the care economy and in the market, to which they add the state sector for public goods supply. They demonstrate the reallocation gains from shifting production in the care economy to the market and to state provisioning, relying on GDP data, labour force partici-pation rates and labour productivity data from Norway. Iulie Aslaksen, Charlotte Koren and Marianne Stokstad (1998) have suggested, however, that there are limits to the trade-off of labour between the care economy on the one hand and the market and the state on the other, because of people's preferences for being active in all three domains and the built-in need in the economic process to enable them to do so with as much flexibility as possible. Phillip O'Hara has formulated these relationships as follows.

> Stable institutional arrangements are essential for long-term develop-ment and growth. One aspect of this necessary stability is household relations within the family, which has the potential to promote human communication, nutrition, emotional development, preparation for work, population growth, consumption, a latent reserve army of labour, total labour time, and work transfer in supermarkets.
>
> (O'Hara 1995: 89)

His argument is that during the 1950s and 1960s these activities in the care economy generated positive feedbacks to GDP growth, while in the 1970s, 1980s and 1990s, changes within families and households gener-ated mixed or even negative effects on the macro economy. In particular, women's double working day of paid and unpaid activities is found to be disturbing for the stability of economic development.[7] Marital instability, conflict and stress emerging in the family from the 1970s onward are suggested as responsible for macroeconomic instability after the 1960s. Moreover, O'Hara points out that the relationship between the market and the household involves endogenous change.

> In a circular and cumulative fashion it is argued that the post-war boom endogenously set in motion forces that led to family instability; that this helped (along with other factors) to propel long-term macro-economic uncertainty and disarray; and that these macroeconomic problems reciprocally affected family stability in a negative fashion.
>
> (O'Hara 1995: 107)

The accompanying changes in institutional structures have further frag-mented the strength of social relationships according to O'Hara. He has formulated his suggestions in the form of hypotheses, which have not been tested in a model, or substantiated with a sufficiently large data set to operate a model. For a better understanding of the role of institutions in the macro economy and its distinctive domains, I have searched the literature for a suitable case study that would provide relevant data on all three domains in more or less comparable units of measurement. I found such a case study in the work of anthropologist Caroline Moser.

As space is limited, Moser's study will be summarised very briefly, leaving out interesting background information and insights. Moser (1989) has stud-ied the combined impact of recession and adjustment policies on low-income women and their households in a poor community in the city of Guayaquil, Ecuador. I found this case study particularly suitable because it has, first, a clear-cut categorisation of the three types of economic roles and accompany-ing sets of institutions (although Moser's labels differ from mine) and, second, rich anthropological descriptions of role combination and its failure.

Moser describes how, in the years before the structural adjustment of the Ecuadorian economy, life expectancy had increased significantly, infant mortality rates had decreased dramatically, and primary school enrolment was almost 100 per cent. GDP growth followed an increase in oil export revenues. Financing of the expansion of public expenditures in the 1970s became heavily dependent on oil revenues and external borrowing. The years 1982–8 saw a severe recession, with decreasing oil revenues, increasing interest rates on foreign debts, difficulties in obtaining new credit, and intense international competition affecting Ecuadorian industry when protection was diminished. In 1982 a stabilisation policy was introduced. This was followed over subsequent years by economic reforms including devaluation of the currency, control of imports, decrease in public sector expenditures, liberalisation of prices, reductions in food, energy and fuel subsidies, and the liberalisation of imports and exports (this last measure resulted in one success story that emerged in 1986: shrimp production and export). In 1986, interest rates were made flexible, and foreign exchange control was abolished, as required by the International Monetary Fund (IMF). Public sector spending, however, still increased due to the demands of powerful interest groups, though not on behalf of the poor. On top of this, in 1988 agricultural and textile production stagnated because of falling domestic purchasing power.

Guayaquil is an important city and port in Ecuador, attracting rural migrants and with a population of about two million in 1988. The neighbourhood exam-ined in the case study is called Indio Guayas. Earlier research in 1978 had shown that most households were headed by men, on the basis of free unions between men and women, and the average household size was 5.8 people. Most labour was unskilled and low paid. Jobs for men included mechanics, construction, tailoring and factory work. Jobs for women included work as domestic servants, washerwomen, cooks, sales assistants and dressmakers. The community was poor but upwardly aspiring, struggling to improve living conditions, especially for the children. After recession and adjustment measures, the following changes were observed in women's economic roles.

Roles in the domain of freedom

Unemployment increased rapidly and wages decreased. The demand for male labour fell sharply, although the emerging shrimp industry attracted migrant workers who spent only one weekend in three at home. Hence, more women had to seek paid work, increasing female labour market participation rates from 40 per cent in 1978 to 52 per cent in 1988. Many women became the only reliable earners. However, wages had fallen to a third of their 1978 value in female occupations. Because of the decline in wages and the rise in prices of basic commodities such as food, women worked longer hours than before, often sixty hours per week, and combined two or even three jobs in domestic service. The women started to work earlier, when their children were younger than before, sometimes leaving them unattended. The number of female-headed households increased from 12 to 19 per cent, a change related to the out-migration of men and to a decrease in male responsibility for household support when taking up a new household in the rural areas.

Roles in the domain of justice

Cutbacks in infrastructural spending by the government has made room for NGO supply of services, which, however, demands much time from women in negotiating for these non-state provided public services and in actually controlling the service systems. Daughters offer support in the organisation of these new public services by, for example, attending Saturday and Sunday meetings. User fees were introduced in health care but the quality of the services declined. A pre-school programme by UNICEF commanded parents' help in construction of a building and in participating in the programme. The primary school lacked adequate equipment and suffered from low-quality teaching. Both boys and girls were sent to school for as long as possible to gain a qualification, which became more and more essential in the overcrowded labour market.

Roles in the domain of care

Longer hours for women in paid work, with no significant redistribution of unpaid work toward men, resulted in less time available for caring tasks. Some women got up at 4 or 5 a.m. in order to cook a meal for the children, who remained alone the rest of the day. At the same time, household tasks demanded more time than before the crisis. Savings on electricity for refrigerators made it necessary to go out shopping more often and to spend more time on finding the cheapest available food, increasing consumer transaction costs. Cutting down on convenience foods that had short cooking times forced the women to spend more time preparing traditional food. Half of the women suffered from an increase in male violence, often related to their demands for cash for household necessities. Daughters lent substantial support with the more demanding household tasks, so their school attendance and homework suffered, with implications for their future careers. Sons often exhibited the opposite behaviour, hanging around in the streets, dropping out of school and getting involved in street gangs and drug use. This tendency was aggravated when the responsibility of the father also disappeared.

The study concludes that 'the real problem is not the length of time women work but the way in which they balance their time between their reproductive, productive and community management roles' (Moser 1989: 159). The study goes on to conclude that about 30 per cent of the women are just 'coping' with the difficulties, 15 per cent are no longer coping but 'burnt out', while 55 per cent of the women are still 'hanging on', trying to balance their three roles and invisibly at risk. Roles in the domains of freedom and justice appeared to become prioritised over women's caring roles since:

> the need to get access to resources has forced women to allocate increasing time to productive and community management activities, at the expense of reproductive activities, which in many cases have become a secondary priority. This has a significant impact on children, on women themselves and increases the likelihood of disintegration in the household.
>
> (Moser 1989: 159)

This case study description points to an important symbolic institution that mediates the roles of women in the three domains. It is the institution of gender role distribution, assigning roles to men and women according to the symbolic meanings these roles have in terms of masculinity and femininity (for a conceptualisation of symbolic notions of gender, see Sandra Harding 1986, 1995). Moser's own analysis mentioned this gendered institution but she did not refer to it in her explanation of the different situations of the three different groups she researched. The symbolism of gender roles in this particular community in Ecuador (it is recognisable in other places as well) assigns only one role to men – income earning – and three roles to women: unpaid caring at home, community work and (secondary) income earning. Particularly in the one-fifth of households headed by women, women had no other option than to combine all three roles, since they stayed behind with the children, whereas the father left on his own, looking

189

for a job elsewhere. But not only 'necessity', as Perkins Gilman explained, but also social norms supported by the symbolic meanings attached to femininity impelled women to take up all three roles. The idea of the 'good mother' influences their activity, as Martha, Thera and Lucila explained in the focus group discussion in Costa Rica. At the same time men have a strong ideology of masculinity impelling them to specialise in income earning so as to justify their position as heads of their households. When this role fails because of unemployment, as Moser shows, men feel they have no other option than to leave the household in search for work elsewhere and eventually start a new household there. Alternatively, they may remain frustrated at home. In neither case do they take up the other two roles carried out by their wives because these are labelled as feminine. For men also, the symbolic meanings attached to gender roles influence their activity.

In her rich anthropological analysis Moser focused on the women's strategies to provide their households with a minimum livelihood. She attributed the problems involved in these strategies solely to the economic crises and the structural adjustment programme. From an institutional point of view however, recognising endogenous effects, the importance of interaction and path dependency, there is more to be said.

Experimental modelling of institutions

In institutional economics, it is argued that 'institutional adjustment – not the price system – is the "balancing wheel" of the social provisioning (i.e., economic) process' (Charles Whalen and Linda Whalen 1994: 29). Aristotle made a parallel observation on the mean between deficiency and excess in virtuous behaviour: 'The mean is hard to attain, and is grasped by perception, not reasoning' (*NE*: II.9). The rest of this chapter will analyse to what extent it might be possible to model the balancing wheel so that it reflects the Aristotelian mean in the economic process. The modelling effort presented here is only an illustration and does not involve any additional argument or explanation: it serves as a metaphor, that is, to support the understanding of endogenous balancing and institutional mediation that was provided in chapter six. The case study of role combination in Ecuador by poor women after economic crisis and adjustment policies will be used to suggest a way of modelling with endogenous feedbacks that illustrates the balancing between three value domains (see also Boulding 1981, 1985). Such a model should bring out the role of the externalities as feedbacks between the domains and it should explain the mediating role of institutions that help to resolve value conflicts within each domain.[8]

Formalisation of institutions is impossible in conventional, linear economic models that depict mechanical relationships between variables. The main reason why such models do not apply is that institutions operate endogenously, at the level of interaction, as was explained earlier, whereas conventional economic models either picture behaviour at the individual level, with exogenously given preferences, or they picture macroeconomic change through an external shock to the economic system, for example from the international sector or from government policy. These micro and macro modelling conventions do not capture the complexity of endogenous feedbacks and institutional mediation in the economic process. From the limitations deriving from mathematical properties in conventional models, it has been argued that any mathematical representation of institutions would therefore be impossible or undesirable (Philip Mirowski 1989). Nevertheless, I would like to explore here whether it is possible to illustrate institutional balancing of the economic process with the help of a mathematical metaphor. I will argue, in line with Michael Radzicki (1990), that there may be an opportunity for additional understanding of the role of institutions in the economic process, using the metaphorical strength of a distinct type of mathematics and modelling.

Radzicki (1990) has suggested that chaos theory, and the non-linear dynamics on which this theory and its models rest, is a promising candidate for the formalisation of the role of institutions in the economic process. He concludes optimistically that: 'it is possible to envision the institutional dynamics models of the future portraying the processes (or results) of instrumental valuation and social conflict, not with noise, but with structures that produce chaos' Radzicki (1990: 95). I will be a little more cautious though, since there are necessary limitations to the metaphorical use of mathematics in social analyses – including the analysis of economic behaviour – as Mirowski has argued so convincingly. A model is a strong metaphor, which runs the risk of enforcing its methodological constraints on understanding rather than facilitating it (Arjo Klamer and Thomas Leonard 1994). My intention in introducing a model as a metaphor to help understand the role of institutions is to complement the understanding of institutions as mediating values at strategic locations, or the imaginative understanding of institutions as a balancing wheel, with a model-type of understanding of the possible nature of the contextual balancing process. I do not, however, wish to let mathematical properties become a strait-jacket for the analysis. The task of metaphors – including a strong metaphor such as a model – is to help understanding, not to mould and control it into elegant but economically barely relevant masterpieces of mathematics (as has sometimes been the case with neoclassical modelling, where Arrow–Debreu-type models assume the working of a Newtonian-like law of motion that always restores equilibrium).

Non-linear models are much less restrictive on the behaviour of the model and leave the emergence of (an unstable) order to the self-organising capacities of the open system (see also Kenneth Boulding 1985; Paul Krugman 1996; Axel Leijonhufvud 1985). Recent developments in neoclassical and post-Keynesian economics also turn to non-linearity, for example in explaining the business cycle and growth.[9] However, the mathematical properties of chaos theory contradict many standard economic assumptions, such as the assumption of market equilibrium and the independence of self-interested, individual behaviour. These assumptions only fit closed systems and become contradictory in open systems, such as those of social behaviour, in which chaos operates.[10] I agree therefore with Mirowski (1990a: 305) that, if chaos models were followed to their logical conclusions, they would render neoclassical economics meaningless: 'What the chaos literature will not do is augment or save neoclassical economic theory' since, contrary to the basic belief in equilibrium inherent in neoclassical economics, non-linear models may have many equilibrium solutions and in the long run no solution at all. Hence, the models cannot predict events, which renders the main objective of many neoclassical models, as discussed in chapter two, unfeasible. This is related to the fact that 'in all non-linear systems . . . the relationship between cause and effect does not appear proportional and determinate but rather vague and, at best, difficult to discern' (Douglas Kiel and Euel Elliott 1996: 2).

On the other hand, this fuzzy property of non-linear dynamics does not imply that the models are 'chaotic' in the common-sense meaning of the word. On the contrary, chaotic systems have an underlying order, which sustains the dynamic process. Such systems exhibit both chaos and order and the two are intricately related, so that chaos becomes a precondition for order and order becomes a precondition for chaos: they presume each other (Ilya Prigogine and Isabelle Stengers 1984). These insights originated in mathematics and physics and are related to (social) systems theory. Chaos theory has evolved from analyses of non-linear dynamic open systems that reveal unstable behaviour between variables. Although chaos shows unstable behaviour between variables, however, it is *not* stochastic. Therefore, the idea of chaos should not be confused with randomness. Random behaviour is unpredictable and independent of the initial position of the model. Randomness is contingent, without any underlying order, whereas chaotic behaviour, though also unpredictable, is dependent on the initial condition of the model; small changes at time t can have large consequences at time t+1. Chaos thus is not randomness: it hides a pattern.

> In classical dynamics the 'quality' of information is disregarded. This, in a sense, is quite logical if you deal with systems with a finite number of degrees of freedom. For example, we may deal with the system sun–earth–moon. The sun speaks to the moon, the moon speaks to the earth; there is no information escaping from these three actors. But LPS [Large Poincaré Systems or unstable dynamical systems] correspond to multiactor systems where the information is transmitted from one degree to another and finally disappears in a sea of highly multiple conditions.
>
> (Ilya Prigogine 1993: 11)

The pattern in 'chaos' is referred to as a 'strange attractor'. An attractor shapes the dynamic behaviour of a non-linear model into a certain order: *the order in chaos*. Attractors are sets of uncountable points that represent a force of attraction that guides a system's behaviour but does not completely determine it. Paths toward the points of attraction are never followed twice, and the attractors are not reduced to a point, but they embody a 'basin of attraction'. That is why they are labelled *strange* attractors: they are neither stable equilibria nor completely random. Rather, they guide a model's behaviour to one or more points of attraction without it ever coming to rest at a point.

Before I discuss more conceptual links between institutions and non-linear models, I will first elaborate on the notion of non-linearity. Following Kiel and Elliott (1996), I list five basic differences between linear and non-linear models.

1   Linear equations are typified by the 'superposition principle', which implies that two solutions of a linear equation can be added to form a new solution. This allows linear equations to break down problems into pieces (think about the *ceteris paribus* assumption in economics and the modelling of partial equilibria). The superposition principle does not hold for non-linear dynamics: a non-linear equation cannot be broken down into components and then reformulated to obtain a solution.

2   A simple non-linear equation can generate chaotic behaviour over time, within defined parameters. Linear models do not necessarily lead to a stable equilibrium (think of multiple equilibria), but they never result in chaos.

3   Linear systems, characterised by stable relationships between variables, generally change only because of external shocks and typically bring the system back to equilibrium. Non-linear systems may periodically behave like linear systems, but during other time periods the relationships between variables may change. Such a transition is called a 'bifurcation'. Three types of dynamic behaviour can be distinguished:

    i   stability: a fixed point equilibrium,
    ii   oscillation: a periodically stable movement of the system between two or more points,
    iii chaos: a divergence of the system toward one or more attractors.

4   Non-linear systems exhibit 'sensitive dependence on initial conditions': the often referred to example of a butterfly in China causing a hurricane in Jamaica. This feature distinguishes chaotic behaviour from random behaviour, where the latter is insensitive to its initial condition. A stochastic term could be used in a non-linear model as well, but only to add some 'noise'. The irregularity does not come from the error term, but from bifurcations in the model.

5   Even without a stochastic element, non-linear systems exhibit uncertainty. The outcome of subsequent bifurcations that result in changing variable interactions can in practice not be predicted. This implies that a wide variety of possible outcomes are inherent in non-linear systems, which makes prediction impossible, in contrast to linear systems.

Institutions in non-linear models

This short introduction to chaos theory and its non-linear models suggests a conceptual link between institutions and strange attractors, visualised by the icons generated in non-linear phase diagrams. But there are more conceptual links between institutionalism and chaos theory. Basically, four parallels can be distinguished.

Parallel 1: reducing complexity and uncertainty

Institutions reflect human values that guide human behaviour (Granovetter 1985; Hodgson 1997, 1998). In chaos theory, strange attractors guide a system's behaviour, but do not completely determine it. An attractor has zero volume, which may be seen as an analogy to the intangibility of the values shaping institutions (see also a suggestion in this direction in Kenyon De Greene 1996). Kenneth Bailey (1994) refers to strange attractors in terms of entropy (H) (the opposite of which could be regarded as knowledge, technology and social norms) that functions in an open system. According to the second law of thermodynamics, entropy increases to its maximum, thereby lowering the level of organisation and complexity until a system becomes predictable and stabilises in equilibrium. Entropy in this sense is similar to the development of an egg (low entropy but much potential) into an adult chicken and through various stages until its death (no potential any more but high entropy). Kenneth Boulding (1966) has illustrated the dynamics of the economic system with the help of entropy from an ecological point of view. He argued that the economy is an open system that needs constant energy inputs to survive, a resource that will sooner or later become exhausted. 'In the energy system there is, unfortunately, no escape from the grim second law of thermodynamics; and if there were no energy inputs into the earth, any evolutionary or developmental process would be impossible' (Boulding 1966: 301).

However, the increase of entropy to its maximum and a stable equilibrium only counts for closed systems, in which there is no import and export of entropy, information/energy (negentropy) and matter. Social systems are open systems. In such systems it seems that human behaviour is able to offset the increase in entropy by importing negentropy into the open system, which makes the system more organised, contrary to the prediction of the second law of thermodynamics. 'If all human action were random, with no replication, then H would be maximum. If all human actions were identical, then H would be the minimum, or zero' (Bailey 1994: 247). Bailey explicitly connects this to institutions, arguing that the level of entropy is somewhere in between maximum and minimum, since it is human action which guides systems, not return to equilibrium. He refers to customs, laws, five-year plans and short-term goals, as guiding this purposive action, in part intentionally, but in part imperfectly and subject to error (ibid.: 247).

It is this property of chaotic systems in particular that suggests strange attractors as suitable candidates for modelling institutions: they keep the economic system evolving on a path somewhere between static equilibrium and randomness, by balancing the economy with the lower and upper thresholds of each of the three economic value domains. This idea is similar to the balancing in my Aristotelian analysis: the delicate process of finding the virtuous mean between excess (maximum entropy) and deficiency (low entropy).

Parallel 2: path dependence

In institutional economics, change in economic processes is embedded in a historical and cultural context; history matters. In chaos theory, systems exhibit sensitive dependence on initial conditions. This path dependence makes change unique and not reproducible; to remind the reader, this has to be distinguished from randomness, which is not dependent on initial conditions. Sensitive dependence on initial conditions occurs because the distance between two neighbouring trajectories of a variable through time with only slightly different initial positions increases exponentially when we use a quadratic model. The difference – of one butterfly in China inducing a hurricane in Jamaica and another butterfly not even causing a bit of wind – occurs because each trajectory develops dynamic behaviour that is orientated by its past behaviour. Each stage in the process may move the evolution of one trajectory further away from the development occurring in the other.

Parallel 3: endogenous change

In institutionalism, dynamics emanate not only from external shocks, but also from inside the system. The movement of business cycles may be reflected in changes of attractors from fixed equilibria (recessions) to chaotic behaviour (booms) by an increasing level of information and knowledge. The new cognitive field that emerges from these increases may function as an informal institution, guiding learning and the further growth of knowledge (De Greene 1996). In chaos theory, dynamics are endogenous and are reflected in changes in the attractors. They can move from a stable point to periodic oscillation or to chaos – and back again. Changing relationships between the model's variables cause endogenous change: parameter values change from one stage to another. Such shifts in the parameters may be substantial and result in bifurcations of the model from stable equilibrium to oscillations or chaos.

Parallel 4: meso level of interaction

In institutionalism, the level of analysis is social. The aggregation of partial analyses is impossible, since parts are not independent of the whole. In chaos theory, the level of analysis is an open system. The focus is not on a dependent variable, but on phase space and, with higher dimensions of a system, the analysis is of a 'manifold'.[11] The degrees of freedom determine the dimensions. Equations cannot be broken down since the superposition principle does not hold. It is impossible to break down the level of analysis from the system as a whole to individual relationships within the system, keeping other variables constant.

The four parallels between institutions and non-linearity as introduced here suggest a close analogy between the two. Together, the four conceptual parallels provide some basic ingredients for non-linear modelling of institutions. Below, a possible, experimental model will be suggested illustrated with help of the case study of household behaviour at a time of economic crisis in Ecuador.

An illustration of non-linear modelling of institutions

The case study that was introduced earlier in this chapter is particularly interesting for non-linear modelling since it suggests that 'chaos' occurs for one of the groups of women studied. The models will indicate however, that the type of chaos that takes place is very different from the one suggested by the author of the case study, Moser (1989).

I will use a simulation model and not a 'real' model because there is not enough quantitative data available for the generation of a full model. That is, I will set the variables for period t = 0 at levels that illustrate best the differences between the three groups that Moser researched, to see what happens in the model in the transition from one group to another.

The three groups that Moser distinguished were:

- 55 per cent of women 'hanging on',
- 30 per cent of women 'coping' with the difficulties,
- 15 per cent of women who are 'burnt out'.

I will use a one-dimensional quadratic map:

$$f(X_t) = \alpha X_t(1 - X_t) \tag{1}$$

where X = economic activity by women in their three roles, α = women's capacity to balance their three roles, and t = months: 120 periods from January 1978 until December 1988.

Low α implies easy combination and high α difficult combination. This parameter changes over the time period in the model: endogenous change. Note that this is very different from how a budget or time constraint functions in conventional models: these remain fixed and only change through external shocks. In this non-linear model however, the parameter values change over the course of the dynamics, inducing endogenous change.

Parameter α represents the capability of women to balance their three roles.[12] These parameters thus reflect the thresholds and the positive and negative feedbacks occurring at these thresholds for each role in their respective value domains. It is in this parameter that the non-linear model captures the role of institutions, linking the value domains.

Below, the model will be discussed through the parameter value of α in various stages. The division into three groups, each representing a particular stage in the dynamics, is derived from Moser.

$2 < \alpha \leq 3$:   Oscillations between the three attractors but moving toward a new, lower level equilibrium, illustrating the 55 per cent group.

$3 < \alpha < 4$:   Continuing oscillations between the three attractors, illustrating the 30 per cent group.

$\alpha \geq 4$:   Transition to chaos, illustrating the 15 per cent group. For this group, pressure on women's balancing capability has become overwhelming. Women in this group are no longer able to combine their roles adequately. They fail to provide a reliable standard of living for their families.

The attractor could be thought of as representing some balance between women's three roles, although no stability. The balance in this case study is very unstable. The effects of the macro-economic recession and reform policies undermine the attracting forces of the model. Thus provisioning is insecure – the system is highly unstable – leading 15 per cent of the women in Indio Guayas to destitution, resulting in disintegrating households, absolute poverty and negative effects on children. The model suggests an unstable but nevertheless *patterned* movement of the model between the institutions representing women's roles in the value domains of freedom, justice and care.

In Moser's case study, women in the third group were no longer able to balance their roles. They were labelled as 'casualties and burnt out' (Moser 1989: 160). Moser characterised them as victimised and as abandoning their role commitments. But the pattern of the attractors in the simulation model suggests something else. Although the behaviour of this group may look 'chaotic' – the term used in daily language – the pattern suggests that this group of women still adheres to their roles. The women still feel responsible for earning money, contributing to public services in the community, and childcare and care for others. But they cannot cope anymore with the unfavourable economic circumstances, the lack of co-operation from their husbands, and the subsequent tensions created by other members of the family.

The simulation model therefore provides some additional insights into the mediating role of institutions in the economic process. First, a seemingly 'chaotic' process, as for example occurs in an economy undergoing crisis, appears not to be a random one. Non-linear modelling suggests that it is inadequate to characterise the disequilibrium situation of economic crisis and periods of severe adjustment as 'chaotic' in the ordinary sense of the word, as used by Moser and others (see for example Gerald Dwyer 1992). The patterned dynamics of the non-linear simulation models of Moser's case study points out that the gendered commitment to the three economic roles still operates among the women responsible for providing livelihood for their households. The women in Moser's study *do adhere* to their roles and *do try* to live up to their commitments, but they fail to do this well enough. Contrary to Moser's assessment of this group of women as 'casualties' and 'victims', non-linear simulation modelling of their economic activity suggests that their behaviour still follows the institutional guidance for their roles in the market, public services supply and caring labour; they still try to live up to their commitments but the constraints on their time and the complexities of role combination allow little chance of success. Institutions thus continue to play a mediating role in the economy, even when the economy undergoes a period of severe instability.

However, the extent to which institutions are able to mediate economic actors' behaviour depends on the strength of the endogenous effect implied in the institutional feedback (William Brock and Steven Durlauf 1997; Durlauf 1996). In Moser's example, it seems that role commitment is stronger for women than for men, who seem to lose their commitment to their single role in income earning once they find themselves unemployed: they abandon the household and their responsibilities altogether. On the other hand, her data suggest that men's adherence to the prevalent gender role ideology is so strong that they do not take up roles in public service supply and caring labour – 'feminine' roles – when unemployed. This is so even when that would increase the household's level of well-being as the wife would be enabled to devote more time to the paid jobs that are still available for women. These contradictory value interpretations underlying the economic roles of women and men need further empirical analysis.

The simulation provides a further insight in the way it models the thresholds and institutional feedbacks occurring at these thresholds. Moser's description of the three groups of women does not say anything about the boundaries between the groups. As a consequence, she does not analyse the transition between 'coping', 'hanging on' and 'failure' in combining the three roles for each group of women. The simulation models suggest that the transition between these stages is not gradual but rather occurs when thresholds are crossed. These sudden changes in the system are labelled as bifurcations and are reflected in changes in the model's parameters. The bifurcations in turn determine the external effects between roles: positive feedbacks and negative feedbacks (Brock and Durlauf 1997). This characteristic of non-linear modelling suggests that institutions do not gradually exert their influence on economic behaviour but rather rely on a critical mass in the expression of its underlying values before they will have external effects on other value domains. The feedbacks that occur are thus endogenous to the process. This endogeneity did not emerge in Moser's analysis. Moser attributed the negative effects on well-being that she perceived directly to the external factors of crisis and adjustment, thereby ignoring interaction effects in economic actors' roles.

Moreover, it seems that it is women's commitment to their roles and the conscious shifts between and within these roles that help to accommodate the effects of the economic crisis and adjustment policies. This strong adherence to role combination rather than specialisation ensures the occurring of the externalities between the roles. The effects appear to be positive in the sense that the combination of roles helps the continuation of the household and its livelihood. I have labelled this effect as a positive externality or enabling institution, whereas Durlauf (1996) uses the notion of a 'social multiplier' to explain the accommodating effect of the institutions in times of economic hardship. In a linear model it would be impossible to capture these insights from Moser's study, since any mediation between an external shock and individual behaviour is absent from such models. Non-linear models however, provide an insight to the mediating role of institutions, by bringing out the positive feedbacks between economic roles accommodating and dampening the negative effects of macroeconomic instability.

A third insight that the simulation model offers is that it suggests an important role for associational distribution (Durlauf 1996) underlying each economic value domain. In Moser's case study, the crucial distributive element is gender roles: women are active in all three domains, men only in one. Socialisation of girls and boys into the traditional gender patterns ensures continuation of the same distributional association of economic actors over roles, creating path dependence in the distribution of gender roles. In the case study, the gendered distributional association appears very unequal. Durlauf argues that an unequal associational distribution limits the success of the accommodating and dampening effect on economic instability. This is illustrated by Moser's data: the very unequal gender role distribution for caring and public service supply make it more difficult for the women to adapt to difficult circumstances. If roles were distributed more equally between men and women, macroeconomic instability might be accommodated more easily at the household level. Men's adherence to a single gender role prevents them from taking up the other two. Both at the household level and in the aggregate, this unequal role distribution is suboptimal, since with high male unemployment some households would probably have done better with women doing more paid work and men taking up activities in caring and public service supply. Again, specialisation seems neither rational nor efficient.

Fourth, the simulation model suggests that without the mediating role of institutions, which help to accommodate and dampen the effects of economic instability, it will be very difficult and probably take a long time for the economy to regain its balance (for this argument see for example, Paul Krugman 1996). This risk of the economic process transcending its upper thresholds and moving toward chaos is known as the 'edge of chaos', a term which has been applied to ecological and political economic problems. The edge of chaos refers to a delicate balance in a system between local stability and full chaos. When a system crosses the edge, or threshold, it requires a lot of 'over-undoing' by policy measures. This is indeed what Moser's case study suggests, when one looks at the negative long-term effects of the endogenous process, such as the decline of child nutrition, the decrease in girls' human capital formation, and the tendency of boys to gravitate towards criminality and drug abuse. In Moser's study (and other research on the effects of economic crisis and structural adjustment on the poor in the same volume published by UNICEF), policy advice suggests complementing structural adjustment measures with social funds for the poor. My non-linear modelling exercise, focusing on endogenous dynamics, suggests that it might be more effective if attention were given to the gender distribution of roles and to support for women *and* men to carry out these roles of provisioning. Hence, policy might better focus on the institutional feedbacks between the economic roles endogenous to the economic process rather than assume that the exogenous effect of a social fund will protect the poor and help restore equilibrium. Politically, however, it is probably much easier to set up and endow a social fund than to change the symbolic institution of gender role distribution.

In conclusion, the non-linear dynamic simulation model presented in the second part of this chapter does not provide the level of formalisation that linear models provide in neoclassical economics. Nor was it possible to run the model against data, because non-linear models require large data sets that are not available in the type of analyses that I am pursuing and of which Moser's case study is an example. There is no behavioural algorithm to be found in the dynamics of non-linearity, nor is any prediction possible. The value added by the use of simulation models for institutional analysis rests in clarifying the endogenous role that institutions play in mediating economic behaviour toward an Aristotelian mean within and between value domains. After all, what more is a *simulation* model than merely a metaphor?

Conclusion

Whereas the notion of externalities is helpful in explaining the relationships between value domains, the notion of institutions appears useful to show how incommensurabilities are resolved between the values belonging to a domain and those that have been transferred from another domain as external effects. Institutions thus express a simultaneous commitment to different values and provide the routines for behaviour that help economic actors to deal with the ambiguities and conflicts involved. The routines thus help actors to behave rationally in a meaningful way: they help them to uphold different commitments simultaneously; they diminish emotional ambiguities; they guide deliberation; and they operate at the social level, enabling actors in their interaction to share the routines that reduce uncertainty. This happens because institutions have two simultaneous functions: enabling and constraining behaviour through positive and negative external effects between the domains. My interpretation of Moser's case study has illustrated the workings of endogenous institutional mediation in the case of household provisioning. The case study provides various insights into the process of institutional mediation between values that are expressed in the roles that these women perform. A modelling exercise was added to illustrate the endogenous process of balancing. This led to the insights that, even in times of high instability, institutions may still operate, although not effectively; that it may take a long time before institutions adapt to new circumstances; and that institutions may create enabling or constraining circumstances depending on threshold values in each domain, a process which is related to underlying distributive norms within each value domain. However, the simulation model exercise has only illustrative value. The main insight developed in this chapter is that institutions seem to be able to mediate different economic value domains, in an Aristotelian balancing way, finding a mean between a value domain's deficiency and excess.

8

CONCLUSION

Today, in contrast to the days of classical economics, economic theory cherishes its belief in value-neutrality. Present-day economics relegates value to ethics, politics, or psychology – disciplines that are disregarded by many economists as 'normative' – whereas classical economics from Adam Smith and John Stuart Mill until the time of John Maynard Keynes presumed the social and moral embeddedness of economic behaviour. If the preceding argument amounts to anything, values prove to be at the core of any economic analysis.

First and foremost I have asserted that modernist economic methodology is constructed on the basis of dualisms: utility is defined as economic, morality is not; reason is regarded as part of economics, emotion not; choice is seen as economic whereas the attributed opposite, coercion, is not; finally, independent behaviour is included in economic theory, while interdependent relationships between actors are not. Because of this dualistic construction of economic theory it is generally assumed that economics need not pay attention to values: they are assumed to be subjective and exogenously given in actors' preferences. However, I have shown that much economic explanation relies on assumptions and concepts that draw on one important human value: the value of *freedom*. This value shows in the enthusiasm of many economists for free choice, free exchange and the idea of the free individual.

Having thus pointed out that the value of freedom – or liberty – is at the core of modernist economics, I continue to argue that this value can only be sustained with a minimum guarantee of *justice* available in an economy. Before people will agree to enter freely into market exchanges they need to believe that the outcomes of free exchange conform to their standards of justice. Moreover, the voluntary interactions between actors in the economy rely on actors' capabilities to relate to each other. Voluntary interaction will only occur when actors succeed in persuading others to relate to them. In other words: economic actors need to *care*.

What follows from the methodological contradictions inherent in modernist economic methodology is that values *do* matter in the economy.

202

Values are not merely subjective ends that can be defined as preferences in individual and independent objective functions. The three major values that underlie economic behaviour are widely shared – and contested – among the actors in an economy. The values of freedom, justice and care are tightly interwoven in economic behaviour. I have pointed out that they are endogenous in the economic process, influencing economic behaviour and at the same time being influenced by the process of economic interaction.

Each type of value has its own form of interaction in the economy: freedom through exchange, justice through redistribution, and care through giving. Each has its own locational source of interaction where transactions take place: the market, the state and the care economy, although each value can be observed to function in each of these places. The values also have distinct virtues such as prudence, propriety and benevolence; and they have distinct emotions and forms of deliberation that characterise each type of value. Because of the differences between the three values I have defined each of them as operating within a distinct value domain: the domains of freedom, justice and care.

I have indicated that the social and moral embeddedness of economic behaviour that has been recognised by a significant number of economists (not coincidentally a significant proportion of them being women) undermines the dualistic axioms underlying the dominant methodology. This re-discovery of the role of values in the economy necessitates a very different conceptualisation of economic behaviour and processes. I found such a conceptual framework in Aristotle's ethics.

Central to Aristotle's ethics are the virtues. Virtue is understood as a contextual mean between deficiency and excess of a value that is important in itself. The mean cannot be found through moral rules or by following an algorithm such as constrained maximisation. Virtue requires from actors that they possess the necessary ethical capabilities to make their behaviour meaningful. These ethical capabilities are core elements of actors' rationality. I have postulated these ethical capabilities as being commitment, emotion, deliberation and interaction. Without these, actors are unable to pursue their valuable ends. Without commitment actors have no reason to hold on to given and unchanging preferences. Without emotion actors would not sustain their commitments and signal them to others. Without the capability to deliberate actors are unable to make free and meaningful choices, but follow an algorithm instead. Without interaction actors cannot persuade each other to enter into transactions.

Each value domain that I found to be operating in the economy has its own type of valuable ends and requires its own specific ethical capabilities. It is not rational, for example, to beg for mercy in the negotiation of one's labour contract, or to defend one's autonomy when in need of care. Each value domain is characterised by its own type of commitments, its own emotional attachments to these commitments, its own forms of deliberation and interaction, as I illustrated in Figure 2.2. Only when actors apply these ethical capabilities in an appropriate value domain do they behave rationally in a meaningful sense.

An Aristotelian picture of economic behaviour raises the question of how the three value domains are related in the economy, and how economic actors combine their activities in each domain, that is, in their different economic roles. The values of care, justice and freedom are distinct from each other, and cannot be aggregated into one value as is the case in utilitarianism. Human values are incommensurable. Nor is there an instrumental relationship between them that makes one value more important than another. Value commitment is intrinsic, not instrumental. Economic theory has a well-known concept for such non-instrumental relationships: the idea of unintended consequences, or externalities. Hence, whereas within their own domain values are furthered intentionally and for their own sakes, in a different domain they are not developed instrumentally but arise as external effects of their functioning in their own domain. For example, a value like trust is developed and nurtured within the domain of care. In the domain of free exchange, trust is needed to make exchange transactions happen but trust cannot be furthered through exchange: it is not an intended part of exchange transactions. Trust cannot be bought and sold (when people try this we tend to call it a bribe). So within its own domain trust is an end that is furthered for its own sake, whereas outside its own domain it is an important value but cannot be developed there: it needs to be transferred from the domain of care. These external effects that occur between each of the three value domains are very important for an economy to function well. The market for example, cannot function without trust. Likewise, distributive rules will not be followed without actors' responsibility, and care will no longer be given unless care givers have self-esteem and there are regulations that prevent them from being exploited.

This Aristotelian conceptualisation of the role of values is very different from recent attempts to include values as endogenous preferences in utility functions. When subordinated to utility, values lose their ethical meaning as commitments that are deliberated in the search for the virtuous mean. In utility functions values are made into preferences that are commensurable, that can be traded off against one another subject to budgetary constraints and according to their contribution to total utility. In an Aristotelian understanding of the economy, however, I have taken values to be the underlying social and ethical influences that guide rational behaviour and make it meaningful. I have interpreted values as the invisible and immeasurable but crucial capabilities that embody meaningful rational action; and I have conceptualised them as the endogenous linkages between the value domains that keep the domains in balance. In this way, I was able to respect the ethical meaning of values and at the same time to conceptualise their role in economic behaviour. In other words, from an Aristotelian perspective economic behaviour relies on distinct but connected values that are *not* instrumental and *not* commensurable.

This conceptualisation of freedom, justice and care implies that where these values come together they create ambiguities and tensions: they may conflict. I have recognised this ethical conflict that is so common in social life. The conflicts arise particularly in individual actors' combination of different economic roles. Because these roles and their underlying values are widely shared in a particular economy, the conflicts are also shared, which generates shared solutions. Through interviews with actors who excel in role combination I found out that there are indeed such shared resolutions to value conflicts. I also found a parallel notion that seemed suitable for characterising this phenomenon: the notion of institutions. This concept is not applied here, however, in its popular interpretation as instrumental to people's interests or as constraints. Rather, I have come to describe institutions as the formal and informal shared routines that help to mediate different types of values in economic actors' interaction. The conflicts between different values occurring in daily economic practices in each value domain are resolved through routines that actors develop to cope with conflicting value commitments and that they share with others who experience similar value conflicts. Institutions mediate actors' deliberations, diminish the emotional ambiguities, and are widely shared with others as common routines.

As an illustration I applied a non-linear simulation model to a case study of household provisioning. From this exercise the influence of values as feedbacks between the different domains in the economy became visible, as did the mediating role of institutions. The exercise suggests that less rigorous models may contribute to a fuller understanding of economic processes than conventional modelling, although much needs to be done to elaborate the type of model that I have used as an illustration only.

My Aristotelian perspective has shown that economic behaviour and economic processes can be understood as ethically grounded rational behaviour rather than through the detached algorithms of *Rational Economic Man*. As a consequence, I have been able to go beyond the dualities of dominant economic methodology. An understanding of the economy that acknowledges the role of values in economic life is not forced to choose between reason or emotion but sees the connection between the two; it does not restrict itself to utilitarianism or give in to the opposite formulated as normative or principled evaluation, but recognises actor's commitments; it does not need to define choice in an algorithmic way as opposed to coercion, but recognises the deliberative character of choices, involving complexity and uncertainty; finally, the acknowledgement of the role of values in economic life rejects the duality between individual autonomy and determinism: value commitments are neither subjective nor universal structures but emotional and highly contextual, shared and contested and above all subject to individual deliberation and interdependent human interaction.

Before I was able to develop this Aristotelian perspective I had to employ a diversity of research methods to develop my hypotheses. I needed to go into the philosophy of economics to find out about the three value domains and their logical connection. I had to undertake an exploration into the history of economic thought, since it was there that I found most clues to how the different value domains are related in the practices of economic life. For the generation of concrete hypotheses on the why and how of the role of the three value domains, however, there was no theory to guide me. I found no other option than to go and ask economic actors themselves in interviews. I could have chosen other approaches, but any of the possible methods of generating hypotheses on the conceptualisation of the three value domains lies outside economics (elsewhere they are common). It was only when these threads came together that this web of methods could provide me with an initial understanding of what values mean in economic life and how the major economic values of freedom, justice and care may be conceptualised in economic theory.

The different threads of the web that I have woven are not new. Aristotle's ethics has existed for over two millennia, and the other methods are common in other disciplines. The classical economists asserted the three different types of values and Hume and Smith recognised the role of virtues. What is new however, is the weaving of a web from all these different threads to contribute to economic understanding. But it is only a beginning. I have mapped one possible way out of the modernist paradoxes in which neoclassical economics has ended up. Other routes can also be followed. Besides, along the path I suggest, many questions remain unanswered. I hope that the outline of the conceptual framework that I have provided can guide further theoretical enquiry into the role of care and other values in economics. I also hope that these concepts appear helpful for empirical research that may come up with meaningful explanations for the many economic phenomena that have so far remained unclear.

Although my research did not go into the consequences of an Aristotelian economic analysis for policy, I would think that the perspective might be relevant for policy makers as well. Much economic policy design is neither rule-bound nor algorithmic but dependent on social, historical and political context and on decision making processes. It is only in concrete cases and in response to concrete policy questions that an Aristotelian perspective makes sense; I cannot provide any general advice. The proof of the pudding is in the eating; an application to policy making was not part of this study but would certainly be an important follow-up. Having worked in the Ministry of Foreign Affairs of the Netherlands while carrying out this research project, I would like to make some suggestions for reflection, based on my own experience with bilateral development co-operation policy.

First, policy makers could try to find out what type of values they want to further in their policy. In the case of bilateral development co-operation: do we want to further poor people's self-reliance in Africa, do we want to strengthen their rights, or do we want to provide emergency aid? Whatever end we pursue, the scarcity of means urges us to pursue it as efficiently as possible.

Second, the form of the co-operation and transfer of resources is important. Each type of value is connected to a particular form of transfer of resources between a developed and a developing country: if we opt for supporting people's free choices in markets we may want to provide loans (soft and commercial ones); if we choose to support people's rights to education we may want to provide grants to express international redistribution of resources from the North to the South (international 'taxes' through the UN system or through bilateral donors); if we aim to provide care we may want to send gifts (development aid). Again the question of contextual evaluation comes up. For example, if we want to support primary education, should we do this through a loan, assuming that it will be paid back with the increased tax revenues that will result after a generation as a government's return on investment? Or should the transfer of resources be a grant as a redistribution from North to South, for example through increasing endowments from the North to UNICEF, UNESCO and UNDP? Or should the transfer in support of primary education in a developing country be a gift? That is, an unconditional transfer of funds to the budget of a Ministry of Education of a recipient country, or transfers in kind such as books or sending teachers who will work on a voluntary basis?

Third, to make things more complex, there are always more domains involved. To follow on with my example of education, it contributes to all three values, but to each in a different way. It provides more freedom to choose among job opportunities; it furthers justice since in various international conventions equal access to education has been agreed upon as a universal right; it furthers care since education responds to the needs of children to share in the world around them and belong to a larger community than just their own family and neighbourhood. Therefore, transfers of resources in development co-operation involve careful deliberation about what development in all its aspects means to people.

In the case of education there are good reasons to distinguish primary education from secondary and tertiary levels. For development co-operation policy I would advise transferring the means necessary to support primary education in the form of grants and gifts, not loans. It is only from the level of secondary education onwards that human capital returns to the individual and, through tax revenues to the government, becomes economically significant. It is primarily equal access to education that matters for economic development since it provides high marginal benefits to those who did not previously have access to education. Care is also important, in aspects such as the building of an intrinsically motivated community and future workforce. Of course such contextual evaluation of policy should be done within the overall discourse on development policy and in close interaction with all stakeholders, in both developed and developing countries. The underlying deliberations thus take a plurality of dimensions into account in evaluating how to support, for example, primary education in developing countries, one of the evaluative dimensions being efficiency.

The art of Aristotelian policy making lies in finding a delicate balance between relying on the market, improving equality of access and providing adequate care. My focus group interviews demonstrated how important balanced policies are for the support of actors in their daily practices in each of the economic value domains. Elmira pointed out that in South Africa there is an urgent need for a straightforward implementation of recent ANC government policies to counter the many injustices against blacks, and particularly black women, in the past. She emphasised equal access to education, health and pension systems. The Dutch group participants indicated that emancipation policy has rightly supported women's position in the labour market but neglected to promote men's responsibility in childcare: women increasingly have a double day whereas men continue their full-time jobs as before with very little time spent on childcare. In Yemen the group participants explained to me how important the freedoms are that are granted to women under Islamic law, but how little women are aware of and make use of them: they call for a more proactive policy to ensure all Yemeni women these rights. Finally, in the focus group in Costa Rica it appeared that the participants expected much from changes in family law, labour laws and social welfare policies. In fact, as Lili told me, without support from government policy it is impossible to live up to the ideal images of their roles as Mother Theresas, as Joans of Arc, or (borrowing Milton and Rose Friedman's metaphor) as Ladies of Liberty.

It is not that the images of Lady Liberty, Joan of Arc and Mother Theresa are too idealistic – they are the symbolic expressions of these women's economic roles – nor is it merely that these women's budget and time constraints need to be relaxed in due course through economic growth. The point is that they need a policy environment that understands and supports their efforts to fulfil their roles as well as they can, contributing to the values of freedom, justice and care for themselves and for their families as they perceive these and share these with others in their community. An Aristotelian perspective to economics is a promising way to make sense of these roles. It allows economists to care.

NOTES

1 THE MISSING ETHICAL CAPABILITIES OF RATIONAL ECONOMIC MAN

1 The case studies and neuro-biological analyses are taken from Antonio Damasio (1994).
2 The place of emotional experience and socialisation into moral rules is located in the thalamus in the forebrain, which is connected to the amygdala in the dorsal brain, which is responsible for evaluation (Damasio 1994).
3 Consistent with standard economic texts, *Rational Economic Man* will be referred to here as a 'he' since in the rhetoric of economics, he has always been constructed as masculine (Ferber and Nelson 1993; Folbre 1994; Lloyd 1984; Mansbridge 1990). Folbre (1994) therefore uses the expression of 'Mr REM'.
4 It is important to note here that metaphysics should not be understood in its unfortunate common interpretation of supernatural, or beyond knowing. Rather, metaphysics in the philosophical meaning of the word, as ontology, the philosophy of being, should be understood as the theory that recognises the existence of things before our knowledge of them. In the Aristotelian interpretation of metaphysics, a distinction is made between the things, the substances, that exist before we know them, and their attributes, which may vary from situation to situation.
5 For a recent misinterpretation of Aristotle by an economist, but now not as a utilitarian but as an ill-defined communitarian, see Alan Peacock (1999).
6 An implication of Groenhout's assessment is that neoclassical economics, based as it is on utilitarianism, has no content, since it has no account of economic actors' ends; these are deemed to be purely subjective.
7 For a Catholic priest, sexuality may not necessarily be part of a good human life. A Catholic priest may rather derive self-realisation, or relatedness to God, or pride from celibacy. In other words, the ends that human beings have, like self-realisation or relatedness to others, are not necessarily fulfilled for every one in the same way, as Nussbaum assumes in her list.
8 Except when one assumes auxiliary preferences for fighting but then it is not clear why the man would prefer to risk his life on the street rather than trying to excel in boxing matches.
9 For this argument, among many others, see Val Plumwood's (1993) discussion on Cartesian dualism and Paul Ricoeur's (1992) *Oneself as an Other*.
10 Martha Nussbaum remarks about this point: 'We do not know how we would talk about an agent who kept improvising himself from moment to moment and was never willing to identify himself with any general commitments' (Nussbaum 1986: 48).
11 In psychology and neurobiology, cognitive processes are not only understood

as thoughts, memory, reasoning and knowledge, but also as the cognition of emotions and evaluative processes informed by both reasoning and emotions.

12 The intuition behind this result can be found in economists from Smith to Boulding. Boulding for example, suggests that unilateral disarmament would help to reduce the arms race, instead of the accepted retaliation strategy of both sides during the Cold War. Adam Smith argued in his *Theory of Moral Sentiments* (1759 Part II, II.iii: 86) that society 'cannot subsist among those who are at all times ready to hurt and injure one another. The moment that injury begins, the moment that mutual resentment and animosity take place, all the bands are broken asunder'.

13 Thorstein Veblen (1919: 73) therefore, called *Rational Economic Man* a 'lightning calculator'.

14 There are rather precise grounds in experience and in history for the reasonable man to expect that certain virtues, which he admires and values, can only be attained at the cost of others, and that the virtues typical of several different ways of life cannot be freely combined, as he might wish. Therefore a reasonable and reflective person will review the separate moral injunctions, which intuitively present themselves as having force and authority, as making a skeleton of an attainable, respectworthy and preferred way of life. He will reject those that seem likely in practice to conflict with others that seem more closely part of, or conditions of, the way of life that he values and admires, or that seem irrelevant to this way of life.

(Stuart Hampshire 1983: 91)

15 Standard micro-economic theory assumes that *Rational Economic Man* maximises his utility function. For this to be technically feasible in economic analysis, the following requirements are needed:

- utility functions are subjective: utility cannot be compared between persons,
- utility functions are independent: the utility of person A is not influenced by the utility of person B,
- utility functions are complete: they contain all possible preferences,
- utility functions are transitive: if X is preferred to Y and Y to Z, then X is preferred to Z,
- utility functions are continuous: at the margin all different combinations of goods can be attained and traded-off against one another.

16 In fact, the technical restrictions on utility functions are merely consequences of the particular mathematical formulation chosen to model rationality in neoclassical economics, not implications of the concept of rationality (Peeters 1987: 445).

2 PARADOXES OF VALUE

1 Following Isaiah Berlin and major economists such as John Stuart Mill and Milton Friedman, the terms 'liberty' and 'freedom' will be used synonymously here.

2 Economic theory was developed mainly but not exclusively by white men living in nineteenth- and twentieth-century western societies, cherishing the ideal of liberty which was dominant over that period in those societies (expressed in the US for example by the Statue of Liberty).

3 John Stuart Mill has argued that such an interpretation of freedom is too limited: even negative freedom may be augmented with some state support, so as to enable people to pursue their own ends: 'When a government provides

means for fulfilling a certain end, leaving individuals free to avail themselves of different means if in their opinion preferable, there is no infringement of liberty, no irksome or degrading restraint' (Mill 1848: 944).

4 Here, Hayek attributes the capacity for taking responsibility for other people's welfare more to women than to men: 'It is part of the ordinary nature of men (and perhaps still more of women) and one of the main conditions of their happiness that they make the welfare of other people their chief aim' (Hayek 1960: 78). His quote also indicates that where Hayek uses the word 'men', he indeed only refers to the male half of the population, contrary to the popular belief among many scholars that the use of the word 'men' implies men and women.

5 Of course, neoclassical theory allows other-regarding preferences in the objective function. But the theory does not acknowledge other-regarding values for other than utilitarian reasons, i.e. as values for their own sake, irrespective of personal utilitarian gain, as implied by Hayek.

6 In most economic theories where justice plays a role, the principles of justice are instrumental for liberty. Justice is not valued for its own sake but regarded as a means to attain either higher liberty or the enjoyment of liberty for a larger group of people. See for example the entitlement theory of Amartya Sen (1987, 1992) in which entitlements help to secure positive freedom for a larger group of people. Even Marxism is actually more concerned with liberty than with justice *per se*. 'Marx's theory of exploitation denies that propertyless workers are actually free when they rent out their labour force for a wage. This is certainly a fair use of the term "freedom" when the wage is at subsistence level and the workers' alternative is starvation' (Serge-Christophe Kolm 1996: 351).

7 The same assumption as for neoclassical economic rationality excluding participation in the negotiation of the social contract by children, weak or aged people, sick persons and the mentally handicapped.

8 This conceptualisation however, brings in a gender-bias in favour of 'fathers', of breadwinners of the family who are implicitly assumed to be male: Rawls constructs his rational individual negotiating the social contract as masculine.

9 This inconsistency between the assumptions of self-interest on the one hand and patriarchal care on the other hand causes another problem for Rawls' construction of the initial position. Family life never assures a fair distribution among its members, particularly not in a patriarchal setting that can be characterised as one of a 'benevolent dictator' (Naila Kabeer 1994: 99–100). Hence, justice in the distribution of primary goods is also needed *within* and not only *between* households, as Moller Okin remarks. However, Rawls excludes intra-household relations from his theory.

> Unless the households in which children are first nurtured, and see their first examples of human interaction, are based on equality and reciprocity rather than on dependence and domination – and the latter is too often the case – how can whatever love they receive from their parents make up for the injustice they see before them in the relationship between these same parents? How, in hierarchical families in which sex roles are rigidly assigned, are we to learn, as Rawls' theory of moral development requires us, to 'put ourselves into another's place and find out what we would do in his position'?
>
> (Moller Okin 1989: 99–100)

10 It is important to note the difference between ethics and morality as used in this study. Morality is understood as particular views on how one should live, whereas ethics is understood as a reflection on morality, in which the question

is put more broadly, that is, on what constitutes the good life (see, for example, Bernard Williams 1985 and Paul Ricoeur 1992).

11 Just for reasons of clarity I want to state here that I do not share the ideas attributed by some to Gilligan's position, that the ethical position expressed by the women in Gilligan's research points to a natural, sexual difference from male moral development. I agree with most interpreters of the ethic of care that caring is a human characteristic, for men and women alike, but one which has become attributed to women because of the gendered division of labour in many societies. See for a critique: Mary Brabeck 1993; Carol Gilligan 1995; Bill Puka 1993; and Joan Tronto 1993.

12 Here we encounter a problem with caring for the self. I will briefly discuss this issue later in this chapter.

13 The substantial difference in measuring unpaid labour in hours and in money can be attributed to the low wage rates applied in the accounting of fictional wages for unpaid labour.

14 Though today's economics tends to equate the economy with the domain of the market (*agora*) the root of the word economy derives from *oikos* and *oikonomia*, as the household and the art of providing for the household.

15 For example today, men's acquiring capabilities of caring is a recurrent topic within the women's movement. Some argue that men are able to and should care just as well and often as women do and have done so during many centuries (even though sons are generally treated differently than daughters and urged to independence at an earlier age than their sisters). Others think that men may be good at caring too, but that inviting them to do so would undermine the expertise and accompanying status that women have gained in this territory over so many years. Or their masculinity would suffer too much from this shift to an attributed feminine sphere. Most sociologists today would agree that care, like liberty and justice, implies human capabilities present in both women and men (see for a Dutch study on men and their practices and subsequent positive valuation of caring labour: Vincent Duyndam 1997).

16 Note that this interpretation of intrinsic motivation contradicts Bruno Frey's (1997) distinction between intrinsic and extrinsic motivation. In his view wage increases crowd out intrinsic motivation, whereas in the case of nursing and other care-sector jobs it is rather underpayment that may partially be responsible for crowding out nurses' intrinsic motivation. I would argue that Frey's argument only counts after a minimum level of payment is reached, a level that coincides with workers' values of fairness, an argument that finds support in George Akerlof (1982).

17 This bias is probably not unrelated to the fact that most studies on the gift have been carried out by men, who, on average, suffer from low levels of experience with care giving.

18 The anthropologist Alfred Schütz has characterised this feature in terms of 'unquestioned constructs'.

> We come, therefore, to the conclusion that 'rational action' on the common-sense level is always action within an unquestioned and undetermined frame of constructs of typicalities of the setting, the motives, the means and ends, the courses of action and personalities involved and taken for granted. They are, however, not merely taken for granted by the actor but also supposed as being taken for granted by the fellow-man.
>
> (Schütz 1953: 18).

19 In economics, hermeneutics has been employed as an alternative method of analysis only recently. Its use is suggested in the interpretation of (historical)

economic texts, or as a strategy for understanding economic processes in the real world (Don Lavoie 1990: 2). Hermeneutics may as well apply to the image of the rational economic actor as an interpretative being (Lawrence Berger 1990: 270; Mark Addleson 1995).

3 *LIBERTÉ, ÉGALITÉ, FRATERNITÉ*

1 The masculine linguistic expression for affective human relationships in the French Revolutionary maxim is unnecessarily gender-biased and should be read here as referring both to brotherhood *and* to sisterhood.
2 Albert Hirschman has argued that after the French Revolution:

> it often turned out, to much surprise, that the reform, that famous 'leap in the dark', could be lived with. The result was enormous relief among owners of capital, political stabilization, and a period of sustained economic growth and prosperity.
>
> (Hirschman 1994: 346–7)

3 How little this contradiction is understood is illustrated by Sheila Dow in a reference to the respected historian of economic thought, Mark Blaug. 'A conflict between methodology and practice is expressed by Blaug (1980) as a failure to live up to principle; perhaps rather it is the result of conflict between "in principle" dualism, and a non-dualistic reality' (Dow 1990: 146).
4 Although others argue that Smith's concern with care was only superficial and not grounded in a thorough understanding of what it is to care for people. His understanding would particularly ignore female experience in the domain of care (Edith Kuiper 1997).
5 Smith used interchangeably the wordings of justice and propriety on the one hand, and the notions of benevolence and beneficence on the other.
6 Two hundred years later, the institutional economist Clarence Ayres (1961) presents freedom, equality and security, as the core human values of all times. According to him, these three values 'are representative. I think that it is reasonable to suppose that what is true of them is true of value in general' (Ayres 1961: 170).
7 The Smithian value of sympathy is different from today's extension of self-interest in the new home economics where 'altruism' is included in one's individual utility function if, and only if, it generates psychological utility.
8 Hirschman's three types of values are often reduced to the first two in most references to his work. This may be seen as another demonstration of the marginalisation of the care values in today's economics, reifying the dualistic liberty versus justice canons.
9 On this distinction between exit as a market force, inducing change indirectly through leaving the less beneficial option, and voice as a political force, inducing change directly through demanding improvement, Hirschman argues that Milton Friedman's exposition of the market strategy is misleading. In an article arguing for the introduction of the market mechanism in state schools through vouchers, Friedman (1955) states that this is a direct strategy, compared to the political strategy of demanding better quality from the school where one's children are. Hirschman cites Friedman's view as

> a near perfect example of the economist's bias in favour of exit and against voice. In the first place, Friedman considers withdrawal or exit as the 'direct' way of expressing one's unfavourable views of an organization. A person less well trained in economics might naively suggest that the direct way of expressing views is to express them! Secondly, the decision to voice

one's views and efforts to make them prevail are contemptuously referred to by Friedman as a resort to 'cumbrous political channels'. But what else is the political, and indeed the democratic, process than the digging, the use, and hopefully the slow improvement of these very channels?

(Hirschman 1970: 17)

10 Twenty years later he admitted how true this was when he analysed the relationships between exit, voice and loyalty with the opening of the Berlin Wall and the subsequent collapse of the German Democratic Republic (Hirschman 1993).

11 In fact, Epicurus was quite sceptical about marriage and friendship. On the first he advised men 'never yield to the charms of love; it never came from heaven, its pleasures have nothing valuable in them' (*Morals:* 24). On the second he said that 'friendship ought to be contracted for the utility we expect therefrom' (ibid.: 57).

12 Jeremy Bentham had a strong normative view of utility and argued that utility (pleasure) is right and disutility (pain), is wrong (Bentham 1789: 16). Among the pleasures he lists pleasures of sense, wealth, skill, amity, good name, power, piety, benevolence, malevolence, memory, imagination, expectation, association and relief. Among the pains Bentham mentions an overlapping list of pains of privation, sense, awkwardness, enmity, ill name, piety, benevolence, malevolence, memory, imagination, expectation and association.

13 For example by Alfred Marshall, who expected women not to undertake paid work since 'it tempts them to neglect their duty of building up a true home, and of investing their efforts in the personal capital of their children's character and abilities' (Marshall 1890 VI.xii.11: 684).

14 The canon in the history of economic thought has almost exclusively focused on Mill alone, as has been argued by Michèle Pujol (1992). She gives the examples of Mark Blaug (1962) and E. K. Hunt (1979) as historians of economic thought who ignore Taylor's influence completely. Pujol mentions Jacob Oser (1970) among those who did acknowledge Harriet Taylor's role but who doubt its extent. When we ask Mill's own view he clearly acknowledges Taylor's influential role. In his *Autobiography*, he describes their intellectual partnership, stating that 'not only during the years of our married life, but during many of the years of confidential friendship which preceded, all my published writings were as much her work as mine' (Mill 1873: 204–5). Pujol (1992: 24) argues that the *Principles of Political Economy* is jointly written by Mill and Taylor, as appears from the dedication to the first edition and other evidence. In the dedication to *On Liberty*, which appeared the year after Taylor's death, Mill writes the following: 'To the beloved and deplored memory of her who was the inspirer, and in part the author, of all that is best in my writings.'

15 It is strange that their texts have been published under Mill's name only. It was probably social expediency which ruled out Taylor's co-authorship, later combined with the pragmatic insight that Mill's well-known name would probably draw a wider readership (Alice Rossi 1970).

16 'Women are as capable as men of appreciating and managing their own concerns' (Mill 1848 Book V.xi.9: 959).

17 In the home, they refer to

the almost despotic power of husbands over wives [which] needs not to be enlarged upon here, because nothing more is needed for the complete removal of the evil than that wives should have the same rights and should receive protection of law in the same manner as all other persons.

(Mill 1859: 175)

18 For my argument here, I will not rely on my own, very incomplete, under-

standing of Marx, but will rather follow some of the recent literature on Marx's view of justice.

19 See, for an extensive discussion of Reid's position and influence, a special issue of *Feminist Economics* in 1996 (2) 3, dedicated to her memory.

20 Yun-Ae Yi (1996: 20) mentions Theodore Schultz, Milton Friedman, Franco Modigliani (who memorialised Reid's influence on his work in his 1985 Nobel Lecture) and Gary Becker. Only in 1980 was her work rewarded with her selection as American Economic Association 'Distinguished Fellow', the first such award to a female economist. See also van Staveren (1998).

21 Interestingly, Reid obviously refers in this quote not to self-interest but to the interest people have in each other.

22 One could think of, for example, the tons of waste circling around in space as left-overs of human space activity.

23 This quote also involves a confusing element: the wording of reciprocity. It is not clear in what sense Smith used the word here. Earlier he rejected sympathy as self-interested and conditional upon a return, but instead regarded sympathy as beneficent and as a free gift. This suggests that Smith used the word reciprocity here to refer to the sharing of sympathy in a community, not as exchange. What he seems to imply – but such an interpretation is of course debatable – is that a society with a shared commitment among its members to care for each other, furthering the belief that everyone will contribute to this value, is happier and more prosperous than a society without the presence of such caring values as sympathy, benevolence and responsibility.

4 BEYOND THE HIGHWAY OF MODERNIST ECONOMICS

1 Arjo Klamer and David Colander warn us that we must not be too optimistic about economists' willingness to understand economic life outside economic textbooks and computable general equilibrium models (Klamer and Colander 1990).

2 The assumed 'value-neutrality' does not refer to the values held by economists but to the values present in economic behaviour: value-neutrality denies the role that values play in the economy. See, among many others, Bruce Caldwell 1994; Marianne Ferber and Julie Nelson 1993; Wade Hands 1985a, 1985b; Geoffrey Hodgson 1988; Harvey Leibenstein 1976; Deirdre McCloskey 1985; Jane Mansbridge 1990; Philip Mirowski 1989, 1993.

3 Becker's reference to 'neglected behaviour' probably refers to his own attitude, since various economists throughout time (see also in the previous chapter) did acknowledge the behavioural characteristics he mentions as being 'neglected'.

4 It is not clear however, how P and S are to be exchanged or distributed within the household, particularly among men and women. Will they specialise on comparative advantage in accumulating P and S? Or do they share an even accumulation in P and S because they share membership of the same household, assuming that they experience the same social and historical networks? And is that possible when they employ a division of labour along the lines of gender outside and within the household?

5 But one could just as well argue that easy divorce possibilities are an incentive to invest in love: you'd better take care that the other feels loved so that she does not exit. The option of divorce makes the voluntary choice of marriage even more convincing than if there is no exit option available. I did not expect to find such a non-liberal reasoning here in Becker's analysis. His position against divorce laws (the exit option) does not fit easily with the rest of his analysis.

6 I can illustrate my point with the help of a story told by a friend of mine, an Englishman who recently went on his honeymoon to New York. Every time he entered a shop he was welcomed with a nice 'how do you do' and similar welcoming phrases. At first, he was surprised and guiltily thought he should change his prejudices against Americans. Being a well-educated Englishman, he tried to answer the salespersons as well and honestly as he could. Sometimes he said 'Thank you very much! I am doing fine, having my honeymoon here with my beautiful wife, we are having a wonderful time and . . .', other times he said 'I am fine, thank you and how do you do madam, . . . had a nice day today? . . . '. But he never got an appropriate reply in return, and not one meaningful conversation evolved. He did not feel treated with respect, but subject to prudence instead.

7 This use of Simon's ideas does not include the option he himself suggested, namely that the social norms which arise are not only instrumental but may also reflect human values, for their own sake, as reflecting a sense of right.

8 Over time, North's views seem to get nearer to a social value theory and away from methodological individualism (John Groenewegen, Frans Kerstholt and Ad Nagelkerke 1995).

9 Marc Tool (1977: 43) points out an ethical dimension once. He states that the notion of instrumental value implies appropriateness of the means to serve the ends.

10 At the end of his article, Williamson puts it almost in terms of the idea of distinct value domains between which no trade-offs are appropriate:

> Personal trust is made nearly noncalculative by switching out of a regime in which the marginal calculus applies into one of a discrete structural kind. That often requires added effort and is warranted only for very special personal relations that would be seriously degraded if a calculative orientation were 'permitted' Commercial relations do not qualify.
>
> (Oliver Williamson 1993: 486)

11 Others have argued from this position as well (see, for example, Margaret Jane Radin's 1996 *Contested Commodities* and Kenneth Arrow's 1997 comprehensive review of her book) but I cannot discuss them all.

12 Anderson forcefully rejects utilitarianism but it is not clear whether she rejects it for both moral and pleasure motives or only for the moral values.

> Thus, consequentialism demands that the instrumental self aim at and care about what isn't really important, deliberate in terms that don't authentically justify its actions, accept false beliefs and value judgements, and have motivations that it would be wrong to act on . . . in addition, consequentialism tells people to have emotions and attitudes that aren't really warranted by their objects, to abandon any robust conception of personal responsibility, and to repudiate (via adoption of the rule to ignore sunk costs) any attempt to construct meaningful connections between its past and future actions.
>
> (Anderson 1993: 42)

13 Although I should admit that in situations of very unequal distribution the resources for potential redistribution to the least well-off seem almost limitless. In such situations scarcity is a less relevant concept than power or interest.

5 HYPOTHESES ON ECONOMIC ROLE COMBINATION

1 In a critique of *Rational Economic Man*, Jane Mansbridge illustrates one of the complexities involved in my quest, which I recognise in my own multiple roles.

In my own case, I have a duty to care for my child, and I am made happy by his happiness, and I get simple sensual pleasure from snuggling close to him as I read him a book. I have a principled commitment to work for women's liberation, and I empathise with other women, and I find a way to use some of my work for women as background to a book that advances my academic career. Duty, love (or empathy), and self-interest intermingle in my actions in a way I can rarely sort out.

(Jane Mansbridge 1990: 133–4)

2 As a consequence the method forces the interviewer to step down from the position of the objective and detached scientist who claims to be confident that she always asks the right questions. The focus group method allows the researcher to move from weak or postulated objectivity to 'strong objectivity' (Sandra Harding 1995) or 'positional objectivity' (Sen 1993b). 'When values and interests constitute conceptual frameworks in the first place, one can come to identify them and then decide which to retain and which to discard only by staring off thought from outside those dominant frameworks' (Sandra Harding 1995: 27).

3 As in any other field method it is impossible to exclude inequalities constructed in social life, such as those along the lines of class, gender, ethnicity, rural/urban positions and so on. It is important to be aware of such inequalities within groups, since they may influence the discussion. Also, group dynamics may induce participants to conform with a dominant norm, even when the interviewer tries to get more diverse views; again, the facilitator should be aware of this risk.

4 Of course, potential misunderstanding can be reduced by learning about the particular culture beforehand. Even so, as an outsider (which I was in two of the four group's contexts and to a lesser extent in another) it is necessary to remain aware of one's ignorance and to seek help from group participants during the discussion, and from others after transcription of the interview, for the interpretation of certain parts of the discussion.

5 The transcriptions of the interviews presented below have been summarised with only minor grammatical adaptations, so as to connect the different parts of the discussions.

6 For anthropologists such a maximisation of diversity is clearly overdone. Economists, however, have no problem in bringing data from countries from all over the world together in a single (regression) analysis. I hereby apologise for this rudeness to the anthropologists among the readers of my book.

7 The notion of empowerment was not unfamiliar, however, because of the involvement of the group participants in political activism and its links to the international women's movement which became very strong in the period just before and after the largest UN conference ever organised (in Beijing in 1995). For a historical overview of interpretations of women's economic empowerment in the global realm, various sources of literature are available, such as Rounaq Jahan (1995), Caroline Moser (1993) and Geertje Lycklama à Nijeholt, Virginia Vargas and Saskia Wieringa (1998).

8 Louise Tilly and Joan Scott argue that 'women were seen to play at least two roles – the biological and the economic' (1978: 3). On page 55 they add: 'The wife's role in providing food could lead to her involvement in public, political actions'. They refer to bread riots which were often led by women, for example the one in Northampton in 1693 where women went to the market 'with knives stuck in their girdles to force corn at their own rates'.

9 In terms of the range of class difference the group in the developed country in Western Europe was fairly similar to the groups in developing countries.

The class background within the western European group was from lower to middle class, whereas in the other groups the range was even larger, including the upper middle class.

10 At a conference of anthropologists at the University of Leiden where I presented my empirical research an African anthropologist suggested this point to me. Particularly in relation to the utterance in the Nairobi focus group that 'we don't challenge the men'. The African scholar's hypothesis was that this statement may express a defence against masculine fears of women's empowerment and feminism in Africa. I am very grateful for this and other interdisciplinary insights gained at the conference.

11 See, for example, Janneke Plantenga (1993) and Hettie Pott-Buter (1993). In the 1950s and 1960s, and in some elderly families in the Netherlands today, men were proud to say that 'my wife need not go out to work'.

12 This paradox was later double checked by phone with Anneke.

13 The Kenyan scholar and political activist Maria Nzomo has argued both against simple acceptance of western or universal categories, and against post-modern extreme positions which completely dismiss the possibility of local adaptations of established categories of value.

> Within the postmodernist approach, the concept of *democracy*, and the principles that hinge upon it, namely *social justice*, *freedom* and *equality*, cannot be treated as universal *ideals* or principles, but should instead be defined and applied only in the specific historic and social context in which the concept is being used. . . . For while acknowledging that there are historical and socio-cultural differences that distinguish Kenyan society, it is difficult to justify a dismissal of the basic principles of democracy as irrelevant to Kenya, simply because they were developed in ancient Greece by political philosophers who knew nothing about Kenya. From past (failed) experiences with imported democracy during African decolonization, one recognises the need to adapt democratic principles developed elsewhere to the specificities of the Kenyan situation. However, taking postmodern thought to its extremes would involve rejecting the outlines of democratic thinking and practice as they have been developed in other parts of the world.
>
> (Maria Nzomo 1995: 134)

14 English translation of the Quran by M. M. Pickthall (1996 AC/1417 AH).

6 TOWARD AN ARISTOTELIAN ECONOMICS

1 Nobody came.

2 In a study on the self, Paul Ricoeur (1992) has developed this insight further. He argues that the autonomy of the self is tightly bound up with care for one's fellow human beings and with justice for everybody. In fact, particular and general others are implied in any image of the self.

3 With this argument Perkins Gilman argues not only against the traditional gender division of labour but also against a specialised division of labour along other lines of distinction, for example along the line of ethnicity.

4 Entitlements refer to the command that economic actors have over goods and services: in the market through exchange entitlements, in the unpaid care economy through subsistence production entitlements (such as land rights, see Bina Agarwal 1994) and finally also through state-guaranteed entitlements such as income transfers, public insurance, food stamps, or public goods.

5 Sen's interpretation of virtues as limited to the capabilities of the domain of freedom is surprising since he refers to Aristotle's *Nicomachean Ethics* as a basic source (Sen 1987: chapter one).

6 In Van Staveren (1994) I similarly suggested an extension of the capability approach to the issue of fertility, in particular women's reproductive freedom.

7 This relationship between some of the Aristotelian virtues and the ethics of care is disputed because of the dichotomous split Aristotle proposes between private life in the household and public life in the *polis* (Aafke Komter 1995; Joan Tronto 1995). I will not enter into this debate and cannot do so, since I am only referring to the economic part of caring values, not to care in general. I would see economic dimensions of care reflected in Aristotle's interpersonal virtues, though it must be recognised that Aristotle himself did not relate any of these virtues to an ethics of care, nor to the practices of caring so widely ascribed and delegated to slaves and women, whom he did not include in his scheme of the good life.

8 Unfortunately, some have interpreted Aristotle as defining a single list of the good. See for one such example Martha Nussbaum (1995: 74–85). In her otherwise very open, inter-subjective approach to human capabilities, she has tried to define a list of core human capabilities important for all human beings irrespective of time and place.

9 'A radically laissez-faire economy would be like a totalitarian state, invading every other sphere, dominating every other distributive process' (Walzer 1983: 119).

10 Mark Addleson (1995) argues in an interpretative approach to economics that there is no such thing as equilibrium. He posits interpretation against equilibrium, as mutually exclusive. I do not agree, as will become clear in the text which follows. I still believe in the possibility of equilibrium, though a very different one from neoclassical economics: an interpretative, contextual balance, arising out of people's interdependent interactions in the economy.

11 Becker's famous 'rotten kid' theorem illustrates his misunderstanding of the Aristotelian mean: virtuous parenthood would not have created a rotten kid in the first place.

12 Boulding (1981) nevertheless suggests that the equilibrium can be found with help of linear algebra and geometry. I do not believe that such a formulaic approach is possible, but rather think that it is a matter of deliberation, in line with Aristotelian contextual ethics.

13 Of course GDP growth is a limited indicator of economic efficiency.

14 Unlike gift-exchange in traditional societies, there is in the free gift of blood to unnamed strangers no contract of custom, no legal bond, no functional determinism, no situations of discriminatory power, domination, constraint or compulsion, no sense of shame or guilt, no gratitude imperative and no need for the penitence of a Chrysostom.

(Titmuss 1970: 239)

7 INSTITUTIONAL MEDIATION BETWEEN VALUE DOMAINS

1 From here on, the label of 'old-institutional school' will be disregarded and the term institutionalism will refer to the tradition established by the 'old-institutional', or Veblenian, institutionalists.

2 These characteristics draw particularly but not exclusively on Hodgson (1988, 1998), Hodgson, Samuels and Tool (1994), Mirowski (1990b), Samuels (1995b).

3 The demand effect is anticipated but cannot be predicted. The example derives from large producers of baby food, such as Nutricia, who have announced to their customers that they will not use genetically manipulated soya in baby food.

4 I want to remind the reader that in the new institutional economics institutions are defined more narrowly as only constraining human behaviour, not as also enabling it. Moreover, new institutional economists conceive institutions as constraints on individual behaviour similar to budget and time constraints. In my analysis however, institutions are enabling or constraining at the social level, that is, in the interaction between economic actors.

5 In many societies however, care giving is not wholly voluntary. The task of care giving is assigned to particular social groups, particularly women, ethnic minorities and migrants.

6 According to Margaret Reid (1943), in 1929 in over half the farms in the United States at least 33 per cent of agricultural production was kept off the market and used for satisfaction of household needs, as subsistence production.

7 'It is one thing to have a spouse (e.g. the husband) come home demoralized and exhausted from working in an undemocratic and uninspiring workplace, while a supportive partner (e.g. the wife) eases some of his pain; but quite another to have both partners in the same situation of subordination and demoralization, with the wife still having to do most of the household labor as well' (Phillip O'Hara 1995: 109).

8 Kenneth Boulding, particularly in the final chapter in *A Preface to Grants Economics* (1981), seems to suggest a stable equilibrium between the different domains. He also pictures linear relationships between each domain and implies commensurability between the domains, although suggesting the possibility of multiple equilibria. My Aristotelian and institutional analyses of the economic process as consisting of incommensurable value domains and of the institutional mediation between domains points in a different direction for modelling the domains. This will be elaborated later on in this chapter.

9 Over the past decade, there has been a flourishing literature on chaos theoretic models for neoclassical queries and Keynesian studies, often of general equilibrium models or models with various kinds of expectations (see, for example, William Barnett, John Geweke and Karl Shell 1989; William Brock, D. A. Hsieh and B. LeBaron 1991; Jean-Michel Grandmont 1985; Jean-Michel Grandmont and Pierre Malgrange 1986; Cars Hommes 1991; Hashem Pesaran and Simon Potter 1993). The mathematics is sophisticated and detailed, as in much linear econometrics. In evolutionary economics, chaos theory has been introduced in close connection with the use of systems theory (Richard Day and Ping Chen 1993; Elias Khalil and Kenneth Boulding 1996). The Keynesian economics use of chaos theory enables models to endogenise the dynamics of business cycles, sometimes called 'deep modelling' (William Barnett and Seugmook Choi 1989: 143).

10 For example, a chaos theoretic article in econometrics clings to the view that 'markets will be assumed to clear in the Walrasian sense at every date, and traders will have perfect foresight along the cycles' (Grandmont 1985).

11 A vector or a set of vectors in a matrix represents a two-dimensional space for mathematical representations in linear economic models. Non-linear models include higher dimensions and even broken dimensions.

12 Parallel parameters for men do not exist, since traditional gender role distribution ascribes only one role to men, which they either perform when having paid work, or do not perform, as in the case of unemployment. Women's gender role commitment requires them to seek a balance between three roles. Men's gender role commitment is different and takes the shape of a discrete value, depending on the availability and location of paid work.

BIBLIOGRAPHY

Addleson, Mark (1995) *Equilibrium Versus Understanding*, London: Routledge.

Agarwal, Bina (1994) *A Field of One's Own. Gender and Land Rights in South Asia*, Cambridge: Cambridge University Press.

Akerlof, George (1982) 'Labour Contracts as Partial Gift Exchange', *Quarterly Journal of Economics* 47 (4), pp. 543–69.

Amariglio, Jack (1988) 'The Body, Economic Discourse, and Power: An Economist's Introduction to Foucault', *History of Political Economy*, 20 (4), pp. 583–613.

Anderson, Elizabeth (1993) *Value in Ethics and Economics*, Cambridge, Mass.: Harvard University Press.

Argyle, Michael (1991) *Cooperation. The Basis of Sociability*, London: Routledge.

Aristotle, *Nichomachean Ethics*, translation by David Ross, revised by J. L. Ackrill and J. O. Urmson, 1980, Oxford: Oxford University Press.

—— *Politics*, edited by Stephen Everson, 1988, Cambridge: Cambridge University Press.

Arrow, Kenneth (1972) 'Gifts and Exchanges', *Philosophy and Public Affairs*, 1 (4), pp. 343–62.

—— (1997) 'Invaluable Goods', *Journal of Economic Literature*, vol. 35, June, pp. 757–65.

Aslaksen, Iulie, Olav Bjerkholt, Charlotte Koren and Stig-Olof Olsson (1997) 'Care Work in the Household and Market: Productivity, Economic Growth, and Welfare', paper presented at IAFFE Summer Conference, 20–2 June, Taxco (Mexico).

Aslaksen, Iulie, Charlotte Koren and Marianne Stokstad (1998) 'Care Work in the Household and Market: Cost of Child Care, Employment and Welfare', paper presented at the IAFFE Conference/Out of the Margin Conference in Amsterdam, 3–5 June.

Aubel, Judi (1994) *Guidelines for Studies Using the Focus Group Interview Technique*, Geneva: International Labour Organisation.

Ayres, Clarence (1961) *Toward a Reasonable Society. The Values of Industrial Civilisation*, Austin: University of Texas Press.

Badgett, Lee and Nancy Folbre (1999) 'Assigning Care: Gender Norms and Economic Outcomes', *International Labour Review*, 138 (3), pp. 311–26.

Baerends, Els (1994) *Changing Kinship, Family and Gender Relations in Sub-Saharan Africa*, Leiden: Leiden University, Women and Autonomy Series.

Baier, Annette (1987) 'Hume, the Women's Moral Theorist?', in Feder Kittay and Diana Meyers (eds) *Women and Moral Theory*, Totowa: Rowman and Littlefield, pp. 37–55.

—— (1993) 'What Do Women Want in Moral Theory?', in Mary Jeanne Larrabee (ed.) *An Ethic of Care. Feminist and Interdisciplinary Perspectives*, London: Routledge, pp. 19–32.

—— (1995) 'The Need for More than Justice', in Virginia Held (ed.) *Justice and Care. Essential Readings in Feminist Ethics*, Boulder: Westview, pp. 47–58.

Bailey, Kenneth (1994) *Sociology and the New Systems Theory: Toward a Theoretical Synthesis*, New York: State University of New York Press.

Baker, Wayne (1984) 'The Social Structure of a National Securities Market', *American Journal of Sociology*, 89 (4), pp. 775–811.

Bakker, Diny de, Cordula Wagner and Emmy Sluijs (1996) 'Kwaliteitssystemen in de Thuiszorg, de Verpleeghuiszorg en de Zorg voor Mensen met een Verstandelijke Handicap', Rapport van het Onderzoeksprogramma Kwaliteit van Zorg (NOW), Utrecht: NIVEL.

Barker, Drue (1995) 'Economists, Social Reformers, and Prophets: A Feminist Critique of Economic Efficiency', *Feminist Economics*, 1 (3), pp. 26–39.

Barnett, William A., John Geweke and Karl Shell (eds) (1989) *Economic Complexity: Chaos, Sunspots, Bubbles and Nonlinearity*, Cambridge: Cambridge University Press.

Barnett, William A. and Seugmook S. Choi (1989) 'Comparison Between the Conventional Econometric Approach to Structural Inference and the Nonparametric Chaotic Attractor Approach', in William Barnett, John Geweke and Karl Shell (eds) *Economic Complexity: Chaos, Sunspots, Bubbles and Nonlinearity*, Cambridge: Cambridge University Press, pp. 141–212.

Barro, Robert (1991) 'Economic Growth in a Cross-Section of Countries', *Quarterly Journal of Economics*, 106, pp. 407–43.

Batson, Daniel (1997) 'Self–Other Merging and the Empathy–Altruism Hypothesis: reply to Neurberg *et al.*', *Journal of Personality and Social Psychology*, 73 (3), pp. 517–22.

Batson, Daniel, Karen Sager, Eric Garst, Misook Kang, Kostia Rubchinsky and Karen Dawson (1997) 'Is Empathy-Induced Helping Due to Self–Other Merging?', *Journal of Personality and Social Psychology*, 73 (3), pp. 495–509.

Bazerman, Charles (1993) 'Money Talks: The Rhetorical Project of the "Wealth of Nations"', in Willie Henderson, Tony Dudley-Evans and Roger Backhouse (eds) *Economics and Language*, London: Routledge, pp. 173–99.

Becker, Gary (1991) *A Treatise on the Family*, enlarged edition, Cambridge, Mass.: Harvard University Press.

—— (1993) 'Nobel Lecture. The Economic Way of Looking at Behaviour', *Journal of Political Economy*, 101 (3), pp. 385–409.

—— (1996) *Accounting for Tastes*, Cambridge, Mass.: Harvard University Press.

Beijing Platform for Action (1995) Document of the UN Fourth Conference on Women, Geneva: United Nations.

Bentham, Jeremy (1789) [1970] *An Introduction to the Principles of Morals and Legislation*, London: Athlone.

Berlin, Isaiah (1969) *Four Essays on Liberty*, Oxford: Oxford University Press.

Berger, Lawrence (1990) 'Self-Interpretation, Attention, and Language: Implications for Economics of Charles Taylor's Hermeneutics', in Don Lavoie (ed.) *Economics and Hermeneutics*, London: Routledge, pp. 262–84.

222

Bergmann, Barbara (1986) *The Economic Emergence of Women*, New York: Harper Collins.

Bethke Elshtain, Jean (1981) *Public Man Private Woman. Women in Social and Political Thought*, Oxford: Martin Robertson.

Birdsall, Nancy, David Ross and Richard Sabot (1995) 'Inequality and Growth Reconsidered: Lessons from East Asia', *World Bank Economic Review*, 9 (3), pp. 477–508.

Blaug, Mark (1962) *Economic Theory in Retrospect*, Homewood, Ill.: Richard D. Irwin.

—— (1980) *The Methodology of Economics*, Cambridge: Cambridge University Press.

—— (ed.) (1991) *Aristotle (384–322 BC)*, Aldershot: Elgar.

Blumberg, Rae Lesser (1991) *Gender, Family and Economy. The Triple Overlap*, New Delhi and London: Sage.

Bok, Sissela (1995) *Common Values*, Columbia: University of Missouri Press.

Boon, Leo (1998) 'Zorg en Toekomst', *Ontwikkelingen in de Gezondheidszorg*, no. 27. Amstelveen: SYMPOZ.

Boserup, Esther (1970) *Women's Role in Economic Development*, New York: St. Martin's and Allen and Unwin.

Bordo, Susan (1986) 'The Cartesian Masculinization of Thought', *Signs*, 11 (3), pp. 439–56.

Boulding, Kenneth (1966). 'The Economics of the Coming Spaceship Earth', in Herman Daly and Kenneth Townsend (eds) *Valuing the Earth. Economics, Ecology, and Ethics*, Cambridge, Mass.: MIT Press, pp. 297–309.

—— (1970) *A Primer on Social Dynamics. History of Dialectics and Development*, New York: Free Press.

—— (1981) *A Preface to Grants Economics. The Economy of Love and Fear*, New York: Praeger.

—— (1985) *The World as a Total System*, Beverly Hills: Sage.

Bowden, Peta (1997) *Caring. Gender-Sensitive Ethics*, London: Routledge.

Bowles, Samuel (1998) 'Endogenous Preferences: The Cultural Consequences of Markets and Other Economic Institutions', *Journal of Economic Literature*, 36, March, pp. 75–111.

Brabeck, Mary (1993) 'Moral Judgement: Theory and Research on Differences between Males and Females', in Mary Jeanne Larrabee (ed.) *An Ethic of Care. Feminist and Interdisciplinary Perspectives*, London: Routledge, pp. 33–48.

Brock, William and Steven Durlauf (1997). 'Discrete Choice with Social Interactions II', unpublished paper, Department of Economics, University of Wisconsin.

Brock, William, David Hsieh and Blake LeBaron (1991). *Nonlinear Dynamics, Chaos and Instability. Statistical Theory and Economic Evidence*, Cambridge, Mass.: MIT Press.

Brown, Vivienne (1993) 'Decanonizing Discourses: Textual Analysis and the History of Economic Thought', in Willie Henderson, Tony Dudley-Evans and Roger Backhouse (eds) *Economics and Language*, London: Routledge, pp. 64–83.

—— (1994a) 'The Economy as Text', in Roger Backhouse (ed.) *New Directions in Economic Methodology*, London: Routledge, pp. 368–82.

—— (1994b) *Adam Smith's Discourse, Canonicity, Commerce and Conscience*, London: Routledge.

Bruyn-Hundt, Marga (1996a) *The Economics of Unpaid Work*, Amsterdam: Thesis Publishers.

—— (1996b) 'Scenarios for a Redistribution of Unpaid Work in the Netherlands', *Feminist Economics*, 2 (3), pp. 129–33.

Buchanan, Allen (1982) *Marx and Justice. The Radical Critique if Liberalism*, Totowa: Rowman and Allenheld.

Buchanan, James (1969) 'Is Economics the Science of Choice?', in Erich Streissler (ed.) *Roads to Freedom. Essays in Honour of Friedrich A. von Hayek*, London: Routledge and Kegan Paul, pp. 47–64.

—— (1972) 'Rawls on Justice as Fairness', *Public Choice*, no. 13, pp. 123–8.

Caldwell, Bruce (1994) [1982] *Beyond Positivism: Economic Methodology in the Twentieth Century*, London: Routledge.

Carrier, James (1995) *Gifts and Commodities. Exchange and Western Capitalism Since 1700*, London: Routledge.

CBS (1991) *De Tijdsbesteding van de Nederlandse Bevolking. Kerncijfers 1988*, Voorburg/Heerlen: Centraal Bureau voor de Statistiek.

—— (2000) *Kerncijfers*, Voorburg/Heerlen: Centraal Bureau voor de Statistiek.

Cheal, David (1988) *The Gift Economy*, London: Routledge.

Chick, Victoria (1995) '"Order out of Chaos" in Economics?', in Sheila Dow and John Hillard (eds) *Keynes, Knowledge and Uncertainty*, Aldershot: Elgar, pp. 25–42.

Code, Lorraine (1995) *Rhetorical Spaces. Essays on Gendered Locations*, London: Routledge.

Commissie Toekomstscenario's (1995) *Gedeelde Zorg. Toekomstscenario's voor Herverdeling van Onbetaalde Zorgarbeid*, Den Haag: Ministerie van Sociale Zaken en Werkgelegenheid.

Commons, John R. (1961) *Institutional Economics. Its Place in Political Economy*, Madison: University of Wisconsin Press.

Dahrendorf, Ralf (1958) *Homo Sociologicus: ein Versuch zur Geschichte, Bedeuting und Kritik der Kategortie der Sozialen Rolle*, Köln: Westdeutscher Verlag.

Dawes, Robyn, Alphons van de Kragt and John Orbell (1990) 'Cooperation for the Benefit of Us – Not Me, or My Conscience', in Jane Mansbridge (ed.) *Beyond Self-Interest*, Chicago: University of Chicago Press, pp. 97–110.

Day, Richard and Ping Chen (eds) (1993) *Nonlinear Dynamics and Evolutionary Economics*, Oxford: Oxford University Press.

Damasio, Antonio (1994) *Descartes' Error. Emotion, Reason and the Human Brain*, New York: Putnam.

De Greene, Kenyon B. (1996) 'Field-Theoretic Framework for the Interpretation of the Evolution, Instability, Structural Change, and Management of Complex Systems', in Douglas Kiel and Euel Elliott (eds) *Chaos Theory in the Social Sciences. Foundations and Applications*, Ann Arbor: University of Michigan Press, pp. 273–94.

Denzau, Arthur and Douglass North (1994) 'Shared Mental Models: Ideologies and Institutions', *Kyklos*, 47 (1), pp. 3–31.

Devaux, Monique (1995) 'Shifting Paradigms: Theorizing Care and Justice in Political Theory', *Hypathia* 10 (2), pp. 115–19.

Dimand, Mary Ann, Robert W. Dimand and Evelyn L. Forget (1995) *Women of Value. Feminist Essays on the History of Women in Economics*, Aldershot and Brookfield: Elgar.

Dixit, Avinash and Barry J. Nalebuff (1991) *Thinking Strategically. The Competitive Edge in Business, Politics, and Everyday Life*, New York: Norton.

Dixon-Mueller, Ruth and Richard Anker (1988) *Assessing Women's Economic Contributions to Development*, paper no. 6, Geneva: ILO.

Dolfsma, Wilfred and Irene van Staveren (1998) 'Khalil versus Smith: Do Moral Sentiments Differ from Ordinary Tastes?', *De Economist*, 146 (4), pp. 606–13.

Douglas, Mary (ed.) (1973) *Rules and Meanings*, Harmondsworth: Penguin.

Douglas, Mary and Baron Isherwood (1979) [1996] *The World of Goods. Towards an Anthropology of Consumption*, London: Routledge.

Dow, Sheila (1985) *Macroeconomic Thought. A Methodological Approach*, Oxford: Blackwell.

—— (1990) 'Beyond Dualism', *Cambridge Journal of Economics*, vol. 14, pp. 143–57.

Durkheim, Émile (1915) *The Elementary Forms of the Religious Life*, London: Allen and Unwin.

—— (1992) *Professional Ethics and Civic Morals*, London: Routledge.

Durlauf, Steven (1996) 'Associational Redistribution: A Defense', SSRI paper, University of Wisconsin, Social Systems Research Institute.

Duyndam, Vincent (1997) *Zorgende Vaders. Over Mannen en Ouderschap, Zorg, Werk en Hulpverlening*, Amsterdam: Van Gennip.

Dwyer, Gerald (1992) 'Stabilization Policy Can Lead to Chaos', *Economic Inquiry* 39, pp. 40–6.

Editorial Mujeres (1995) *Feminismo en Costa Rica. Testimonios, Reflexiones, Ensayos*, San José: Editorial Mujeres.

Elson, Diane (ed.) (1995) *Male Bias in Economic Development*, Manchester: University of Manchester Press.

—— (2000) *Progress of the World's Women 2000*, New York: UNIFEM.

Elson, Diane and Barbara Evers (1998) 'Sector Programme Support: The Health Sector. A Gender-Aware Analysis', paper published by the Graduate School of Social Sciences, Genecon Unit, Manchester: University of Manchester.

Elster, Jon (1983) *Sour Grapes. Studies in the Subversion of Rationality*, Cambridge: Cambridge University Press.

—— (1985) *Making Sense of Marx*, Cambridge: Cambridge University Press.

—— (1986) 'Self-Realization in Work and Politics: The Marxist Conception of the Good Life', *Social Philosophy and Policy*, 3 (2), pp. 97–126.

—— (1992) *Local Justice: How Institutions Allocate Scarce Goods and Necessary Burdens*, Cambridge: Cambridge University Press.

—— (1998) 'Emotions and Economic Theory', *Journal of Economic Literature*, vol. 36, pp. 47–74.

England, Paula (1993) 'The Separative Self: Androcentric Bias in Neoclassical Assumptions', in Marianne Ferber and Julie Nelson (eds) *Beyond Economic Man. Feminist Theory and Economics*, Chicago: University of Chicago Press, pp. 37–53.

England, Paula and Nancy Folbre (1999) 'The Cost of Caring', *Annals of the American Academy of Political and Social Science*, 561 (0), pp. 39–51.

Epicurus, *Morals*, translated by John Digb, 1975, New York: AMS Press.

Esim, Simel (1997) 'Can Feminist Methodology Reduce Power Hierarchies in Research Settings?', *Feminist Economics*, 3 (2), pp. 137–9.

Esposito, John (1982) *Women in Muslim Family Law*, Syracuse: Syracuse University Press.

Etzioni, Amitai (1988) *The Moral Dimension. Toward a New Economics*, New York: Free Press.

Fapohunda, Eleanor (1983) 'Female and Male Work Profiles', in Christine Oppong (ed.) *Female and Male in West Africa*, London: Allen and Unwin, pp. 32–53.

Feiner, Susan (ed.) (1994) *Race and Gender in the American Economy. Views from Across the Spectrum*, Englewood Cliffs: Prentice Hall.

Ferber, Marianne and Julie Nelson (eds) (1993) *Beyond Economic Man. Feminist Theory and Economics*, Chicago: University of Chicago Press.

Festinger, Leon (1957) *A Theory of Cognitive Dissonance*, White Plains: Row, Peterson.

Fisher, Berenice and Joan Tronto (1990) 'Toward a Feminist Theory of Caring', in Emily Abel and Margaret Nelson (eds) *Circles of Care*, Albany: State University of New York Press, pp. 35–62.

Fitzgibbons, Athol (1995) *Adam Smith's System of Liberty, Wealth, and Virtue. The Moral and Political Foundations of 'The Wealth of Nations'*, Oxford: Clarendon.

Fleetwood, Steve (1997) 'Aristotle in the 21st Century', *Cambridge Journal of Economics*, vol. 21, pp. 729–44.

Folbre, Nancy (1994) *Who Pays for the Kids? Gender and the Structures of Constraint*, London: Routledge.

—— (1995) '"Holding Hands at Midnight": The Paradox of Caring Labour', *Feminist Economics*, 1 (1), pp. 73–92.

Folbre, Nancy and Heidi Hartmann (1988) 'The Rhetoric of Self-Interest: Ideology of Gender in Economic Theory', in Arjo Klamer, Deirdre McCloskey and Robert Solow (eds) *The Consequences of Economic Rhetoric*, Cambridge: Cambridge University Press, pp. 184–203.

Folbre, Nancy and Thomas Weisskopf (1998) 'Did Father Know Best? Families, Markets, and the Supply of Caring Labour', in Avner Ben-Ner and Louis Putterman (eds) *Economics, Values and Organization*, Cambridge: Cambridge University Press, pp. 171–205.

Foley, Caroline (1893) 'Fashion', *Economic Journal*, no. 3, pp. 458–74.

Foot, Philippa (1978) *Virtues and Vices and other Essays in Moral Philosophy*, Oxford: Blackwell.

Foucault, Michel (1971) 'Orders of Discourse', inaugural lecture delivered at the College de France, 2 December, 1970. Translation: Rupert Swyer, in *Social Science Information*, 10 (2), pp. 7–30.

Frank, Robert (1988) *Passions Within Reason. The Strategic Role for the Emotions*, New York: Norton.

Freeland, Cynthia (1998) *Feminist Interpretations of Aristotle*, Pennsylvania: Pennsylvania State University Press.

Frey, Bruno (1997) *Not Just for the Money. An Economic Theory of Personal Motivation*, Cheltenham: Elgar.

Friedman, Marilyn (1989) 'Feminism and Modern Friendship: Dislocating the Community', in *Ethics*, vol. 99, pp. 275–90.

Friedman, Milton (1953) 'The Methodology of Positive Economics', in Milton Friedman, *Essays in Positive Economics*, Chicago and London: University of Chicago Press and Cambridge University Press, pp. 3–43.

—— (1955) 'The Role of Government in Education', in Robert Solow (ed.) *Economics and the Public Interest*, New Brunswick: Rutgers University Press, pp. 123–44.

Friedman, Milton and Rose Friedman (1980) *Free to Choose. A Personal Statement*, New York: Harcourt Brace Jovanovich.

Fukuyama, Francis (1995) *Trust. The Social Virtues and the Creation of Prosperity*, London: Penguin.

Fullbrook, Edward (1998) 'Caroline Foley and the Theory of Intersubjective Demand', *Journal of Economic Issues*, 32 (3), pp. 709–31.

García Quesada, Ana Isabel (1996) 'Ajuste Estructural Y Politicas de Genero en el Inicio de la Era Post-Beijing', *Revista Centroamericana de Economía*, 1 (46, 47), pp. 86–102.

Gardiner, Jean (1997) *Gender, Care and Economics*, London: Macmillan.

Gauthier, David (1977) 'The Social Contract as Ideology', *Philosophy and Public Affairs*, no. 2, pp. 130–64.

Geertz, Clifford (1973) *The Interpretation of Cultures*, New York: Basic.

—— (1977) 'From the Native's Point of View: On the Nature of Anthropological Understanding', in Janet Dolgin, David Kemnitzer and David Schneider (eds) *Symbolic Anthropology. A Reader in the Study of Symbols and Meanings*, New York: Columbia University Press, pp. 480–92. Reprint from 1974.

Gilligan, Carol (1982) *In a Different Voice. Psychological Theory and Women's Development*, Cambridge, Mass.: Harvard University Press.

—— (1995) 'Moral Orientation and Moral Development', in Virginia Held (ed.) *Justice and Care. Essential Readings in Feminist Ethics*, Boulder: Westview.

Glover, Jonathan and Martha Nussbaum (eds) *Women, Culture and Development. A Study of Human Capabilities*, Oxford: Clarendon.

Goffman, Erving (1959) *The Presentation of Self in Everyday Life*, Garden City: Doubleday.

Goldschmidt-Clermont, Luisella and Elisabetta Pagnossin-Agilisakis (1995) *Measures of Unrecorded Economic Activities in Fourteen Countries*, New York: Human Development Report Office, UNDP.

Goodman, Nelson (1979) *Fact, Fiction and Forecast*, Cambridge, Mass.: Harvard University Press.

—— (1983) 'Notes on the Well-Made World', *Erkenntnis*, vol. 19, pp. 99–107.

Grandmont, Jean-Michel (1985) 'On Endogenous Competitive Business Cycles', *Econometrica*, no. 5, pp. 995–1045.

Grandmont, Jean-Michel and Pierre Malgrange (1986) 'Nonlinear Economic Dynamics', *Journal of Economic Theory*, no. 40, pp. 3–12.

Granovetter, Mark (1985) 'Economic Action and Social Structure: The Problem of Embeddedness', *American Journal of Sociology*, 91 (3), pp. 481–510.

Gregory, Chris (1982) *Gifts and Commodities*, London: Academic Press.

Griffin, James (1986) *Well-being. Its Meaning, Measurement and Moral Importance*, Oxford: Clarendon.

Groenewegen, John, Frans Kerstholt and Ad Nagelkerke (1995) 'On Integrating New and Old Institutionalism: Douglass North Building Bridges', *Journal of Economic Issues*, 29 (2), pp. 467–75.

Groenewegen, Peter (ed.) (1996) *Economics and Ethics?*, London: Routledge.

Groenhout, Ruth (1998) 'The Virtue of Care: Aristotelian Ethics and Contemporary Ethics of Care', in Cynthia Freeland (ed.) *Feminist Interpretations of Aristotle*, Pennsylvania: Pennsylvania State University Press, pp. 171–200.

Groot, Wim and Henriette Maassen van den Brink (1997) *Verlate Uittreding. Oorzaken van Uitttreding uit het Arbeidsproces Ruim na de Geboorte van het Eerste Kind*, Den Haag: VUGA, Ministerie van Sociale Zaken en Werkgelegenheid.

Grupo Agenda Política de Mujeres Costarricenses (1997) *Agenda Política de Mujeres Costarricenses*, San José.

Gudeman, Stephen (1986) *Economics as Culture. Models and Metaphors of Livelihood*, London: Routledge and Kegan Paul.

Hampshire, Stuart (1983) *Morality and Conflict*, Oxford: Blackwell.

Hands, Wade (1985a) 'Karl Popper and Economic Methodology: A New Look', *Economics and Philosophy*, vol. 1, pp. 83–99.

—— (1985b) 'Second Thoughts on Lakatos', *History of Political Economy*, vol. 17, pp. 1–16.

Harding, Sandra (1986) *The Science Question in Feminism*, Milton Keynes: Open University Press.

—— (ed.) (1987) *Feminism and Methodology*, Bloomington and Milton Keynes: Indiana University Press and Open University Press.

—— (1995) 'Can Feminist Thought Make Economics More Objective?', *Feminist Economics*, 1 (1), pp. 7–32.

Harding, Sandra and Merrill Hintikka (eds) (1983) *Discovering Reality. Feminist Perspectives on Epistemology, Metaphysics, Methodology, and Philosophy of Science*, Dordrecht: Reidel.

Hargreaves Heap, Shaun (1989) *Rationality in Economics*, Oxford: Blackwell.

Hargreaves Heap, Shaun, Martin Hollis, Bruce Lyons, Robert Sugden and Albert Weale (1992) *The Theory of Choice. A Critical Guide*, Oxford: Blackwell.

Harsanyi, John (1975) 'Can the Maximin Principle Serve as a Basis for Morality? A Criterion of John Rawls' Theory', *American Political Science Review*, 69 (2), pp. 594–606.

Hausman, Daniel and Michael McPherson (1993) 'Taking Ethics Seriously: Economics and Contemporary Moral Philosophy', *Journal of Economic Literature*, vol. 31, pp. 671–731.

—— (1996) *Economic Analysis and Moral Philosophy*, Cambridge: Cambridge University Press.

Hayek, Friedrich A. (1960) *The Constitution of Liberty*, London: Routledge and Kegan Paul.

Heilbroner, Robert (1988) *Behind the Veil of Economics. Essays in Worldly Philosophy*, New York: Norton.

Held, Virginia (1987) 'Feminism and Moral Theory', in Feder Kittay and Diana Meyers (eds) *Women and Moral Theory*, Totowa, N.J.: Rowman and Littlefield, pp. 111–28.

—— (ed.) (1995) *Justice and Care. Essential Readings in Feminist Ethics*, Boulder: Westview.

Herrnstein Smith, Barbara (1988) *Contingencies of Value. Alternative Perspectives for Critical Theory*, Cambridge, Mass.: Harvard University Press.

Hewitson, Gillian (1999) *Feminist Economics. Interrogating the Masculinity of Rational Economic Man*, Cheltenham: Elgar.

Himmelweit, Susan (1995) 'The Discovery of "Unpaid Work": The Social Consequences of the Expansion of "Work"', *Feminist Economics*, 1 (2), pp. 1–19.

—— (1999) 'Caring Labour', *Annals of the American Academy of Political and Social Science*, 561 (0), pp. 27–38.

Hirschman, Albert (1970) *Exit, Voice and Loyalty. Responses to Decline in Firms, Organizations, and States*, Cambridge, Mass.: Harvard University Press.

—— (1993) 'Exit, Voice, and the Fate of the German Democratic Republic: An Essay in Conceptual History', *World Politics*, 4–5 (2), pp. 173–202.

—— (1994) 'The On-and-Off Connection between Political and Economic Progress', *American Economic Review*, 84 (2), pp. 343–8.

Hochschild, Arlie (1989) *The Second Shift*, New York: Avon.

—— (1997) *The Time Bind*, New York: Metropolitan.

Hodgson, Geoffrey M. (1988) *Economics and Institutions. A Manifesto for a Modern Institutional Economics*, Cambridge: Polity.

—— (1997) 'The Ubiquity of Habits and Rules', *Cambridge Journal of Economics*, vol. 21, pp. 663–84.

—— (1998) 'The Approach of Institutional Economics', *Journal of Economic Literature*, vol. 36, pp. 166–92.

Hodgson, Geoffrey M., Warren J. Samuels and Marc R. Tool (1994) *The Elgar Companion to Institutional and Evolutionary Economics*, Aldershot: Elgar.

Hollis, Martin (1987) *The Cunning of Reason*, Cambridge: Cambridge University Press.

Hommes, Cars (1991). *Chaotic Dynamics in Economic Models. Some Simple Case Studies*, Groningen: Wolters-Noordhoff.

Hunt, E. K. (1979) *History of Economic Thought. A Critical Perspective*, Belmont, Calif.: Wadsworth.

Hume, David (1741) [1985] *Essays, Moral, Political and Literary*, Indianapolis: Liberty Fund.

INSTRAW (1995) *Measurement and Valuation of Unpaid Contribution. Accounting Through Time and Output*, Santo Domingo: INSTRAW.

Jahan, Rounaq (1995) *The Elusive Agenda. Mainstreaming Women in Development*, Dhaka and London: Dhaka University Press (Bangladesh) and Zed Books.

Janssen, Maarten (1993) *Microfoundations. A Critical Inquiry*, London: Routledge.

Jennings, Ann (1993) 'Public or Private? Institutional Economic and Feminism', in Marianne Ferber and Julie Nelson (eds) *Beyond Economic Man. Feminist Theory and Economics*, Chicago: University of Chicago Press, pp. 111–29.

Kabeer, Naila (1994) *Reversed Realities. Gender Hierarchies in Development Thought*, London: Verso.

Keddie, Nikki (1991) 'Introduction: Deciphering Middle Eastern Women's History', in Nikki Keddie and Beth Baron (eds) *Women in Middle Eastern History. Shifting Boundaries in Sex and Gender*, New Haven: Yale University Press, pp. 1–22.

Keynes, John Maynard (1936) *The General Theory of Employment, Interest and Money*, London: Macmillan.

Khalil, Elias L. and Kenneth E. Boulding (1996) *Evolution, Order and Complexity*, London: Routledge.

Kiel, Douglas and Euel Elliott (1996) *Chaos Theory in the Social Sciences. Foundations and Applications*, Ann Arbor: University of Michigan Press.

Kittay, Feder and Diana Meyers (eds) (1987) *Women and Moral Theory*, Totowa, N.J.: Rowman and Littlefield.

Klamer, Arjo (1983) *Conversations with Economists. New Classical Economists and Their Opponents Speak Out on the Current Controversy in Macroeconomics*, Savage, Md.: Rowman and Littlefield.

—— (1989) 'A Conversation with Amartya Sen', *Journal of Economic Perspectives*, 3 (1), pp. 135–50.

—— (1996) *The Value of Culture. On the Relationship Between Economics and Arts*, Amsterdam: Amsterdam University Press.

Klamer, Arjo and David Colander (1990) *The Making of an Economist*, Boulder: Westview.

Klamer, Arjo and Thomas Leonard (1994) 'So What's an Economic Metaphor?', in Philip Mirowski (ed.) *Natural Images in Economic Thought*, Cambridge: Cambridge University Press, pp. 20–51.

Klamer, Arjo, Deirdre McCloskey and Robert Solow (eds) (1988) *The Consequences of Economic Rhetoric*, Cambridge: Cambridge University Press.

Knight, Frank (1921) *Risk, Uncertainty and Profit*, Chicago: University of Chicago Press.

Kolm, Serge-Christophe (1996) *Modern Theories of Justice*, Cambridge, Mass.: MIT Press.

Komter, Aafke (1995) 'Justice, Friendship, and Care: Aristotle and Gilligan – Two of a Kind?', *European Journal of Women's Studies*, 2 (1), pp. 151–69.

—— (ed.) (1996) *The Gift. An Interdisciplinary Perspective*, Amsterdam: Amsterdam University Press.

Kroeger-Mappes, Joy (1994) 'The Ethic of Care *Vis-à-vis* the Ethic of Rights: A Problem for Contemporary Moral Theory', *Hypatia*, 9 (3), pp. 108–31.

Krugman, Paul (1996) *The Self-Organizing Economy*, Cambridge and Oxford: Blackwell.

Kuiper, Edith (1997) 'The Construction of Masculine Identity in Adam Smith's "Theory of Moral Sentiments"', paper presented at IAFFE Summer Conference, 20–2 June, Taxco (Mexico).

Kuiper, Edith and Jolande Sap (eds) (1995) *Out of the Margin. Feminist Perspectives on Economics*, London: Routledge.

Lange, Lynda (1983) 'Woman is Not a Rational Animal: On Aristotle's Biology of Reproduction', in Sandra Harding and Merrill Hintikka (eds) *Discovering Reality. Feminist Perspectives on Epistemology, Metaphysics, Methodology, and Philosophy of Science*, Dordrecht: Reidel, pp. 1–15.

Langlois, Richard and László Csontos (1993) 'Optimization, Rule-Following, and the Methodology of Situational Analysis', in Uskali Mäki, Bo Gustafsson and Christian Knudsen (eds) *Rationality, Institutions and Economic Methodology*, London: Routledge, pp. 113–32.

Larrabee, Mary Jeanne (ed.) (1993) *An Ethic of Care. Feminist and Interdisciplinary Perspectives*, London: Routledge.

Laslier, Jean-François, Marc Fleurbaey, Nicolas Gravel and Alain Trannoy (1998) *Freedom in Economics. New Perspectives in Normative Analysis*, London: Routledge.

Lavoie, Don (1990) *Economics and Hermeneutics*, London: Routledge.

Lawson, Tony (1997) *Economics and Reality*, London: Routledge.

—— (1999) 'Feminism, Realism, and Universalism', *Feminist Economics*, 5 (2), pp. 25–59.

Leibenstein, Harvey (1976) *Beyond Economic Man. A New Foundation for Microeconomics*, Cambridge, Mass.: Harvard University Press.

Leijonhufvud, Axel (1985) 'Ideology and Analysis in Macroeconomics', in Peter Koslowski (ed.) *Economics and Philosophy*, Tübingen: Mohr, pp. 182–207.

Lévi-Strauss, Claude (1949) *Les Structures Elémentaires de la Parenté*, translation: *The Elementary Structures of Kinship*, Boston: Beacon, 1969.

Lewis, Alan and Karl-Erik Wärneryd (eds) (1994) *Ethics and Economic Affairs*, London: Routledge.

Little, Margaret Olivia (1995) 'Seeing and Caring: The Role of Affect in Feminist Moral Epistemology', in *Hypatia*, 10 (3), pp. 117–37.

Lloyd, Genevieve (1984) *The Man of Reason*, London: Methuen.

Lucas, Robert (1981) 'Econometric Policy Evaluation: A Critique', in Robert Lucas, *Studies in Business Cycle Theory*, Oxford: Blackwell, pp. 104–30.

Lycklama à Nijeholt, Geertje, Virginia Vargas and Saskia Wieringa (1998) *Women's Movements and Public Policy in Europe, Latin America, and the Caribbean*, New York: Garland.

McCloskey, Deirdre (1982) *The Applied Theory of Price*, New York: Macmillan.

—— (1985) *The Rhetoric of Economics*, Madison: University of Wisconsin Press.

—— (1994a) *Knowledge and Persuasion*, Cambridge: Cambridge University Press.

—— (1994b) 'Bourgeois Virtue', *American Scholar*, 63 (2), pp. 177–91.

—— (1996) *The Vices of Economists. The Virtues of the Bourgeoisie*, Amsterdam: Amsterdam University Press.

McCloskey, Deirdre and Arjo Klamer (1995) 'One Quarter of GDP Is Persuasion', *American Economic Review*, 85 (2), pp. 191–5.

McElroy, Marjorie and Mary Jean Horney (1981) 'Nash-Bargained Household Decisions: Towards a Generalization of the Theory of Demand', *International Economic Review*, 22 (2), pp. 333–49.

MacIntyre, Alisdair (1987) [1981] *After Virtue. A Study in Moral Theory*, second edition, London: Duckworth.

Mäki, Uskali, Bo Gustafsson and Christian Knudsen (eds) (1993) *Rationality, Institutions and Economic Methodology*, London: Routledge.

Malinowski, Bronislaw (1922) *Argonauts of the Western Pacific. An Account of Native Enterprise and Adventure in the Archipelagoes of Melanesian New Guinea*, London and New York: Routledge and Dutton.

Mansbridge, Jane (ed.) (1990) *Beyond Self-Interest*, Chicago: University of Chicago Press.

Marshall, Alfred (1890) [1961] *Principles of Economics*, London: Macmillan.

Marx, Karl (1855) [1960] 'Value, Price and Profit', in *The Essential Left*, London: Allen and Unwin, pp. 49–101.

—— (1867) [1969] *Das Kapital. Kritik an der Politischen Oekonomie*, translation: *Capital. A Critique of Political Economy*, edited by Friedrich Engels, Hamburg: Meissner.

Mauss, Marcel (1923) *Essai sur le Don. Forme Archaique de l'Echange*, translation: *The Gift. The Form and Reason for Exchange in Archaic Societies*, London: Routledge, 1990.

Mead, George (ed.) (1934) *Mind, Self, and Society: From the Standpoint of the Social Behaviourist*, Chicago: University of Chicago Press.

Mehta, Judith (1993) 'Meaning in the Context of Bargaining Games – Narratives in Opposition', in Willie Henderson, Tony Dudley-Evans and Roger Backhouse (eds) *Economics and Language*, London: Routledge, pp. 85–99.

Meikle, Scott (1995) *Aristotle's Economic Thought*, Oxford: Clarendon.

Merton, Robert (1949) [1968] *Social Theory and Social Structure*, enlarged edition, New York: Free Press..

Merton, Robert, Marjorie Fiske and Patricia Kendall (1956) *The Focused Interview: A Manual of Problems and Procedures*, Glencoe, Ill.: Free Press.

Mill, John Stuart (1848) [1917] *Principles of Political Economy*, edited by W. J. Ashley, London: Longmans Green.

—— (1859) [1975] *On Liberty*, Middlesex: Penguin.

—— (1869) [1970] 'On the Subjection of Women', in John Stuart Mill and Harriet Taylor Mill, *Essays on Sex Equality*, edited by Alice S. Rossi, Chicago: University of Chicago Press, pp. 125–242.

—— (1873) [1935] *Autobiography*, Oxford: Oxford University Press.

Miller, Arthur (1949) [1961] *Death of a Salesman*, London: Penguin.

Mirowski, Philip (1989) *More Heat than Light. Economics as Social Physics: Physics as Nature's Economics*, Cambridge: Cambridge University Press.

—— (1990a) 'From Mandelsbrot to Chaos in Economic Theory', *Southern Economic Journal*, no. 57, pp. 289–307.

—— (1990b) 'The Philosophical Bases of Institutionalist Economics', in Don Lavoie, *Economics and Hermeneutics*, London: Routledge, pp. 76–112.

—— (1993) 'Mathematical Formalism and Economic Explanation', in Philip Mirowski (ed.) *The Reconstruction of Economic Theory*, Dordrecht: Kluwer-Nijhoff, pp. 179–240.

Mohanty, Chandra (1991) 'Under Western Eyes: Feminist Scholarship and Colonial Discourses', in Chandra Mohanty, Ann Russo and Lourdes Torres (eds) *Third World Women and the Politics of Feminism*, Indianapolis: Indiana University Press, pp. 51–80.

Moller Okin, Susan (1979) *Women in Western Political Thought*, Princeton: University of Princeton Press.

—— (1989) *Justice, Gender and the Family*, New York: Basic.

Morgan, David (1988) *Focus Groups as Qualitative Research*, London and New Delhi: Sage.

Moser, Caroline (1989). 'The Impact of Recession and Adjustment Policies at the Micro Level: Low Income Women and Their Households in Guayaquil, Ecuador', UNICEF, *The Invisible Adjustment. Poor Women and the Economic Crisis*, second revised edition. Santiago: UNICEF, pp. 137–66.

—— (1993) *Gender Planning and Development*, London and New York: Routledge.

Navias, Martin and Susan Willet (eds) (1996) *The European Arms Trade*, New York: Nova Science Publishers.

Nelson, Julie (1993a) 'Value-Free or Valueless? Notes on the Pursuit of Detachment in Economics', *History of Political Economy*, 25 (1), pp. 121–45.

—— (1993b) 'The Study of Choice or the Study of Provisioning? Gender and the Definition of Economics', in Marianne A. Ferber and Julie A. Nelson, *Beyond Economic Man. Feminist Theory and Economics*, Chicago: University of Chicago Press, pp. 23–36.

—— (1996) *Feminism, Objectivity and Economics*, London: Routledge.

—— (1999) 'Of Markets and Martyrs: Is it OK to Pay Well for Care?', *Feminist Economics*, 5 (3), pp. 43–59.

Nieuwhof, Martijn (1998) 'Solo of Niet Solo? Dat is de Vraag! Een Onderzoek naar de Motieven van Thuiszorg-organisaties om Niet te Participeren in Strategische Allianties', doctoral thesis, Rotterdam: Erasmus University.

North, Douglass (1990) *Institutions, Institutional Change and Economic Performance*, Cambridge: Cambridge University Press.

—— (1991) 'Institutions', *Journal of Economic Perspectives*, 5 (1), pp. 97–112.

—— (1992) *Transaction Costs, Institutions, and Economic Performance*, International Centre for Economic Growth, Occasional Paper no. 30.

Nussbaum, Martha (1986) *The Fragility of Goodness. Luck and Ethics in Greek Tragedy and Philosophy,* Cambridge: Cambridge University Press.

—— (1990) *Love's Knowledge. Essays on Philosophy and Literature,* Oxford: Oxford University Press.

—— (1995) 'Human Capabilities, Female Human Beings', in Jonathan Glover and Martha Nussbaum (eds) *Women, Culture and Development. A Study of Human Capabilities,* Oxford: Clarendon, pp. 61–104.

—— (1998) 'Aristotle, Feminism, and Needs for Functioning', in Cynthia Freeland (ed.) *Feminist Interpretations of Aristotle,* University Park: Pennsylvania State University Press.

Nussbaum, Martha and Amartya Sen (eds) (1993) *The Quality of Life,* Oxford: Clarendon.

Nzomo, Maria (1995) 'Women and the Democratisation Struggles in Africa: What Relevance to Postmodernist Discourse?', in Marianne H. Marchand and Jane L. Parpart (eds) *Feminism Postmodernism Development,* London and New York: Routledge, pp. 131–41.

Oakly, Justin (1992) *Morality and the Emotions,* London: Routledge.

OECD (1996) *Employment Outlook,* Paris: OECD.

O'Hara, Phillip Anthony (1995) 'Household Labour, the Family, and Macroeconomic Instability in the United States: 1940s–1990s', *Review of Social Economy,* no.1, pp. 89–120.

Oliner, Samuel and Pearl Oliner (1988) *The Altruistic Personality. Rescuers of Jews in Nazi Europe,* New York: Free Press.

Olson, Mancur (1975) *The Logic of Collective Action. Public Goods and the Theory of Groups,* Cambridge, Mass.: Harvard University Press. Reprint of 1965.

O'Neill, John (1998) *The Market. Ethics, Knowledge and Politics,* London: Routledge.

Oppong, Christine (ed.) (1983) *Female and Male in West Africa,* London: Allen and Unwin.

Oser, Jacob (1970) *The Evolution of Economic Thought,* second edition. San Diego: Harcourt, Brace and World.

Ott, Notburga (1992) *Intrafamily Bargaining and Household Decisions,* New York: Springer.

Peacock, Alan (1997) *The Political Economy of Economic Freedom,* Cheltenham: Elgar.

—— (1999) 'The Communitarian Attack on Economics', *Kyklos,* 52 (4), pp. 497–510.

Peeters, Marcel (1987), 'A Dismal Science: An Essay on New Classical Economics', *De Economist,* 135 (4), pp. 442–66.

Perkins Gilman, Charlotte (1899) [1920] *Women and Economics. A Study of the Economic Relation between Men and Women as a Factor in Social Evolution,* ninth edition, London: Putnam.

—— (1903) [1972] *The Home. Its Work and Influence,* Urbana: University of Illinois Press.

Pesaran, Hashem and Simon M. Potter (1993) *Nonlinear Dynamics, Chaos and Econometrics,* Chichester: Wiley.

Picchio, Antonella (1992) *Social Reproduction. The Political Economy of the Labour Market,* Cambridge: Cambridge University Press.

Pickthall, M. M. (1996 AC/1417 AH) *The Meaning of the Glorious Quran,* explanatory translation, revised and edited by Arafat K. El-Ashi, Beltsville, Md.: Amana.

Pigou, Arthur (1929) *The Economics of Welfare,* third edition, London: Macmillan.

Plantenga, Janneke (1993) *Een Afwijkend Patroon. Honderd Jaar Vrouwenarbeid in Nederland en (West-) Duitsland*, Amsterdam: SUA.

Plato, *The Republic*, translated by Desmond Lee, second edition, 1987, London: Penguin.

Plumwood, Val (1993) *Feminism and the Mastery of Nature*, London: Routledge.

Polanyi, Karl (1944) *The Great Transformation*, New York: Rinehart.

—— (1957) 'The Economy as Instituted Process', in Karl Polanyi, Conrad Arensberg and Harry Pearson (eds) *Trade and Markets in the Early Empires. Economies in History and Theory*, Glencoe: Free Press, pp. 243–70.

—— (1968) *Primitive, Archaic and Modern Economies. Essays of Karl Polanyi*, edited by George Dalton, New York: Anchor.

Pott-Buter, Hettie (1993) *Facts and Fairy Tales about Female Labour, Family and Fertility*, Amsterdam: Amsterdam University Press.

Prigogine, Ilya (1993) 'Bounded Rationality: From Dynamical Systems to Socio-economic Models', in Richard H. Day and Ping Chen (eds) *Nonlinear Dynamics and Evolutionary Economics*, Oxford: Oxford University Press, pp. 3–13.

Prigogine, Ilya and Isabelle Stengers (1984) *Order out of Chaos. Man's New Dialogue with Nature*, New York: Bantam.

Pruzan, Elliot (1988) *The Concept of Justice in Marx*, New York: Peter Lang.

Pujol, Michèle (1992) *Feminism and Anti-Feminism in Early Economic Thought*, Aldershot: Elgar.

Puka, Bill (1993) 'The Liberation of Caring: A Different Voice for Gilligan's "Different Voice"', in Mary Jeanne Larrabee (ed.) *An Ethic of Care. Feminist and Interdisciplinary Perspectives*. London: Routledge.

Putnam, Robert with Robert Leonardi and Raffaella Naretti (1992) *Making Democracy Work. Civic Traditions in Modern Italy*, Princeton: Princeton University Press.

Radin, Margaret Jane (1996) *Contested Commodities*, Cambridge, Mass.: Harvard University Press.

Radzicki, Michael (1990) 'Institutional Dynamics, Deterministic Chaos, and Self-Organizing Systems', *Journal of Economic Issues*, no. 1, pp. 57–102.

Rawls, John (1971) *A Theory of Justice*, Cambridge, Mass.: Harvard University Press.

—— (1985) 'Justice as Fairness: Political Not Metaphysical', *Philosophy and Public Affairs*, 14 (3), pp. 223–52.

Reid, Margaret (1934) *Economics of Household Production*, New York and London: Wiley and Chapman and Hall.

—— (1942) *Consumers and the Market*, third edition, New York: Appleton-Century-Crofts.

—— (1943) *Food for People*, New York and London: Wiley and Chapman and Hall.

Ricoeur, Paul (1991) *From Text to Action. Essays in Hermeneutics, II*, translated by Kathleen Blamey and John Thompson from *Du Texte à l'Action. Essais d'Hermen-eutique, II*, 1986, London: Athlone.

—— (1992) *Oneself as Another*, translation: Kathleen Blamey, Chicago: University of Chicago Press.

Robbins, Lionel (1935) [1952] *An Essay on the Nature and Significance of Economic Science*, second edition, London: Macmillan.

Robinson, Joan (1962) *Economic Philosophy*, London: Watts.

—— (1970) *Freedom and Necessity. An Introduction to the Study of Society*, London: Allen and Unwin.

Roemer, John (1982) *A General Theory of Exploitation and Class,* Cambridge, Mass.: Harvard University Press.
—— (1996) *Theories of Distributive Justice,* Cambridge, Mass.: Harvard University Press.
Rossi, Alice (1970) 'Sentiment and Intellect. The Story of John Stuart Mill and Harriet Taylor Mill', in John Stuart Mill and Harriet Taylor Mill *Essays on Sex Equality,* edited by Alice S. Rossi, Chicago: University of Chicago Press, pp. 1–64.
Sahlins, Marshall (1972) *Stone Age Economics,* New York: Aldine.
Salanti, Andrea and Ernesto Screpanti (eds) (1997) *Pluralism in Economics. New Perspectives in History and Methodology,* Cheltenham: Elgar.
Samuels, Warren (1995a) 'The Instrumental Value Principle and its Role', in Charles Michael Andres Clark (ed.) *Institutional Economics and the Theory of Social Value: Essays in Honor of Marc R. Tool,* Dordrecht: Kluwer, pp. 97–112.
—— (1995b) 'The Present State of Institutional Economics', *Cambridge Journal of Economics,* no. 19, pp. 569–90.
—— (1997) 'Instrumental Valuation', in Warren Samuels, Steven Medema and Allan Schmid (eds) *The Economy as a Process of Valuation,* Cheltenham: Elgar, pp. 1–71.
Saxonhouse, Arlene (1985) *Women in the History of Political Thought. Ancient Greece to Machiavelli,* New York: Praeger.
Schelling, Thomas (1978) *Micromotives and Macrobehaviour,* New York: Norton.
Schmidtz, David (1996) 'Reasons for Altruism', in Aafke Komter *The Gift. An Interdisciplinary Perspective,* Amsterdam: Amsterdam University Press, pp. 164–75.
Schütz, Alfred (1973) [1953] 'The Frame of Unquestioned Constructs', in Mary Douglas (ed.) *Rules and Meanings,* Harmondsworth: Penguin, pp. 18–20.
Sen, Amartya (1977) 'Rational Fools: A Critique of the Behavioural Foundations of Economic Theory', *Philosophy and Public Affairs,* 6 (4), pp. 317–44.
—— (1981) 'Rights and Agency', *Philosophy and Public Affairs,* 11 (1), pp. 3–39.
—— (1987) *On Ethics and Economics,* Oxford: Blackwell.
—— (1990a) 'Gender and Cooperative Conflicts', in Irene Tinker (ed.) *Persistent Inequalities. Women and World Development,* Oxford: Oxford University Press, pp. 123–49.
—— (1990b) 'Justice: Means Versus Freedoms', *Philosophy and Public Affairs,* 19 (2), pp. 111–21.
—— (1992) *Inequality Reexamined,* Oxford: Clarendon.
—— (1993a) 'Capability and Well-Being', in Martha Nussbaum and Amartya Sen (eds) *The Quality of Life,* Oxford: Clarendon, pp. 30–53.
—— (1993b) 'Positional Objectivity', *Philosophy and Public Affairs,* 22 (2), pp. 126–45.
—— (1995) 'The Formulation of Rational Choice', *American Economic Review,* 84 (2), pp. 385–90.
—— (1998) 'Human Development and Financial Conservatism', *World Development,* 26 (4), pp. 733–42.
—— (1999) *Development as Freedom,* Oxford: Oxford University Press.
Sen, Amartya and Martha Nussbaum (1993) 'Introduction', in Martha Nussbaum and Amartya Sen (eds) *The Quality of Life,* Oxford: Clarendon, pp. 1–6.
Sen, Amartya and Bernard Williams (eds) (1982) *Utilitarianism and Beyond,* Cambridge: Cambridge University Press.
Sevenhuijsen, Selma (1991) 'The Morality of Feminism', *Hypathia,* 6 (2), pp. 173–91.

—— (1998) *Citizenship and the Ethics of Care. Feminist Considerations on Justice, Morality and Politics*, London: Routledge.

Shiller, Robert (1989) *Market Volatility*, Cambridge, Mass.: MIT Press.

—— (1995) 'Conversation, Information, and Herd Behaviour', *American Economic Review*, 85 (2), pp. 181–5.

Simmel, Georg (1908) [1950] *The Sociology of George Simmel*, edited by K. Wolff, New York: Free Press.

Simon, Herbert A. (1982) *Models of Bounded Rationality*, Cambridge, Mass.: MIT Press.

—— (1983) *Reason in Human Affairs*, Oxford: Blackwell.

Smith, Adam (1759) [1984] *The Theory of Moral Sentiments*, Indianapolis: Liberty Fund.

—— (1766) [1978] *Letters on Jurisprudence*, edited by R. L. Meek, D. D. Raphael and P. G. Stein, Oxford: Oxford University Press.

—— (1776) [1981] *An Inquiry into the Nature and Causes of the Wealth of Nations*, Indianapolis: Liberty Fund.

Solomon, Robert (1996) 'Corporate Roles, Personal Virtues: An Aristotelian Approach to Business Ethics', in Thomas Donaldson and Patricia Werhane (eds) *Ethical Issues in Business. A Philosophical Approach*, fifth edition, Upper Saddle River, N.J.: Prentice Hall, pp. 45–59.

Spelman, Elizabeth (1983) 'Aristotle and the Politization of the Soul', in Sandra Harding and Merrill Hintikka (eds) *Discovering Reality. Feminist Perspectives on Epistemology, Metaphysics, Methodology, and Philosophy of Science*, Dordrecht: Reidel, pp. 17–30.

Staveren, Irene van (1994) 'A Political Economy of Reproduction', *Development*, no. 3, pp. 20–3.

—— (1997) 'Focus Groups: Contributing to a Gender-Aware Methodology', *Feminist Economics*, 3 (2), pp. 131–5.

—— (1998) 'Economie van het Huishouden: Margaret Reid', *ESB*, 9 September, pp. 675–7.

—— (1999) *Caring for Economics. An Aristotelian Perspective*, Delft: Eburon.

Swaay, Agnes van (1997) 'Thuiszorg in Beweging. Welke Koers Vaart het Vrijwilligerswerk?', Een Discussiestuk, Utrecht: NIZW.

Taylor, Charles (1992) *Philosophy and the Human Sciences*, philosophical papers 2, Cambridge: Cambridge University Press.

Thomson, Dorothy Lampen (1973) *Adam Smith's Daughters*, New York: Exposition.

Tilly, Louise and Joan Scott (1978) *Women, Work and Family*, London: Routledge.

Tirman, John (1997) *Spoils of War. The Human Cost of America's Arms Trade*, New York: Free Press.

Titmuss, Richard (1970) *The Gift Relationship. From Human Blood to Social Policy*, London: Allen and Unwin.

Tool, Marc (1977) 'A Social Value Theory in Neo-Institutional Economics', *Journal of Economic Issues*, 11 (4), pp. 823–46.

—— (1979) *The Discretionary Economy. A Normative Theory of Political Economy*, Santa Monica: Goodyear.

—— (1986) *Essays in Social Value Theory. A Neo-Institutionalist Contribution*, New York: Sharpe.

Tronto, Joan (1993) *Moral Boundaries. A Political Argument for an Ethic of Care*, London: Routledge.

—— (1995) 'Caring for Democracy: A Feminist Vision', inaugural speech, Utrecht: Humanist University, 6 June.

UNDP (1995) *Human Development Report*, Oxford: Oxford University Press.

—— (1996) *Human Development Report*, Oxford: Oxford University Press.

—— (1997) *Human Development Report*, Oxford: Oxford University Press.

—— (2000) *Human Development Report*, Oxford: Oxford University Press.

Van Lear, William and Lynette Fowler (1997) 'Efficiency and Service in the Group Home Industry', *Journal of Economic Issues*, 31 (4), pp. 1039–50.

Veblen, Thorstein (1899) [1931] *The Theory of the Leisure Class. An Economic Study of Institutions*, edited by B. W. Huebsch, New York: Viking.

—— (1919) [1961] *The Place of Science in Modern Civilisation. And Other Essays*, New York: Rusell and Rusell.

Vromen, Jack (1995) *Economic Evolution. An Enquiry into the Foundations of New Institutions Economics*, London: Routledge.

Waller, William (1995) 'Compulsive Shift or Cultural Blind Drift? Literary Theory, Critical Rhetoric, Feminist Theory and Institutional Economics', in Charles Michael Andres Clark (ed.) *Institutional Economics and the Theory of Social Value. Essays in Honor of Marc R. Tool*, Dordrecht: Kluwer, pp. 153–78.

Walzer, Michael (1983) *Spheres of Justice*, New York: Basic.

Waring, Marilyn (1988) *If Women Counted*, New York: HarperCollins.

Whalen, Charles and Linda Whalen (1994) 'Institutionalism: A Useful Foundation for Feminist Economics?', in Janice Peterson and Doug Brown (eds) *The Economic Status of Women Under Capitalism*, Aldershot: Elgar, pp. 19–34.

Williams, Bernard (1971) 'The Idea of Equality', in H. Bedau (ed.) *Justice and Equality*, Englewood Cliffs: Prentice-Hall, pp. 116–37.

—— (1985) *Ethics and the Limits of Philosophy*, London: Fontana and Collins.

Williamson, Oliver (1993) 'Calculativeness, Trust, and Economic Organization', in *Journal of Law and Economics*, vol. 36, pp. 453–86.

Wolf, Eric (1982) *Europe and the People Without History*, Berkeley and Los Angeles: University of California Press.

Wood, Allan (1972) 'The Marxian Critique of Justice', *Philosophy and Public Affairs*, 1 (3), pp. 244–82.

Woolley, Frances (2000) 'Degrees of Connection: A Critique of Rawls' Theory of Mutual Disinterest', in *Feminist Economics*, 6 (2), pp. 1–21.

World Bank (1998) *Gender, Growth, and Poverty Reduction. 1998 Status Report on Poverty in Sub-Saharan Africa*, Special Program of Assistance for Africa, Washington D.C.: World Bank.

Yi, Yun-Ae (1996) 'Margaret R. Reid: Life and Achievements', in *Feminist Economics*, 2 (3), pp. 17–36.

Young, Iris (1990) *Justice and the Politics of Difference*, Princeton: Princeton University Press.

Zey, Mary (ed.) (1992) *Decision Making. Alternatives to Rational Choice Models*, London and New Delhi: Sage.

Ziekenfondsraad (1998) 'Onderzoek Modernisering in de Thuiszorg', rapport no. 777, Amstelveen: Ziekenfondsraad.

INDEX

Addleson, Mark 109
Agarwal, Bina 118
Akerlof, George 51–2, 169
Amariglio, Jack 114
Anderson, Elizabeth 102–6
Anker, Richard 49
Argyle, Michael 17, 170
Aristotle 6–11, 38, 42, 47, 79–83, 96, 145, 150–9, 171–3, 190, 203–6
Arrow, Kenneth 51, 55, 91
Aslaksen, Iulie, 186
Aubel, Judi 111
Ayres, Clarence 100

Badgett, Lee 41, 46
Baerends, Els 140
Baier, Annette 36, 38, 40, 53, 101
Bailey, Kenneth 194–5
Baker, Wayne 49
Bakker, Diny de 167
Barker, Drue 10
Barro, Robert 169
Batson, Daniel 13
Bazerman, Charles 60
Becker, Gary 43, 56, 77, 90–8, 102, 106
Bentham, Jeremy 65–9, 181
Bergmann, Barbara 45
Berlin, Isaiah 27
Bethke Elshtain, Jean 10
Birdsall, Nancy 169
Bjerkholt, Olav 186
Blaug, Mark 9
Blumberg, Rae Lesser 140
Bok, Sissela 57
Boon, Leo 167

Bordo, Susan 4
Boserup, Esther 140
Boulding, Kenneth 52, 62–3, 96, 163–4, 172, 184, 190–1, 194
Bowden, Peta 38, 47, 55
Bowles, Samuel 5, 94
Brock, William 198–9
Brown, Vivienne 59, 60, 108
Bruyn-Hundt, Marga 44, 49, 141
Buchanan, Allen 73–4
Buchanan, James 17, 35

Caldwell, Bruce xi
capabilities 1–4, 6, 8, 10, 11, 21–5, 28, 36, 47, 52–3, 55, 57, 70, 72, 86, 94, 104, 107–8, 112, 114, 122, 133, 137–9, 144–5, 148–60, 164, 171, 179, 182, 202–3
capital 55, 67 158, 165, 181, 207
Carrier, James 50
CBS 49, 141
chaos theory xi, 192–8, 200
Cheal, David 50
Chick, Victoria 59, 89, 90
Code, Lorraine 38
Colander, David 110
commensurability 6, 9, 21, 47, 54, 79, 104–8, 144, 152, 174–7, 185, 204
Commissie Toekomstscenario's 141
Commons, John 100, 177–8
Csontos, László 13, 17
culture 24, 34, 53, 54, 62, 96, 101, 108, 111, 112, 116, 118, 119, 125, 136, 140, 144, 163, 175, 177, 195

Dahrendorf, Ralf 109

Damasio, Antonio 3–4, 15, 20
Dawes, Robyn 14
De Greene, Kenyon 194–5
Denzau, Arthur 100
deontology *see* justice theories
Devaux, Monique 38
Dimand, Mary Ann 64
Dimand, Robert 64
distribution 20, 32–5, 38–40, 43, 45–8,
    52–58, 62, 77–8, 80, 81, 86–7, 108,
    113, 121, 123, 128, 130, 138, 141, 143,
    149, 150–3, 158–9, 165, 169, 172, 175,
    182–3, 199–204
Dixit, Avinash 15, 17
Dixon-Mueller, Ruth 49
Dolfsma, Wilfred 161
Douglas, Mary 55, 105
Dow, Sheila 59, 188–9
Durkheim, Émile 16
Durlauf, Steven 198–200
Dwyer, Gerald 192

Editorial Mujeres 143
efficiency 2, 12, 29, 30, 57, 67, 71, 73,
    77–9, 86, 98–101, 133, 165–73, 183,
    200, 207, 208
Elliott, Euel 192–3
Elson, Diane 44, 167
Elster, Jon 5, 14, 16, 40–1, 54, 73–5, 90,
    93, 160–1, 164
emotion x, 4–8, 12, 15–16, 20–9, 30, 36,
    44, 46, 53–5, 63–5, 69, 81–4, 88, 90,
    94, 117, 119, 134–8, 143, 147–55,
    174–9, 201–6
England, Paula 14, 41, 44, 46
Epicurus 65–6, 96, 72
Esim, Simel 111
Esposito, John 142
ethics of care 38–42, 81
Etzioni, Amitai 21, 54, 102–6
Evers, Barbara 167
exchange 8–9, 20, 26, 29–30, 35, 38, 39,
    44–62, 73, 75, 79–82, 85–7, 99, 101,
    107–8, 138–9, 149–51, 159–60, 164–5,
    170–1, 175, 181–2, 185, 202–4

Fapohunda, Eleanor 140
Feiner, Susan 5
femininity 4, 89, 90, 113, 142, 181, 189,
    190, 198
feminism xii, 10, 11, 38, 41, 46, 89, 112,
    135, 136, 143

Ferber, Marianne 4, 5
Festinger, Leon 16
Fisher, Berenice 39
Fiske, Marjorie 109
Fitzgibbons, Athol 16
Fleetwood, Steve 9
Fleurbaey, Marc 26, 30, 53
Folbre, Nancy 4, 5, 12, 14, 21, 36, 38,
    41, 44, 46, 185
Foley, Caroline 20
Foot, Philippa 10
Forget, Evelyn 64
Foucault, Michel 108
Fowler, Lynette167
Frank, Robert 5, 16–17, 41, 90, 93
Freeland, Cynthia 10–11
Frey, Bruno 13
Friedman, Marilyn 58
Friedman, Milton 22, 23, 26–32, 38, 96,
    157, 164, 183
Friedman, Rose 26–32, 38, 164, 183
Fukuyama, Francis 43, 162–3
Fullbrook, Edward 21

García Quesada, Ana Isabel 142
Gardiner, Jean 5, 45, 185
Gauthier, David 35–8, 53
Geertz, Clifford 109–10
gender 4, 23, 44, 46, 85, 90, 113, 117,
    119, 140, 167, 181, 184, 189–90,
    198–200
gift 20, 44–56, 62, 81–4, 108, 117, 146,
    151, 159, 164, 165, 168–71, 181–2,
    203, 207
Gilligan, Carol 38, 41
Goffman, Erving 109
Goldschmidt-Clermont, Luisella 49
Goodman, Nelson 13, 55
Granovetter, Mark 11, 21, 25, 177, 194
Gravel, Nicolas 26, 30, 53
Gregory, Chris 50
Griffin, James 106
Groenewegen, Peter 106
Groenhout, Ruth 11, 81
Groot, Wim 141
Grupo Agenda Política de Mujeres
    Costarricenses 142
Gudeman, Stephen 110
Gustafsson, Bo 4, 19

Hampshire, Stuart 19, 152
Harding, Sandra 64, 176

Hargreaves Heap, Shaun 3, 4, 12, 19, 21, 23, 110
Harsanyi, John 35
Hartmann, Heidi 36
Hausman, Daniel 5, 35, 55, 106
Hayek, Friedrich 27–32, 38, 96, 157, 164, 182
Heilbroner, Robert 4
Held, Virginia 38
Herrnstein Smith, Barbara 14, 19
Hewitson, Gillian 5
Himmelweit, Susan 41, 44
Hirschman, Albert 63–4, 96, 158, 165, 182
Hochschild, Arlie 106
Hodgson, Geoffrey 17, 21, 177, 194
Hollis, Martin 13, 19, 21
Horney, Mary Jean 118
household 6, 36, 44, 45, 53, 78–81, 84, 92, 121, 124, 131–3, 137, 140, 146, 167, 175, 183–90, 196–201
Hume, David 38, 40, 42, 60, 80, 96, 150, 153

IMF 187
incommensurability see commensurability
institution 24, 29, 36, 48, 98–100, 106, 137, 139, 140, 162, 174–5, 177–8, 180–5, 189–201, 205; institutional mediation 139, 144, 174–7, 179–82, 184–5, 190, 201, 205
INSTRAW 49
Isherwood, Baron 105

Janssen, Maarten 5, 21
Jennings, Ann 89
justice theories 32–4, 40–2, 75, 76, 80

Kabeer, Naila 183
Kant, Immanuel 38, 41, 42, 50, 81, 103
Keddie, Nikki 142
Kendall, Patricia 109
Keynes, John Maynard 1, 152, 172
Kiel, Douglas 192–3
Kittay, Feder 38
Klamer, Arjo 4, 13, 19, 21, 49, 89, 110, 191
Knight, Frank 18
Knudsen, Christian 4, 19
Kolm, Serge-Christophe 33, 35, 53
Komter, Aafke 10, 49

Koren, Charlotte 186
Kragt, Alphons van de 14
Kroeger-Mappes, Joy 38
Krugman, Paul 191, 200
Kuiper, Edith xii, 5

labour 9, 24, 41, 44, 46–51, 55, 67, 68, 70, 71, 74–6, 85, 105, 107, 133, 137, 140–3, 148, 150, 158, 160, 164–7, 170, 176, 181–3, 186–8, 203; labour market 6, 13, 44, 46, 48, 49, 71, 76, 85, 105, 123–5, 130, 167, 169, 176, 182, 188, 208; unpaid labour 24, 44, 49, 50, 55, 76–9, 84, 86, 106, 123, 125–6, 141–4, 167, 186, 189
Lange, Lynda 10
Langlois, Richard 13, 17
Larrabee, Mary Jeanne 38
Laslier, Jean-François 26, 30, 53
Lawson, Tony 4–5, 11–12, 17, 21–2
Leibenstein, Harvey 4–5, 22, 169
Leijonhufvud, Axel 191
Leonard, Thomas 191
Lévi-Strauss, Claude 49–50
Lewis, Alan 106
liberalism 26, 29–32, 35, 38, 50, 52, 66, 73, 75, 131, 153, 180–4
Little, Margaret Olivia 38
Lloyd, Genevieve 4
Lucas, Robert 23

Maassen van den Brink, Henriëtte 141
McCloskey, Deirdre 4, 16, 19, 21, 22, 26, 35–6, 49, 60–1, 83, 90, 95–8, 106, 110, 160
McElroy, Marjorie 118
MacIntyre, Alisdair 47, 58
McPherson, Michael 5, 35, 55, 106
Mäki, Uskali 4, 19
Malinowski, Bronislaw 49–50
Mansbridge, Jane 4, 12, 19, 106
market 2, 24, 29–30, 35–9, 44–5, 49, 53–4, 58, 62, 67, 77–9, 92, 95–7, 100–1, 106–7, 137–40, 144, 148–9, 156, 159, 160, 162, 164–73, 181–6, 192, 198, 202–4, 208
Marshall, Alfred 84
Marx, Karl 73–6, 79, 80, 87, 165, 182, 184
masculinity 4, 5, 89, 90, 95, 113, 181, 189, 190
Mauss, Marcel 49–50

Mead, George 109
Mehta, Judith 158
Meikle, Scott 8–9
Merton, Robert 109
Meyers, Diana 38
Mill, John Stuart xi, 10, 26–7, 65, 68–80, 87–9, 96, 114, 164–5, 182–4
Miller, Arthur 145–7
Mirowski, Philip 4, 88, 191, 192
model xii, 3, 18, 90, 190, 191, 195–201, 205
Mohanty, Chandra 136
Moller Okin, Susan 10, 36
moral principle *see* moral rule
moral rule 7, 19, 27, 38, 42, 49, 203
morality 4–8, 11, 12, 19, 22, 26–30, 35, 38–42, 47, 49–50, 53–4, 57, 62, 66, 68, 78, 81, 94, 101–8, 160, 171, 177, 202, 203
Morgan, David 111
Moser, Caroline 187–90, 196–201
motivation x, 4, 13, 14, 17, 44, 46, 48, 50, 51, 61, 90, 103–8, 110, 167–71, 208

Nalebuff, Barry 15, 17
Navias, Martine 105
Nelson, Julie 3–5, 14, 21, 41, 44–5, 56, 89
Nieuwhof, Martijn 167
North, Douglass 98–102
Nussbaum, Martha 11, 16

Oakly, Justin 16
OECD 107, 141
O'Hara, Phillip Anthony 186–7
Oliner, Pearl 13, 42
Oliner, Samuel 13, 42
Olson, Mancur 63
Olsson, Stig-Olof 186
O'Neill, John 8
ontology 8, 9, 47, 52, 84, 107, 155
Oppong, Christine 140
Orbell, John 14
Ott, Notburga 118

Pagnossin-Agilisakis, Elisabetta 49
Peacock, Alan 30, 53
Peeters, Marcel 4
Perkins Gilman, Charlotte 84–7, 96, 138, 150–3, 165, 177, 182, 184, 190
Picchio, Antonella 45
Pigou, Arthur 84, 165

Plato 72–3, 76, 87
Polanyi, Karl 54, 58, 62–3, 96, 110
policy xii, 25, 30, 46, 54, 121, 142, 168, 172, 181, 185, 200, 207–8
Pott-Buter, Hettie 141
Prigogine, Ilya 192
productivity 12, 167, 172, 186
Pruzan, Elliot 73–5
Pujol, Michèle 65, 68
Putnam, Robert 43, 56

Radzicki, Michael 191
rationality 1–6, 10–17, 19, 21–5, 31–2, 36–8, 43, 51, 56–7, 70, 83, 91, 99, 102, 104, 108, 110, 114, 137, 140, 145, 149–52, 157, 162, 165, 171–4, 179, 200–5; *Rational Economic Man* x, 1–6, 12, 15, 17–23, 26, 31, 34, 35, 43, 53, 91, 93, 94, 205
Rawls, John 33–7, 53, 73, 75–7, 109, 137, 152
redistribution *see* distribution
Reid, Margaret 63, 76–9, 84, 87, 139, 166, 182, 184
responsibility 3, 4, 8, 18, 31, 32, 35–43, 46–51, 66, 70, 80, 81, 83, 94–6, 106, 109, 116, 130, 132, 134, 136, 137, 140, 142, 144, 158, 159, 164–71, 175–6, 182, 188–9, 198, 204, 208
Ricoeur, Paul 55
rights 30, 31, 34, 35, 60, 96, 73–6, 79, 114–15, 120, 123, 125, 129, 130–3, 136, 140–4, 148, 149, 159, 164, 176, 181, 207
risk 2, 17, 18, 43, 78, 79, 86, 87, 92, 101, 121, 123, 137–40, 144, 156, 171, 182–5, 189, 200
Robbins, Lionel 56
Robinson, Joan 25–7
Roemer, John 35, 53, 73
Ross, David 169

Sabot, Richard 169
Sahlins, Marshall 49–50
Salanti, Andrea xi
Samuels, Warren 100, 178
Sap, Jolande xii, 5
Saxonhouse, Arlene 10
Schelling, Thomas 5, 21
Schmidtz, David 50
Scott, Joan 113
Screpanti, Ernesto xi

Sen, Amartya xi, 4, 8–9, 13–14, 22, 35, 41–2, 60, 76, 83, 90, 92–3, 106, 143, 151–2, 164, 169, 181
Sevenhuijsen, Selma 38
Shiller, Robert 49
Simmel, Georg 50
Simon, Herbert 19, 99
Sluijs, Emmy 167
Smith, Adam x, 17, 38–9, 42, 46, 59, 60–3, 66–9, 72, 75–6, 79–84, 87, 89, 96–7, 150, 152–3, 164–5, 181–2
social 3–5, 8, 12, 17, 20–3, 27, 31, 34–41, 49, 51, 54, 55, 62, 64, 73, 76–80, 85, 91, 92, 94, 100–4, 107–8, 113, 121, 123, 125, 130, 131, 134, 139, 142, 146, 149, 153, 158, 162–5, 171, 176–8 181–5, 190–6, 199–204, 207
social capital 43, 50, 55, 92, 93, 156, 162, 164, 173
society 3, 25, 28–37, 58–61, 70–5, 83, 95–6, 118–19, 140, 157, 163
Solomon, Robert 8
Solow, Robert 4, 110
Spelman, Elizabeth 10
state x, 24, 32, 44, 46, 53, 72, 73, 77, 90, 107, 126, 138, 140, 142, 149, 156, 159, 166, 168–9, 176, 181, 185–8, 203
Staveren, Irene van xi, 111, 161
Stengers, Isabelle 192
Stokstad, Marianne 186
Swaay, Agnes van 167

Taylor, Charles 47, 55
Taylor, Harriet 68–72, 74–6, 79, 87, 165, 181–4
Thomson, Dorothy Lampen 65
Tilly, Louise 113
Tirman, John 105
Titmuss, Richard 105, 170, 171
Tool, Marc 100, 185
Trannoy, Alain 26, 30, 53
Tronto, Joan 38–9, 43, 46, 55, 58, 84, 155

UN 107, 113, 143
UNDP 49, 113, 143, 169, 207
UNESCO 207
UNICEF 188, 200, 207
utilitarianism see utility
utility 6, 8, 9, 12, 13, 17–23, 27–39, 42, 50, 51, 54, 66–9, 73, 74, 79, 81, 88, 89–95, 100–3, 107, 143, 151–2, 159, 177–8, 202–5

Van Lear, William 167
Veblen, Thorstein 17, 100, 174, 177–8
virtue 6–11, 29, 38, 40, 42, 59–62, 65–7, 76, 80–3, 86, 94–8, 106, 107, 150–4, 157, 162, 163, 172, 190, 203, 206; virtue ethics xi, 5, 6, 11, 38, 79, 80, 107
Vromen, Jack 100

Wagner, Cordula 167
Waller, William 4, 89
Walzer, Michael 157, 185
Waring, Marilyn 44
Wärneryd, Karl-Erik 106
Weisskopf, Thomas 46
Whalen, Charles 190
Whalen, Linda 190
Willet, Susan 105
Williams, Bernard 4, 35
Williamson, Oliver 100–2, 164
Wolf, Eric 110
women x, xii, 2, 4, 5, 10, 33, 41, 44–6, 49, 65, 68–73, 76, 81, 84–6, 89, 92, 97, 113–21, 124–43, 150, 165, 167, 169, 175, 176, 186–90, 196–201, 208
Wood, Allan 73
Woolley, Frances 36
World Bank 107, 169

Young, Iris , 36

Zey, Mary 4
Ziekenfondsraad 167

6315